CHINESE PHILOSOPHY A–Z

Volumes available in the Philosophy A–Z Series
Chinese Philosophy A–Z, Bo Mou
Christian Philosophy A–Z, Daniel J. Hill and Randal D.
  Rauser
Epistemology A–Z, Martijn Blaauw and Duncan Pritchard
Ethics A–Z, Jonathan A. Jacobs
Indian Philosophy A–Z, Christopher Bartley
Islamic Philosophy A–Z, Peter S. Groff
Jewish Philosophy A–Z, Aaron W. Hughes
Philosophy of Language A–Z, Alessandra Tanesini
Philosophy of Mind A–Z, Marina Rakova
Philosophy of Religion A–Z, Patrick Quinn
Philosophy of Science A–Z, Stathis Psillos
Political Philosophy A–Z, Jon Pike

Forthcoming volumes
Aesthetics A–Z, Eran Guter

Chinese Philosophy A–Z

Bo Mou

Edinburgh University Press

To my daughter Yingying (瑩瑩),
who inspired me to explain reflectively worthy things
in a plain way

© Bo Mou, 2009

Edinburgh University Press Ltd
22 George Square, Edinburgh

Typeset in 10.5/13 Sabon by
Servis Filmsetting Ltd, Stockport, Cheshire, and
printed and bound in Great Britain by
CPI Antony Rowe Ltd, Chippenham and Eastbourne

A CIP record for this book is
available from the British Library

ISBN 978 0 7486 3712 6 (hardback)
ISBN 978 0 7486 2241 2 (paperback)

Contents

Series Editor's Preface

Chinese philosophy and Chinese civilization go hand in hand, and the richness of both is spectacularly obvious to anyone who has even a little knowledge about them. Some of the terms for the major philosophical schools in China are unfamiliar to many outside of that culture, and yet the debates that characterize them are rather familiar, as are the strategies for resolving those debates. On the other hand, they also seem to be rather distant from the leading controversies in other cultures, and a good deal of contextual knowledge is required in order to begin to grasp where the conceptual battle-lines actually lie and how the protagonists of different positions understand what they are doing. There can be no doubt, however, about the quality of the work that was carried out under the label of Chinese philosophy, and Bo Mou's account has the advantage of linking it closely with philosophy in general, so that Chinese philosophers are seen very much as part of the general philosophical enterprise as such, and not just as a specific Chinese phenomenon. Nonetheless, it is necessary to know a fair amount about Chinese culture, and about philosophy in general, in order to have a grasp of Chinese philosophy, and this the reader is provided with here. Like the other books in this series, this book offers an introduction to the considerable riches that lie before anyone interested in a particular philosophical tradition, and the detailed bibliography and guide to other relevant material will be very helpful in that respect. Readers are here supplied with the basic building blocks of Chinese philosophy as an introduction to the discipline and so encouraged to delve deeper into the sea of Chinese culture itself.

Oliver Leaman

Introduction

The main objective of this book is to provide a concise, alphabetical guide to the main concepts, issues, topics, figures, and important movements of thought that have shaped Chinese philosophy over the last 3,000 years.

This book has three prominent features. The first, which distinguishes this volume from others, lies in its style and presentation. The entries are written concisely and extensive cross-references allow the reader to easily make and follow connections and pursue themes.

Nevertheless, this feature does not mean turning reflectively profound things in Chinese philosophy into something that is shallow or less reflectively interesting; nor does it mean that the major part of the work just simplifies and summarizes ready-made explanations or descriptions available in the literature. Though brief and concise, the characterizations in many entries concerning main concepts, issues, and topics in Chinese philosophy have been made in ways that more or less reflect this author's critical examinations and research on various issues in the past decade. As far as those parts other than mere matter-of-fact ones are concerned, the book is intended to be reflectively interesting as well as informative, for both beginners and experts in this field, in an accessible way. Nevertheless, how this is made possible involves, or is based on, one methodological consideration.

Indeed, the second feature of this book lies in its underlying methodological approach. The book was completed bearing in mind some general methodological considerations concerning how to examine Chinese philosophy, some substantial understanding of the nature of philosophy and Chinese philosophy, my own research results in this regard, as well as my pedagogic approach and experience of teaching Chinese philosophy in the past decade in American universities. It is true to some extent that, historically speaking, there is no total separation between literature, history, and philosophy in ancient Chinese thought; it is also historically true in part that there seems to be no separation between philosophy and religion in ancient Chinese thought. Nevertheless, this amounts to saying neither that there is no conceptual distinction between these distinct kinds of inquiries, nor that we cannot reflectively and effectively focus on the philosophical dimension of the historical whole. That would depend on the primary purpose and nature of a project in reflective examination. This book emphasizes *core* terms in order to provide a basic grounding in Chinese philosophy. The choice of entries and their explanatory lines emphasize philosophical relevance and constructive engagement. The book pays attention to due explanation of the issue/topic entries, in the context of which relevant major figures' thoughts are identified.

The third prominent feature is that a comprehensive, relatively up-to-date bibliography is provided. To be more informative and sensitive to readers' needs, the bibliography is organized into various subjects of the movements of thought and a variety of across-the-board subjects.

The book is suitable for undergraduate and post-graduate students, teachers of philosophy, and the interested general reader. This book is suitable for use as a supplementary text or convenient reference book for courses including Chinese philosophy, Asian philosophy, or comparative (Chinese–Western) philosophy at introductory level. In view of some of the aforementioned features, this book is also useful to those experts in the relevant areas who are interested in metaphilo-sophical and methodological issues, substantial interpreta-tions, up-to-date bibliographical information, and pedagogic issues in studies of Chinese philosophy.

Using This Book

(1) Term entries in the book are cross-referenced to show the internal connections of Chinese philosophy and their coherent treatment.

(2) Romanized transcriptions are typically given in the *pinyin* system, which is relatively accurate in transcribing actual pronunciation in Chinese common speech and is currently most widely used.

(3) The Chinese originals for important terms/concepts are given in the main text so that the reader can check and examine the originals of required. This also avoids conflations when two important terms have the same English transliteration (even with the same tone): such as *li* 禮 and *li* 理 (in the Confucian tradition) and *yi* 義 and *yi* 易. For the sake of possible reference need in using Chinese source materials, the Chinese originals are given for the style names 字 and honorific names 號 (if any) of those significant figures cited in the book, as well as their family names and given names. It is noted that the term "Zi"/ "子" in each of those figure entries like "Confucius (Kong Zi)", "Lao Zi", "Xun Zi" and "Zhuang Zi", is neither part of the figure's genuine family name nor this figure's given name; its being attached after a figure's family name constitutes a usual respectful form of address in ancient China, whose function in these figures' cases is similar to that of the term "Master" in English.

(4) The volume contains a bibliography in which entries are

organized into subjects on different movements of thought in Chinese philosophy in various periods of its history such as "Classical Daoism (in the pre-*Han* classical period)" and "Enlightenment Movement (in Modern Chinese Philosophy)" and on different aspects of philosophy generally, such as "Metaphysics and Epistemology" and "Language, Mind, and Logic", as they are presented in Chinese philosophy. In this way, the interested reader can look up further reading on her targeted subject(s).

(5) In the Further reading section at the end of some of the entries, the reader will find suggested further readings in reflective studies of Chinese philosophy, rather than relevant source materials. By default, (selections of) relevant source materials available in English, especially those well-established classics like Confucius' *Lun Yü* (the *Analects*) and Lao Zi's *Dao-De-Jing*, are implicitly suggested. The bibliographical information of a source material reading for an entry is given in the "Source Materials" section(s) of the relevant "movement of thought" part(s) in the Subject Bibliography.

(6) In some of the main text entries, passages end with an asterisk. This serves two purposes: first, it indicates that the content of the passage has as a main reference source the further reading entry with a corresponding asterisk in the "Further reading" at the end of this main text entry; second, such cross-referencing acknowledges the source of the content.

(7) Bearing in mind that readers come primarily from the English-speaking world whose philosophical tradition(s) largely fall into the category of Western philosophy and that readers' prior knowledge of philosophy (if any) is basically that of Western philosophy, a comparative chronology of Chinese and Western philosophers is given so that the reader can contextualize the relevant historical timelines.

Acknowledgements

I would like to thank Oliver Leaman, Editor of the A–Z Series, for his invitation to contribute to the series and for his helpful suggestions. Though, generally speaking, I have more interest in working on research papers than introductory writings, I render the current project reflectively stimulating, challenging, and worthwhile, especially for the sake of the second primary feature of this book as indicated in my "Introduction." I have valued the opportunity and taken the project very seriously.

I am grateful to Brenda Hood and Edward Simetz, who read earlier versions of the manuscript, for their helpful feedback.

I am grateful to the house editors at Edinburgh University Press, Carol Macdonald and Máiréad McElligott, for their kindly and timely professional assistance and support.

Bo Mou
Albany, California
30 December 2008

aesthetics: Aesthetics, the reflective study of (appreciation of) beauty and the arts, has a distinct and special place in Chinese philosophy for three reasons. First, in the standard sense of the term as used in the Western tradition, there is a rich literature in the Chinese classics which reflectively examines such questions as: What is a work of art? What makes a work of art successful? What is the difference between understanding a work of art and failing to do so? Second, there has been a tradition in the Chinese arts that takes a work of art (say, a landscape painting) as a means of delivering certain philosophical ideas; exploration and elaboration of philosophical implications of some works of art are a part of philosophical inquiries in Chinese philosophy. Third, Chinese philosophy has a perennial concern with the relation between the beautiful, the good, and the true.

There have been two basic orientations or attitudes in Chinese philosophy: one renders the three *essentially* in accord and emphasizes their connection and unification. This includes **Lao Zi**'s approach in the ***Dao-De-Jing***, which unifies the three on the basis of the metaphysical *dao* primarily in the sense that they capture the way things are (the *dao*) in their distinct modes, though Lao Zi thought that their social or conventional presentations in human society might be, or appear to be, divergent ["Believable [true] words are not beautiful, while beautiful words are not believable [true]" (Ch. 81)]. The other considers the beautiful and the true to be *essentially* opposed, as **Wang Guo-wei**, a modern Chinese philosopher, highlights: "what is believable [to be true] is not lovable [to be appreciated as an object of beauty], while what is lovable is not believable."

See *dao*; *Dao-De-Jing*; **Lao Zi**; **Wang, Guo-wei**

Further reading: Cai 2004 (2.5.1); Dale 2005 (2.5.1); Gier 2001 (1.2.2); Li 1995 (2.5.1); Saussy 1995 (2.5.1); Zhu 2002 (1.5.2)

Ai, Si-qi 艾思奇 (1910–66) was a Chinese Marxist philosopher who played a significant role in the Sinification of **Marxist philosophy** (i.e., **dialectical materialism** and **historical materialism**), that is, interpreting and developing Marxist philosophy in terms of relevant resources in the Chinese philosophical tradition and applying it to specific Chinese situations and practices. Through many of his writings, especially *Da-Zong-Zhe-Xue* (*Philosophy for the Masses*, 1947), he also played an important role in making Marxist philosophy accessible and understandable to ordinary people in China.

See **dialectical materialism and its development in China**; **historical materialism**; **Marxist philosophy**

Further reading: Fogel 1987 (1.12); Tian 2009 (1.12)

Analects see *Lun-Yü* 論語

analysis / analytic methodology / analytic philosophy: The concept of analysis is an important, even indispensable, conceptual resource in the reflective examination and elaboration of classical Chinese philosophy in the following three senses of the term "analysis". (1) The term "analysis", in its technical sense, means a specific instrumental method that examines concepts typified by definition, breaking concepts into components in a complex structure. This is in contrast to "synthesis." (2) An analytic statement is one whose truth derives solely from its meaning or structure, in contrast to a "synthetic" statement. (3) When the term "analysis," or its cognate "analytic," is associated with a style of doing philosophy ("analytic philosophy" or "analytic approach" in philosophy), understood broadly, its meaning is not limited to its technical sense, but often also means a style of methodological approach, i.e., analytic methodology.

Analytic methodology, understood broadly, is a methodological way of doing philosophy, or a general methodological approach in philosophical inquiry. It is not limited to a single and specific instrumental method (i.e., what "analysis" means in its technical sense, in contrast to "synthesis"), but collectively includes (1) a collection of "analytic" instrumental methods and their associated conceptual and explanatory resources, and (2) a generic type of methodological perspectives that is intended to point to and capture something certain, stable, constant, regular, definite, universal, or unchanging (i.e., the **being**-aspect/dimension/layer, understood in the sense of "being" in contrast to that of "becoming") of an object of study (and/or its conceptual characterization). The two are closely related: the analytic methodological perspective or analytic expectation demands such "analytic" instruments as meaning analysis, conceptual clarity, precise formulation, or rigorous argumentation, by means of which to implement the "analytic" being-aspect-concerned methodological perspective. In this sense, and to this extent, the generic type of analytic methodological perspective underlies various analytic instrumental methods.

In view of this characterization of analytic methodology, three notes are due. First, analytic methodology is not intrinsically or conceptually related to any specific philosophical tradition alone, although, historically speaking, it is prominently manifested in a particular tradition – the analytic tradition of Western philosophy. Analytic strands and elements can be identified explicitly or directly in some of the classical Chinese philosophers' works, such as those of **Gong-sun Long** and the **Mohist**, but also, implicitly or indirectly, in almost all of the classical Chinese philosophers' writings, such as **Confucius'** *Lun-Yü* and **Lao Zi'**s *Dao-De-Jing*. Moreover, there is a signficant **analytic movement in modern Chinese philosophy**.

Second, in the analytic tradition of Western philosophy, analytic methodology can be traced back to Socrates' *elenchus* method, which explicitly took the analytic methodological perspective as well as some analytic instrumental methods. The term "analytic philosophy," when used to indicate one mainstream tradition in Western philosophy, refers to a tradition running from Socrates, Plato, and Aristotle via Descartes, British empiricism, and Kant to the contemporary analytic movement in the twentieth and twenty-first centuries. However, the term is sometimes also used in a narrow sense to refer to the contemporary analytic movement in distinguishing "Anglo-American" from "Continental" philosophy in the twentieth and twenty-first centuries.

Third, analytic methodology as a generic type of methodological perspectives, together with a collection of instrumental methods, is not intrinsically or conceptually related to any *ad hoc* methodological guiding principle concerned with how to look at the relationship between such methodological perspectives and instruments and other types of methodological perspectives and instruments. Historically, analytic methodology was applied by philosophers who might hold or presuppose different methodological guiding principles, some of which were arguably adequate while some others were not. Therefore, analytic methodology is not intrinsically or conceptually associated with any *ad hoc* (adequate or inadequate) methodological guiding principles, though the application of analytic methodology should be, or needs to be, regulated by adequate ones.

Analytic philosophy, understood in methodological terms, means analytic methodology; understood in a more substantial way, it means both analytic methodology and the substantial research results that are achieved by employing analytic methodology.

See **analytic movement in modern Chinese philosophy; argumentation; being versus becoming; Fung, Yu-lan; Gong-sun, Long; Hu, Shi; logical argumentation; Mohism; synthesis/synthetic**

Further reading: Mou 2001b (2.1); Searle 2008 (2.1)

analytic movement in modern Chinese philosophy: The analytic movement in modern Chinese philosophy is a remarkable movement which since the nineteenth century, has strive to pursue philosophical studies by reflectively and explicitly employing analytic methodology within the Chinese philosophical tradition. The development of the analytic movement can be classified into three stages, or rather three closely related and mutually promoted dimensions, insofar as kinds of endeavors in the first and second stages have become important dimensions of the multiple-level endeavor in the third stage. The first is the reflective-introduction stage or dimension, beginning in the late *Qing* Dynasty following the Opium War, (1839–42) at which time many classical works in the analytic tradition of the

Western philosophy were translated into Chinese. The second is the reflective-application stage in which many Chinese scholars consciously applied a variety of analytic instrumental methods and conceptual resources to their philosophical studies, including studies of the classical Chinese philosophy. The third creative-development stage marks two kinds of creative research work which have become prominent: the first comprises creative research projects by native Chinese philosophers in the core areas of contemporary analytic philosophy on its various front issues; the second consists of creative research projects by scholars both in and outside geographic China aiming at exploring how the methodological approaches and/or substantial points of view from analytic philosophy and traditional Chinese philosophy can engage each other and make a joint contribution to the common philosophical enterprise. What characteristically distinguishes the analytic movement in modern Chinese philosophy from the analytic movements in other philosophical traditions lies primarily in the second kind of creative research works.

See **analytic analytic/philosophy methodology; Chinese philosophy; constructive engagement in modern Chinese philosophy**

Further reading: Bunnin 2003 (2.1); Mou 2001a, 2009c (2.1)

argumentation/argument: Argumentation is a defining feature of philosophical inquiry, and Chinese philosophy embraces variety of argumentation, though it cannot be identified exclusively in terms of **logical argumentation**; as Chinese philosophy also includes various types of **evocative argumentation**.

Argumentation, a crucial feature of philosophical inquiry, provides justification or reasons for a claim in philosophy. The reason why argumentation is so crucial is that, in taking nothing for granted, *philosophical* inquiry intrinsically requires argumentation for the sake of justification, in both its critical examination and its positive establishment of conclusions. There are two basic modes of argumentation in philosophy. The first is **logical argumentation**, which covers **deductive argument** and inductive argument; the second is **evocative argumentation**, which covers **argument by analogy**, argument by appealing to value, etc. The two modes are sometimes contrasted as "logical vs. rhetoric," "inferential vs. preferential," or "probative vs. prohairetic." It can be argued that each of the two modes of argumentation cannot be totally immune from the other.

See **argument by analogy; evocative argumentation; logical argumentation;**

Further reading: Mou 2009a (2.1); Rescher 1994 (2.1)

argument by analogy: Argument by analogy is among those extensively used representative forms of argumentation in classical Chinese philosophy, although it is often used in combination with other forms of argumentation. An argument by analogy is one sort of **evocative argumentation**. It draws its conclusion by evoking similarity between certain aspects of two (kinds of) things from, or on the basis of, their similarity in other aspects. For example, the argumentation implicit in **Confucius'** version of the Golden Rule (as delivered in 6.28 of the *Lun-Yü*) illustrates argument by analogy and argument by appealing to value. Confucius teaches that one should treat others in a moral way; he also elaborates how one should treat others. One is expected to identify the moral way based in part on how one would like to be treated – our common human identity results in relevant similarities between moral human beings. Confucius' version of the

Golden Rule guides the moral agent to "draw the analogy from oneself [the way one would desire to be treated]" to how to treat others in a moral way (that is, to evoke the similarity in regard to what would be desired, what would be rendered moral, etc., by both the moral agent and the moral recipient). Furthermore, the moral agent is not expected to start from nowhere, but to be a moral agent possessing (a certain degree of) initial moral sensibility (i.e., a certain level of the virtue of *ren*); this initial moral sensibility serves as the internal starting point of how the moral agent is to adequately draw the analogy.

When applying argument by analogy, one needs to be careful to avoid fallacies. Unlike deductive reasoning, there is no formal procedure or manual; instead there are general guidelines whose application needs to be context- or situation-sensitive. One sort of fallacy here is *mistaking relevant dissimilarities as irrelevant*: an argument by analogy could commit this fallacy when it mistakes relevant dissimilarities between two (kinds of) things as irrelevant to the issue under examination, thus exaggerating their similarities.

See **evocative argumentation; Golden Rule**

B

being versus becoming: The issue of the relation between being/unchanging and becoming/changing was addressed as early as in the **Yi-Jing** text; the issue partially overlaps with, but is not the same as, the issue of *you* versus *wu* in classical Chinese philosophy.

The term "being," when used in its original or broad sense, refers to whatever exists (in a broad sense of "exist"). **Metaphysics**, as the reflective study of existence, is called by Aristotle "the study of being" when the term being is used in this broad sense. The term "being" is also used in a narrow and specific sense in the philosophical context, especially when used in contrast to the meaning of the term "becoming" (i.e., unstable, irregular, indefinite, impermanent, accidental, transient, changing aspect or process of existing things). The term "being" is then intended to denote the stable, constant, certain, permanent, regular, definite, **universal**, or unchanging aspect or layer of existing things. A prominent example of the use of the term "being" in this sense is Parmenides (515–450 BCE). In the history of Western philosophy, the two characteristic uses of the term are closely connected in many philosophers' minds. This is because the stable, constant, certain, regular, definite, permanent, universal, or unchanging aspect of an object is considered its defining or crucial aspect and is supposedly the essence of that object. Thus, the metaphysical study of being as existence is viewed as essentially the study of being as the stable, constant, regular, definite, permanent, universal, or unchanging in existence.

Being, understood in this specific way, and becoming are considered as the two most fundamental modes of existence and thus two fundamental metaphysical categories. Their relationship is viewed as fundamental in metaphysics. What is at issue includes: which one – being or becoming – is more (or the most) fundamental with regard to the origin and constitution of the universe? What is the relation between them? There is a wide spectrum of points of view on such issues. At one end of this spectrum is the view of Parmenides which renders becoming as merely illusionary while maintaining that being is only genuinely real. At the other end of the spectrum is the **Buddhist** view to the effect that only becoming/changing is genuinely real while being or permanence is merely an illusion (*anicca*). Buddhism avoids committing to any distinction that is intrinsically associated with being or permanence, but seeks to maintain the middle way (neither this nor that) by making no fixed distinction.

Between those two positions there is a variety of distinct approaches. Plato's position is kindred in spirit to Parmenides', but still significantly different. In contrast to Parmenides, Plato (428–348 BCE) does not deny the real existence of our sensible world which consists of all particular things. Rather, he renders our *becoming* sensible world less real because he considers becoming less fundamental than *being*: our *becoming* world is only an imperfect copy of the perfect *being* world of Forms. Both Parmenides and Plato maintain the overwhelming priority of being over becoming, though to different extents.

On the other hand, also in the Greek tradition, Heraclitus (535–475 BCE) emphasizes the fundamental status of becoming both as a fundamental mode of existence and as a fundamental driving force for the movement and development of things. It is noted that, in contrast to the Buddhist view, Heraclitus also stresses the role played by *logos* as the principle of change – changing and becoming do not happen in chaos but follow *logos*, which remains constant. Nevertheless, his basic orientation emphasizes the priority of becoming over being. At the level of a thing's constitution, everything in the cosmos is in a state of flux. As far as the changing aspect of a thing is concerned, one cannot step into the same river twice; though Heraclitus actually goes further: "We step into and we do not step into the same rivers. We are and we are not." Given that what is being talked about is whether we can step into the same rivers once, there seem to be two interesting points. First, if the changing of a thing can be characterized in terms of contradictions (it is and it is not), it seems that contradictions truly exist.

Second, an object (a river, a person, etc.) truly possesses being (its unchanging aspect) and becoming (its changing aspect). Several questions remain: What is the nature of *logos*? Does it exist prior to things in the universe or does it supervene them? If both becoming and being play an indispensable role, how do they make this joint play? How should we understand the relation between becoming and being? Heraclitus does not explicitly give us answers to these questions.

There are two other figures in Greek philosophy whose thoughts on the issue of being and becoming are worth mentioning. The first is Democritus (460–370 BCE); the other is Aristotle (384–322 BCE). According to Democritus, the unchanging and permanent features of the universe are based on the eternal, immutable features of atoms. The constant motion of the atoms would account for change and alteration in an unchanging world. He seeks to explain apparent changes in terms of different combinations of atoms. Aristotle suggests his doctrine of matter and form to explain the two basic features, change and permanence, of the material world. According to this doctrine, two basic aspects of the material object are matter and form. Matter, in its pure state, would have no specific characteristics but would only have the potential to receive different forms; the form of the material object at any given time is what it has become, its actuality, at that specific moment. The permanent aspect, matter, of a material object never exists independently of its changing aspect, i.e., its form (one form at one time, another at a later time). Each of these thinkers attempts to reconcile both the being (unchanging) and becoming (changing) of a material object in a non-contradictory or non-paradoxical way.

Indeed, Parmenides and Plato represent a tendency to maintain an overwhelming priority of being over becoming, while Heraclitus in the West and the Buddhist account in the East represent a tendency to champion the overwhelming priority of becoming over being. In contrast, the *yin-yang* **metaphysical vision** as delivered in the original *Yi-Jing* text offers a third approach, which can be characterized in terms of "becoming–being complementarity." This approach renders neither absolutely dominant over the other but *yin-yang* complementary in the sense that being and becoming are interdependent, interactive, intertransforming, and interpenetrating in view of their metaphysical status and character. Whether or not it is a correct to characterize some of the schools in Chinese philosophy in terms of the priority of becoming over being, the *yin-yang* metaphysical vision as delivered in the original *Yi-Jing* text is not as mono-simplex as the becoming-concerned perspective alone. Instead, it is a multilayered metaphysical complex which suggests a balanced metaphysical guiding insight that can be characterized in terms of "becoming–being complementarity." It is noted that some of the subsequent interpretations of the *Yi-Jing* text have tended to highlight its becoming/changing-concerned perspective only, resulting in a tendency to celebrate absolute priority of becoming over being among some later interpreters.

See **Buddhism; metaphysics; universals;** *Yi-Jing*; *yin-yang* **metaphysical vision;** *yin-yang* **way of thinking;** *you* **versus** *wu*

Buddha: The *historical* Buddha, Siddhartha Gautama (sixth century BCE) is the founder of **Buddhism.** The *metaphysical* Buddha, according to *Mahayana* **Buddhism,** is the attribute of enlightenment realized or shared by anyone who achieves *nirvana*.

See **Buddhism;** *Mahayana* **Buddhism;** *nirvana*
Further reading: King 1991 (1.8.2)

Buddhism / Buddhist: Buddhism originated in India and has an historical founder, Siddhartha Gautama, known as the **Buddha** (sixth century BCE). "Buddha" is also used as a title, meaning the "Enlightened One." Theoretically, anyone who is enlightened is Buddha, and all beings are potential Buddhas according to Buddhism.

The core ideas of Buddhism include the Buddha's teachings on three signs of being and the Four Noble Truths (*Si-Sheng-Di* 四聖諦). The three fundamental signs of being (*tri-laksana*) are: (1) suffering (*dukkha*): suffering or dissatisfaction is rooted in the very existence of all living beings in this world; (2) impermanence (*anicca*): there is nothing permanent in the universe; (3) non-self (*anatman*): there is no eternal and permanent soul or changeless entity in the person.

Based on such an understanding, the Four Noble Truths are presented as four closely related statements: (1) all life (birth, old age, sickness, and death) is (filled with) suffering/dissatisfaction (i.e., one of three signs of being: suffering *dukkha*); (2) the origin of suffering lies in clinging to or craving for things that cannot be permament (such as sensual pleasures and self-existence) (*trsna*); (3) one can be liberated from suffering or become enlightened (*nirvana*) by eliminating such craving; (4) the way to eliminate such craving and achieve *nirvana* is the Noble Eightfold Path, which holistically consists of eight aspects/layers: right way of viewing, right thinking, right speech, right conduct, right way of living, right effort, right mindfulness, and right meditative concentration.

The three signs of being, the Four Noble Truths, and the Noble Eightfold Path are considered to be the Buddha's central teachings and thus constitute the essence of Buddhist thought. They are (supposed to be) maintained by various subsequent Buddhist schools of thought. The Buddha's (the Gautama's) life, the Buddha's teachings (the *dharma*), and the Buddhist community (the *sangha*) are viewed as the three jewels of Buddhism.

There are two basic types of Buddhism. The first is *Hinayana* Buddhism, which is also called "Small Vehicle" (*xiao-cheng* 小乘) Buddhism. It emphasizes that each individual rides his own "Small Vehicle" to save himself and takes self-enlightenment with wisdom as its ideal. This was the mainstream Buddhism within Indian Buddhism or *Pali* Buddhism (Buddhism delivered in the Indian Pali language). The other type is **Mahayana Buddhism**, also labeled "Great Vehicle" (*da-cheng* 大乘) Buddhism. This stresses that all individuals ride together in the Great Vehicle toward salvation and takes the compassionate salvation of others as its ideal. Various forms of **Chinese Buddhism** belong to the tradition of *Mahayana* Buddhism. Geographically, *Mahayana* spread in north and east Asia and is thus also called "Northern Buddhism," while *Hinayana* (nowaday usually called *Theravada* for some historical reason) is strong in south and southeast Asia and is thus also called "Southern Buddhism." Though a minority trend within Indian Buddhism and in south/southeast Asia, *Mahayana* Buddhism is now the mainstream Buddhism worldwide.

See **Buddha; Buddhist *karma* and *samsara*; *Chan/Zen* Buddhism; Consciousness-Only Buddhism; *Hua-Yan* Buddhism; *Mahayana* Buddhism; Three-Treatise Buddhism; *Tian-Tai* Buddhism**

Further reading: Cheng 2005 (1.8.2); Garfield 2001 (1.8.2); Lai 1997, 2009 (1.8.2); Takakusu 1956 (1.8.2)

Buddhist *karma* and *samsara*: In Buddhism, the term *samsara* means reincarnation, transmigration, or the cycle or chain of birth and death. The term *karma* means law of cause and effect, deed, or action. There is no *samsara* without *karma*; reincarnation takes place due to a causal factor. Whenever a person does anything (acts, speaks, or even thinks), it produces a result, no matter how distant. This result is the effect or retribution of that action as *karma*. According to Buddhism, one's whole existence is made up of a chain of cause and effect; one's present state is determined by one's past *karma*, and one's destiny will be determined by one's present *karma*, good or bad. Consequently, what one does now will bear fruit in one's future life. Because one's birth and death will be repeated again and again, *samsara* itself is considered to be a chain of suffering. The root cause of the chain and all suffering is ignorance (*avidya* or *wu-ming* 無明 in Chinese): the fundamental illusion of the existence of permanence. From ignorance comes a craving for and cleaving to things that cannot be permanent; the individual in a state of ignorance is thus bound to eternal *samsara*. The only hope for escaping this chain of suffering lies in replacing ignorance with enlightenment (*Bodhi*). All the teachings and practices of various Buddhist schools are attempts to contribute to enlightenment. The result of enlightenment is to achieve **nirvana**, on emancipation from the *karma* cycle.

See **Buddhism; *nirvana***

Further reading: Zeuschner 1981 (1.8.2)

C

Chan* (*Zen*) Buddhism** (Chan-Zong*** 禪宗): The Chinese term *Chan* 禪 (*Zen* in Japanese) is the Chinese transliteration of the Sanskrit term *dhyana*, meaning meditation. *Chan* Buddhism is known for its unique characterization of meditation. *Chan* Buddhism is a type of Buddhism that combines **Three-Treatise (Middle-Way) Buddhism**

(i.e., the *Madhyamika* school) in *Mahayana* **Buddhism** with (*philosophical*) **Daoism**. *Chan* Buddhism has been described as a radical re-formation or revolution in **Buddhism** for the following reason. *Chan* is one of the products of traditional Chinese philosophy, largely philosophical Daoism, following its contact with Indian thought, which was introduced into China in the first century CE through the medium of Buddhist teachings. In the early stage of its development, *Chan* Buddhism consisted of the Northern School, whose founder was Shen Xiu 神秀 (605–706), and the Southern School, whose founder was **Hui Neng** 慧能 (638–713). Shen Xiu emphasized gradual enlightenment, while Hui Neng stressed sudden enlightenment. The Southern School was thus also called the "Sudden Enlightenment" School. The Southern School became so influential that the history of *Chan* Buddhism became that of the Southern School from the ninth century.

Chan Buddhism combines Three-Treatise (Middle-Way) Buddhism with Daoism as follows. What is called by **Ji Zang** (a systematic interpreter of Three-Treatise Buddhism), in his double-truth account (*er-di-lun*), "higher-sense truth" at the third/highest level (i.e., the highest truth about which we cannot affirm anything via finite and relative predicates) is identified by *Chan* Buddhism as the first principle. In *Chan* Buddhism's terms, the first principle, like the eternal *dao* as a whole, cannot be exhausted by any finite expressions; and any conceptualization with distinction and definiteness would distort the first principle. Paradoxically, knowledge of the first principle is characterized as knowledge that is non-knowledge; non-paradoxically, knowledge of the first principle is knowledge that is beyond that which is conventionally characterized as consisting of definite concepts and categorized distinctions.

In a paradoxical way, the Chanist method of cultivation is characterized as cultivation that is non-cultivation, or cultivation in terms of non-cultivation: in a nonparadoxical way, it emphasizes cultivating without deliberate effort and a purposeful mind. The practice of cultivation is in itself only a sort of preparatory work; to achieve enlightenment, this sort of cultivation must climax in sudden enlightenment. Sudden enlightenment refers to a kind of qualitative psychological leap to reach comprehension of the *dao* (being one with the *dao*). In such enlightenment, all fixed distinctions are gone (emptiness) to the effect that there ceases to be a fixed distinction between the experiencer and the experienced (like one who drinks water knows by oneself whether it is cold or warm). *Chan* Buddhism also emphasizes the attainment of non-attainment. The attainment of sudden enlightenment does not imply the attainment of anything further or anything else; what is different is the person himself or herself who is enlightened, although what the person does is no different from what everyone else does and from what that person did before.

See **Buddhism; Daoism;** *er-di-lun*; **Hui, Neng; Ji, Zang;** *Mahayana* **Buddhism; Three-Treatise (Middle-Way) Buddhism**

Further Reading: Buswell 1992 (1.8.2); Chan 1963, Ch. 26 (1.8.1); Chang (Chung-yuan) 1971 (1.8.2); Cheng (Chung-yin) 1973 (1.8.2); Cheng (Hsueh-li) 1981 (1.8.2); Dumoulin 1988 (1.8.2); Faure 1991, 1993 (1.8.2); Gimello and Gregory 1983 (1.8.2); Lancaster and Lai 1983 (1.8.2); McRae 1986 (1.8.2); Zeuschner 1981 (1.8.2)

cheng 誠 (**sincerity**): The notion of *cheng*, as emphasized in the **Confucian** tradition, means the virtue of sincerity or truthfulness. Especially in the early Confucian texts, it means an ideal state in which the heart is fully or wholly directed toward being good or moral sensibility. A related notion in the Confucian tradition is *cheng-yi* 誠意, which means making one's thoughts sincere as presented in the *Da-Xue*, along with *ge-wu* (investigating things), *zhi-zhi* (extending knowledge), and *zheng-xin* (rectifying the heart) as four steps in the process of self-cultivation. In **Neo-Confucianism** (say, in **Zhou Dun-yi**'s works), *cheng* is not merely a psychological state or moral virtue, but a metaphysical state that everything is to obtain its correct nature and destiny. *Cheng* is taken as the ultimate metaphysical principle, standing for the way of heaven (the ultimate source of creativity for all things). When it is embodied in humans, it is the virtue that characterizes the moral sage who is in complete union with the way of heaven.*

See **Confucianism**; *Da-Xue*; *ge-wu-zhi-zhi*; **Neo-Confucianism**; **Zhou, Dun-yi**

Further reading: Shun 2003 (1.2.2)*

Cheng, Hao (Ch'eng Hao) 程顥 (style name "Bo-chun" 伯淳; honorific name "Ming-dao" 明道: 1032–85) and his younger brother **Cheng Yi (Ch'eng I)** 程頤 (style name "Zheng-shu" 正叔; honorific name "Yi-chuan" 伊川: 1033–1107) are known as "Er-Cheng" (the two Chengs) for their joint role in founding **Neo-Confucianism**. The two Chengs studied under **Zhou Dun-yi** and paved a new way in **Confucianism** by making *li* 理 the central concept of Neo-Confucianism and thus establishing its metaphysical foundation. Their approach in this regard was influenced by their study of **Daoism** and **Buddhism** prior to their conversion to Confucianism.

There are significant differences between Cheng Hao and Cheng Yi, which led to a fundamental difference between the two basic schools of Neo-Confucianism. Cheng Hao considered (1) the mind-heart (*xin*) to be the sole agent in understanding moral principles; and (2) the goal of learning to be the activation of one's innate ability and the attainment of spiritual enlightenment from within. His approach was further developed into the *xin-xue* of **Lu Jiu-yuan** and **Wang Shou-ren**. In contrast, Cheng Yi rendered the mind-heart and the empirical study of the external world equally important to the discovery of moral principles and emphasized both internal awakening and external conformity to adequate principles of action. Cheng Yi's approach set the stage for the *li-xue* of Cheng Yi and **Zhu Xi**.

The two Chengs' works are collected in *Er-Cheng-Quan-Shu* (*Complete Works of the Two Chengs*).

See **Confucianism**; *li*; *li-xue*; Lu, Jiu-yuan; Neo-Confucianism; Wang, Shou-ren; *xin-xue*; Zhou, Dun-yi; Zhu, Xi

Further reading: Graham 1992 (1.9.2); Hon 2003 (1.9.2)

Cheng, Yi (Ch'eng I) 程頤 see **Cheng, Hao**

Chinese Buddhism see *Chan* Buddhism; *Hua-Yan* Buddhism; *Mahayana* Buddhism; Pure-Land Buddhism; Three-Treatise Buddhism; *Tian-Tai* Buddhism

Chinese language and its related folk way of thinking: It seems that the characteristic features of the Chinese language have influenced or encouraged certain orientations in the Chinese (folk and reflective) way of thinking. There are some well-known facts about certain features of the Chinese ideographic language in comparison and contrast to Western phonetic languages (say, English) that might reflect distinctive orientations or tendencies of the ways of thinking in the two types of linguistic communities. We know how we as English speakers give our names and addresses: we first give our given names or surname (thus they being called our "first name") and then give our family names or surname (thus they being called our "last name"). However, in Chinese, the family name goes first (thus the family name is really the first name), followed by the given name. So, for example, the order of this author's name in Chinese is Mou Bo and not Bo Mou as given on the cover of this book. For, in philosophical terms, the family (name) is both metaphysically and logically prior to the individual (name), and the former provides a necessary holistic background for understanding the latter. By the same token, a postal address when delivered in the Chinese way would be: "USA, California, San Jose, San Jose State University, Department of Philosophy, Mou Bo"; that is, the largest thing comes first while the smallest thing comes last. It is arguably right that the structure of the Chinese language in this respect to some extent bears on the orientation of the way of thinking of the Chinese people as a whole.

Two points are due. First, the relationship between them is bi-directional not one-directional. The actual situation might be this: as the Chinese language originally took shape, it was influenced by the way people at that time thought; when such an influence was eventually manifested through some relatively stable syntactic–semantic features of the Chinese language, the latter conversely influenced the way of thinking of Chinese language speakers. Second, the foregoing influence implies neither that people who speak Chinese tend to put the family or collective interest first nor that English speakers tend to do the opposite. Other relevant elements can also contribute to what is really happening in this connection. Even if such distinctive linguistic ordering indeed influences priority in our mind, it seems that one might actually think about all the things involved simultaneously in some linguistic contexts, though saying them in a certain order.

See **Chinese language and reflective way of thinking in Chinese philosophy; ideographic language**

Further reading: Hansen 1992, Ch.1 (2.5.2); Mou 2006 (2.5.2)

Chinese language and reflective way of thinking in Chinese philosophy: The issue of relating Chinese thought to the structure and functions of the Chinese language has for generations tantalized sinologists and philosophers concerned with the issue. In recent decades, significant progress has been made in this regard. One suspects that the structures (the surface and deep ones together) and uses of different languages might play roles in pushing philosophical theorization in different directions. How one speaks and writes the Chinese language might somehow reveal and reflect Chinese folk ideology and then influence the ways in which certain philosophical questions are posed and certain ontological insights are formed. Among others, some engaging approaches have been suggested.

A mass-noun hypothesis concerning the issue (Hansen 1983) consists of the following points: (1) the (folk) semantics of Chinese nouns are like those of mass-nouns (i.e., those nouns referring to the so-called interpenetrating stuffs, like "water" and "snow"), and naming in Chinese is not grounded on the existence of, or roles for, abstract entities, either on the ontic level or on the conceptual level, but rather on finding "boundaries" between things; (2) influenced by mass-noun semantics, the classical Chinese semantic theorists and ontological theorists view words in ways that are natural to view mass-nouns rather than count-nouns, and Chinese theorists tend to organize the objects in the world in a mereological stuff–whole model of reality (the term "mereology," in its technical sense in mathematics, means the theory of the relation of parts to whole); (3) the language theory of classical Chinese philosophers thus differs fundamentally from the language theory of Western philosophy. This hypothesis has been challenged in several ways.

One way is to challenge the mass-stuff model from the perspective of a holographic process ontology (Cheng 1987; Hall and Ames 1987). They focus on the case analysis of the typical philosophical nouns or terms, such as "*tai-ji*," "*wu*," "*yin-yang*," "*wu-xing*", which constitute the basic lexicon (vocabulary) of Chinese metaphysical systems. They argue that those nouns stand for interpenetrating wholes and parts in a quite different sense from the mass-noun hypothesis: the individual things behave in ongoing patterns and in the events or processes of interaction among them; the universe behaves as an organic whole, with parts exemplifying the structure of the whole. They claim that Chinese words in general share this ontological feature of combining universality and particularity, abstractness and concreteness, activity and the result of activity. In this way, some writers (e.g. Hall and Ames 1987) prefer to consider the relations of "parts" and "wholes" in terms of the "focus" and "field" model and take Chinese ontological views as holographic rather than mereological.

Another way is to directly challenge the mass-noun hypothesis by arguing that there is a clear grammatical distinction in classical Chinese between count-nouns and other nouns (Harbsmeier 1989). It is claimed that there is a clear grammatical distinction in classical Chinese between count-nouns and other nouns (generic nouns and mass-nouns), thus rendering the mass-noun hypothesis "historically implausible and grammatically quite wrong-headed." However, it is noted that the mass-noun hypothesis is not a grammatical claim that classical Chinese nouns have mass-noun grammar but a semantic interpretive hypothesis that the semantics of Chinese nouns may be like those of mass-nouns, and classical Chinese theorists view words in ways that are natural to view mass-nouns. But this criticism is not irrelevant in the following sense: the alleged distinction between count-nouns and other nouns is not merely grammatical but also semantic; the mass-noun hypothesis thus needs to deal with the linguistic (semantic) evidence against it.

Another challenge to the mass-noun hypothesis is presented by the collective-noun hypothesis, though it is also in a semantic perspective and within the mereological-analysis track (Mou 1999). Its main ideas are these. (1) Chinese common nouns typically function, semantically and syntactically, in the way collective nouns (i.e., nouns that denote collections of individual things, like the English nouns "people" and "cattle") function, and the folk semantics of Chinese nouns are like those of collective nouns. (2) Their implicit ontology is a mereological ontology of collection of individuals both with the part–whole structure and with the member–class structure, which does justice to the role of abstraction at the conceptual level. (3) Encouraged and shaped by the folk semantics of Chinese nouns, the classical Chinese theorists of language take this kind of mereological nominalism for granted. As a result, the classical Platonic one–many problem in the Western philosophical tradition has not been consciously posed in the Chinese philosophical tradition; hence, classical Chinese philosophers seem less interested in debating the relevant ontological issues in a way typical of the Western tradition.

See **Chinese language and its related folk way of thinking**

Further reading: Cheng 1987 (2.5.2); Hall 2001 (2.1); Hansen 1983 (2.5.2); Harbsmeier 1989 (2.5.2); Mou 1999 (2.5.2)

Chinese philosophy: Chinese philosophy has been shaped over the last 3,000 years by various movements and thinkers under examination in this book. The history of Chinese philosophy can be classified into two major parts: classical Chinese philosophy (from the *Zhou* Dynasty, roughly the eleventh century to 256 BCE, through to the early *Qing* Dynasty), and modern Chinese philosophy (from the late *Qing* Dynasty through to the twenty-first century). Classical Chinese philosophy can be further classified into three distinctive periods respectively labeled: (1) classical Chinese philosophy in the pre-*Han* period (roughly from the eleventh century to 206 BCE), (2) classical Chinese philosophy from *Han* through to *Tang* (roughly from 206 BCE to 618), (3) classical Chinese philosophy from *Song* through to early *Qing* (roughly from 618 to 1839).

The identity of Chinese philosophy needs explanation and clarification. Some say that ancient Chinese thought lacked any explicit separation between literature, history, and philosophy. If this is the case, then is it legitimate to single out a history of Chinese philosophy? This is true in the sense that writers in the classical period did not make the conceptual distinction between intellectual disciplines that we do. Applying that distinction to ancient Chinese materials reveals about the same degree of overlap and distinctiveness as it does to ancient Western materials, which also did not distinguish what we now call "philosophy" from wisdom or what is called "natural philosophy" (incipient science). In keeping with this consideration, we can soundly and reflectively focus on the philosophical aspects and dimensions of texts which also have historical and literary value and content. So nothing in this observation about Chinese thought prevents us from reflecting on the philosophical significance of an idea or approach in the tradition where its philosophical value and inferential connection with other concerns, issues, ideas, or approaches could also be given an historical or literary description. In giving the philosophical dimension, we legitimately focus on an interest or agenda that we have now in trying to understand an aspect of Chinese culture; we can do this without denying that other kinds of understanding and elaboration are possible. We can answer the familiar charge that ancient Chinese thought makes no distinction between philosophy and religion in the same way. We have the conceptual resources to distinguish between thinkers, themes, ideas, and arguments that are more or less philosophical or religious. Given our understanding of philosophical inquiry and how its methodology differs from a religious methodology, the overlap of subject matter, and the fact that the methods are mixed, do not prevent our highlighting or discussing the philosophical distinctions and reflecting on how the overlap might or might not be relevant to a proper understanding of ancient Chinese philosophy and religion. For these reasons, the current book is called *Chinese Philosophy A–Z* and not *Chinese Thought A–Z* or *Chinese Religious Thought A–Z*.

See **philosophy**

Further reading: Cua 2003 (2.1); Defoort 2001 (2.1); Fung 1948 (2.1); Hall 2001 (2.1); Hansen 1992 (2.1); Mou 2009a (2.1)

Classical (pre-*Qin*) Confucianism 前秦儒學: Classical Confucianism is a school of thought formed during the first major stage of the development of (philosophical) **Confucianism**. Classical Confucianism as a movement with philosophical significance was initially developed by **Confucius** and further developed by **Mencius, Xun Zi**, etc. Its primary texts include the *Lun-Yü, Mencius, Xun-Zi, Yi-Zhuang* (*Ten Wings*, largely Confucian commentaries on the original *Yi-Jing* text), *Da-Xue*, and *Zhong-Yong*. These become the classical texts of the whole Confucian tradition; this school of thought within Confucianism is thus called "classical Confucianism." One central concern among the classical Confucian philosophers is with how one is to carry out moral **sage**; **self-cultivation** to become a *jun-zi* (a morally superior person) or moral **sage** via *nei-sheng-wai-wang* (inner sageliness and outer kingliness); this central concern has become a primary Confucian mission to be fulfilled throughout the Confucian tradition.

See **Confucianism; Confucius;** *Da-Xue; jun-zi; Lun-Yü;* **Mencius;** *Mencius; nei-sheng-wai-wang;* **sage; self-cultivation; Xun, Zi;** *Xun-Zi; Yi-Zhuang; Zhong-Yong*

Further reading: Chong 2007 (1.2.2); Yao 2000 (1.2.2)

Classical Daoism / Lao-Zhuang Daoism / Lao-Zhuang Philosophy 老莊道家哲學: Classical Daoism usually means the philosophical thoughts presented in the two **Daoist** classics, the *Dao-De-Jing* and the *Zhuang-Zi*. As **Lao Zi** and **Zhuang Zi** are usually considered respectively as the legendary authors or proxy figures of the two classics, classical Daoism is also called Lao-Zhuang Daoism or Lao-Zhuang philosophy. Classical Daoism understood in a broad sense also includes **Yang Zhu**'s relevant views and certain basic insights and ideas as presented in those ancient texts, like the original *Yi-Jing* text and the *Lie-Zi*, which are similar to, or kindred in spirit with, some of the basic thoughts in the two basic Daoist classics. The three classical Daoist texts, the *Dao-De-Jing*, the *Zhuang-Zi*, and the *Yi-Jing*, were later collectively labeled the *San-Xue* (三玄 *the Three Profound Treatises*).

See *Dao-De-Jing;* **Daoism; Lao, Zi;** *Lie-Zi;* **Yang, Zhu;** *Yi-Jing;* **Zhuang, Zi;** *Zhuang-Zi* comparative philosophy: Comparative philosophy, understood in a broad, constructive way (see below), is intrinsically related to *philosophical* scholarship of studies of **Chinese philosophy**. A philosopher studying Chinese philosophy is intrinsically interested in distinct approaches (from other philosophical traditions and/or from different styles/orientation of doing philosophy) to those issues, problems, theme, or topics in his or her philosophical inquiries into Chinese philosophy.

The identity and nature of what the phrase "comparative philosophy" is to refer to have been understood in various ways. Understood narrowly, comparative philosophy is sometimes taken to be limited to comparative studies of different philosophical approaches from different ethnic/national traditions or groups; it is sometimes considered to focus merely on the philosophical works of "under-represented" ethnic/national groups. Understood in another narrow or less philosophically interesting way, comparative philosophy as a whole is taken to focus on a historical description of what appear to be similarities and dissimilarities between different ideas or figures from different ethnic traditions of thought. Understood in a broad and constructive way, comparative philosophy considers philosophy in a global context and emphasizes the **constructive engagement** of distinct approaches and resources from different philosophical traditions and/or different styles/orientations of doing philosophy. Generally speaking, the constructive engagement strategy of comparative philosophy is this: to inquire into how, via reflective criticism and self-criticism, distinct modes of thinking, methodological approaches, visions, substantial points of view, or conceptual and explanatory resources from different philosophical traditions and/or from different styles/orientations of doing philosophy (within or without the same tradition), can learn from each other and jointly contribute to a series of commonly concerned issues or topics of philosophical significance. It is noted that *commonly concerned* issues or topics (common concerns for short) are identified in comparative studies through *philosophical interpretation* and for the sake of enhancing our understanding and treatment of the issues and topics in philosophical inquiries, instead of being *exclusively* relied on, or determined by, a historical description of what the (ancient) figures or texts under examination literally said.

There are various orientations together with their distinct methodological approaches in comparative studies that are somehow related to comparative philosophy understood in the foregoing way. Among others, there are three major types: (1) the historical-description-concerned orientation that aims to give accurate descriptions of relevant historical matters of fact and making historical data collection and examination; (2) the interpretation-concerned orientation that aims to enhance our understanding of a thinker's ideas and their relevance to the philosophical issue we are concerned with through elaborating due implications of the text and ideas of the thinker via relevant and effective conceptual and explanatory resources, whether or not those resources were actually used by the thinker; (3) the philosophical-issue-concerned orientation that aims at how thinkers' ideas under comparative examination can make joint contributions to some commonly concerned issues, themes, or topics of philosophical significance. With due understanding of their respective aims, functions, and limits, on the one hand, the three orientations and their related methodological approaches can be complementary. On the other hand, (3) and (2) are closely related and most philosophically relevant to the common philosophical enterprise. The reflective efforts in (3) understand ancient thinkers' views and identify commonly concerned issues or topics through reflective interpretation made in (2). It is noted that comparative philosophy understood in the above broad and constructive way is intrinsically related to **world philosophy**: comparative philosophy via the constructive engagement of philosophies throughout the world moves toward world philosophy.

Comparative Chinese–Western philosophy, theoretically and practically speaking, has been a significant part of comparative philosophy. Theoretically speaking, the Chinese and Western philosophical traditions are both several thousand-year-long traditions with their rich resources subjected to comparative examination. Practically speaking, currently, there are more research personnel and research results in the literature than any other tradition versus tradition comparative studies in philosophy.

See **Chinese philosophy; constructive engagement (methodology/purpose); world philosophy**

Further reading: Allinson 2001 (2.1); Littlejohn 2006 (2.1); Mou 2006b and 2009c (2.1); Wong 2005 (2.1)

conduct ethics: Although the classical Chinese moral philosophy is primarily virtue-concerned and is thus usually characterized in terms of **virtue ethics**, and although there has been a relatively explicit distinction has been made between virtue ethics-oriented and conduct ethics-oriented moral thought in the Western tradition, the Chinese ethical tradition has also paid much attention to conduct ethics, and the conduct concern and the virtue concern in the Chinese tradition are essentially correlated and treated in a complementary way. The relation between *li* 禮 and *ren* in Confucius' teachings well illustrates this point. Nevertheless, the conceptual distinction between virtue ethics and conduct ethics is reflectively illuminating and effective in analyzing the structure and contents of the classical Chinese moral philosophy.

Generally speaking, in contrast to virtue ethics, conduct ethics is a kind of ethics which focuses on and evaluates the actions of a moral agent or things that directly relate his or her actions (actions *per se*, consequence of the action; motive for the action, etc.). The basic questions in conduct ethics are these: What should I do? How should I perform moral actions? There are two basic approaches in conduct ethics: **consequentialism** and non-consequentialism/deontology. Consequentialism means those ethical theories that judge the moral rightness or wrongness of an action according to the desirability or undesirability of the action's consequences. (e.g. ethical **egoism; utilitarianism**). In contrast, non-consequentialist (roughly, deontological) ethics contends that the moral rightness or wrongness of an action is determined by more than, or something other than, the likely consequences of that action. We can take for example, moral evaluation based on the intrinsic moral value of the action itself (e.g. Kantian ethics).

Though being distinct in conception and theoretical elaboration, conduct ethics and virtue ethics can be complementary kinds or aspects of ethics as a whole. This has been shown in some of the prominent movements in classical Chinese moral philosophy.

See **consequentialism; egoism; ethics;** *li* 禮**; morality;** *ren***; utilitarianism; virtue ethics**

Confucianism (*Ru-Jia* 儒家) **/ Confucian**: Confucianism is a major and significant movement in Chinese philosophy. The literal sense of the original Chinese term *ru-jia* for Confucianism is not related to that of the term "Confucianism" but denotes a group of scholars who studied the *Liu-Yi* (六藝 the six classics in liberal arts, such as the *Yi-Jing*)' for '(the Six Classics or six liberal arts). Confucius did not originate the school, which was formed before his time. Nevertheless, he was the key figure in turning the earlier liberal arts school into a major, philosophically significant movement of thought. To this extent, it makes sense to translate the term *ru-jia* as "Confucianism" when *ru-jia* is primarily intended to mean the school as a philosophical movement of thought with regard to humanism.

Even after Confucius, there are three meanings of "Confucianism". (1) *philosophical Confucianism*: the philosophical tradition of those thinkers like **Confucius, Mencius, Xun Zi, Zhu Xi,** and **Wang Shou-ren** which has been revived by contemporary Confucians; (2) *politicized Confucianism*: the tradition of **Dong Zhong-shu** and others which served as the official ideology starting in the *Han* Dynasty and took in ingredients from schools of thought such as **Daoism**; and (3) *popular Confucianism*: beliefs at the grassroots level that emphasize concepts such as family values, diligence, and education and can hardly be separated from other beliefs in popular **Buddhism** and Daoism, including, for example, various superstitions. The term "Confucianism" used in this book primarily means philosophical Confucianism.

The mission of (philosophical) Confucianism can be highlighted in terms of the slogan *nei-sheng-wai-wang* (inner sageliness and outer kingliness) which captures the two intrinsically-related aspects of the Confucian mission: on the one hand, one is to strive to become a *jun-zi*, (morally superior person); on the other hand, one is to actively participate in social transformation to help others and the whole of society improve in accordance with *ren* and *li* 禮.

There are three major stages of the development of (philosophical) Confucianism: (1) **classical Confucianism:**

Confucius, Mencius, Xun Zi, etc.; (2) **Neo-Confucianism** (*Song-Ming* Confucianism): Zhu Xi, Wang Shou-ren, etc. (3) **contemporary Neo-Confucianism** in the twentieth and twenty-first centuries.

See **classical Confucianism; Confucius; Contemporary Neo-Confucianism; humanism;** *jun-zi;* **li** 禮**; Mencius; moral cultivation; Neo-Confucianism;** *ren;* **Wang, Shou-ren; Xun, Zi; Zhu, Xi**

Further reading: Liu 1998 (1.2.2); Nivison 1996 (1.2.2); Shun 2005 (1.2.2); Yao 2000 (1.2.2)

Confucius (Kong Zi) 孔子 (given name "Qiu" 丘; style name "Zhong-ni" 仲尼: 551–479 BCE) was born in the State of *Lu*, a region located in today's Shandong Province, China. Confucius was the key figure in the formation and development of **Confucianism** (*Ru-Jia*) into a movement of thought with philosophical significance (i.e., philosophical Confucianism). Confucius' teachings were written down by his followers over the centuries after his death. This text is called the *Lun-Yü* (the *Analects*).

Confucius' primary concern is how one can morally cultivate oneself into a *jun-zi* (a morally superior person or a gentleman with ideal moral character – the fully achieved virtue *ren*). Behind Confucius' pursuit of the ideal moral character lies his understanding of the fundamental value of the human being that the ultimate concern a person should have, and also the primary worthwhile thing a person can do, is to strive to become a *jun-zi*. Moral **self-cultivation** has to be pursued for its own sake and with complete indifference to success or failure and to rewards, whether after death or in this life.

See **classical Confucianism; Confucianism;** *jun-zi; Lun-Yü; ren;* **self-cultivation**

Further reading: Ames 2003 (1.2.2); Creel 1960 (1.2.2); Fingerette 1972 (1.2.2); Ivanhoe 2002 (1.2.2)

Consciousness-Only Buddhism (*Wei-Shi-Zong*) 唯識宗: It is
also called "the school of *Yogacara*" (瑜伽學), or it is the
Chinese version of *Yogacara* Buddhism as **Xuan Zang**
(玄奘 596–664) translated into Chinese, and interpreted,
many *Yogacara* texts. It is one of the two major schools
in ***Mahayana* Buddhism**.

According to Consciousness-Only Buddhism, all existence is nothing but consciousness; there is nothing
outside the mind. The question that arises asks how this
is possible. Consciousness-Only Buddhism attempted to
answer the question in terms of its central doctrine.
According to this school, there are eight consciousnesses: the five sense consciousnesses (eyes, ears, nose,
tongue, and body); the sixth consciousness is the sense-
center consciousness or perception; the seventh is the
thought-center consciousness which wills and reasons;
and the eighth is the storehouse consciousness. These
eight consciousnesses endlessly evolve through three
kinds of transformation. The first kind of transformation is that of the storehouse consciousness: the storehouse consciousness stores the "seeds" or effects of
good and evil deeds which become the energy to produce
manifestations (現行); it is constantly "perfumed" (薰
influenced) by incoming perceptions and cognitions
from manifestations, while it endows them with the
energy of the seeds, which produce manifestations. Such
simultaneous interaction of the seeds was summarized
by the school in this way:

   (i)   seeds produce manifestations or the external
         world;
   (ii) seeds are perfumed by manifestations/the exter-
         nal world;
   (iii) the three elements (seeds, manifestations, and
         perfuming) turn on and on [seeds produces
         more seeds];

(iv) the cause and effect occur at one and the same time.

The second kind of transformation is that of the seventh consciousness which, unlike the other six consciousnesses and instead of external manifestations, has as its object the eighth consciousness. The third kind of transformation is that of the five sense consciousnesses and the sixth "sense-center" consciousness out of whose roles of discrimination and differentiation the external world appears: each of the five sense consciousnesses has its specific and distinct objects, while the sixth consciousness has the whole external world as its object. All three kinds of transformations simultaneously interact with each other via the law of cause and effect.*

The influence of the school began to decline around the ninth century, but continued to have an impact on subsequent Chinese philosophers. For example, **Xiong Shi-li**, a modern Chinese philosopher, strived to re-establish new **Confucianism**, basing it in part on Consciousness-Only Buddhism.

See **Buddhism**; *Mahayana* **Buddhism; Xiong Shi-li; Xuan, Zang**

Further reading: Chan 1963, Ch. 23 (2.2)*; Jiang 2006 (1.8); Lusthaus 2003 (1.8)

consequentialism: Some strands and thoughts in classical Chinese moral philosophy, such as those in **Yangists'** ethical **egoism** and **Mohists' utilitarianism,** manifest themselves in the orientation or direction of consequentialism. Consequentialism is one approach in **conduct ethics,** which judges the moral rightness or wrongness of an action according to the desirability or undesirability of the action's consequences (also teleological ethics). Consequentialism may be narrow in scope (e.g., egoism or nationalism) or wide in scope (e.g. utilitarianism or **Buddhism**). Different theories may emphasize different outcomes –pleasure, happiness, wealth, etc. In contrast, non-consequentialism (also identified as deontological ethics) maintains that the moral rightness of an action is a function of something *other than* its consequences (e.g. duty, past actions, desire, justice, or merit). Kantian ethics is an example of deontological ethics.

See **Buddhism; conduct ethics; egoism; Mohists; utilitarianism; Yangists**

constructive engagement (methodology/purpose): The constructive-engagement methodology in philosophy is especially relevant to recent developments in Chinese philosophy and comparative Chinese–Western philosophy. It has significantly contributed to the emergence and development of the **constructive engagement movement in modern Chinese philosophy.**

The conception of constructive engagement is a kind of methodological guiding principle and reflective goal in comparative philosophy specifically speaking, and in philosophical inquiry generally speaking. It is to inquire into how, via reflective criticism and self-criticism, distinct modes of thinking, methodological approaches, visions, substantial points of view, or conceptual and explanatory resources from different philosophical traditions and/or from different styles/orientations of doing philosophy (within or without the same tradition), can learn from each other and jointly contribute to the common philosophical enterprise and a series of issues and topics of philosophical significance.

See **comparative philosophy; constructive engagement movement in modern Chinese philosophy; methodology**

Further reading: Mou 2009b (2.1)

constructive engagement movement in modern Chinese philosophy: The constructive engagement movement is a recent trend in modern Chinese philosophy and in comparative philosophy especially in the late twentieth and earlier twenty-first centuries. Its identity can be viewed from different angles. As a collective trend in comparative philosophy, it considers philosophy in a global context and through the **constructive engagement** of philosophies from around the world. As a collective enterprise in modern Chinese philosophy, it emphasizes the **constructive engagement** between Chinese philosophy and Western philosophy (or any other philosophical traditions) and between distinct movements of thought within Chinese philosophy on a series of issues and topics of philosophical significance. They share the same **constructive engagement methodology** as a kind of methodological guiding principle in their reflective pursuits.

The label "the constructive engagement movement" in modern Chinese philosophy can be understood in both a weak sense and a strong sense. In its weak sense, the phrase means a collective trend in recent decades in studies of Chinese philosophy and comparative Chinese–Western philosophy in the direction of the foregoing constructive engagement, whether or not its metaphilosophical and methodological issues have been consciously and systematically examined, whether or not the trend has its explicit systematic agenda in print, and whether or not it has been explicitly promoted by a certain academic organization with an articulate constructive engagement purpose. In its stronger sense, the term means a movement that has emerged especially since the beginning of the twenty-first century: the movement goes with its explicitly specified reflective purpose, some related academic organizations or institutions as a collective driving force, various coordinated systematic efforts for the constructive engagement purpose, etc. Such systematic efforts have brought about some major collective research projects and have already resulted in a large body of scholarship.

In modern Chinese philosophy, the constructive engagement trend, especially in the strong sense, has been considered a movement toward **world philosophy** (or part of comparative philosophy in general as doing philosophy in a global context), instead of a merely local one, in the following two senses. First, the issues and topics under its reflective examination, generally speaking, are cross-tradition ones instead of idiosyncratically holding only for Chinese philosophy. Second, the movement is not limited to its constructive engagement with *Western* philosophy alone, but with other philosophical traditions as well as the constructive engagement between distinct movements within Chinese philosophy. To this extent, the constructive engagement between Chinese and Western philosophy can serve as a methodological *template* for the constructive engagement between any two or more seemingly competing approaches with distinct styles or orientations in philosophical inquiries and between the Chinese tradition and other non-Western philosophical traditions like the Indian, African, Latin-American ones.

See **constructive engagement; modern Chinese philosophy; world philosophy**

Further reading: Angle 2007 (2.1); Fung 1948 (2.1); Mou 2006a, 2008a, 2009c (2.1)

Contemporary Neo-Confucianism (*dang-dai-Xin-Ru-Xue*) 當代新儒學: Contemporary Neo-Confucianism is a specific movement of thought in modern Chinese philosophy which continues the tradition of *Song-Ming* **Neo-Confucianism** 宋明 (新) 儒學 (especially the tradition of its idealistic school of *xin-xue*) in the contemporary context. Its representative thinkers include **Xiong Shi-li, Mou Zong-san,** and **Tang Jun-yi**. The modern Confucian thinkers of this movement have visions and approaches in common: (1) they consider philosophy primarily as **metaphysics**; (2) they maintain that a reconstruction of Confucian metaphysics based on *Song-Ming* studies of heart-mind and nature (*xin-xing-zhi-xue* 心性之學) is the key to revive Confucianism in contemporary society in the face of various challenges; (3) they actively engage Buddhism and modern Western ideas (those of science and democracy as well as those from modern Western philosophy such as Kant's philosophy).*

Three notes are due. First, the English term for this movement is sometimes given in terms of "contemporary (modern) *New* Confucianism" or simply "New Confucianism"; the label "contemporary *Neo*-Confucianism" is considered better to capture its continuity with (*Song-Ming*) Neo-Confucianism. Second, which figures should be included in the movement is controversial; that depends on how one identifies the connection of a figure in question with Neo-Confucianism. Third, the movement is distinguished from modern studies of Confucianism, which include not only the studies of Confucianism by the figures of the movement but also the studies of Confucianism by other scholars who do not share the foregoing approaches of contemporary Neo-Confucians.

See **Confucianism; Mou, Zong-san; Neo-Confucianism; Tang, Jun-yi;** *xin-xue*; **Xiong, Shi-li**

Further reading: Cheng 1991 (1.13.2); Liu 2003 (1.13.2); Makeham 2003 (1.13.2); Tan 2009 (1.13.2)*

"Continental" philosophy study movement in modern Chinese philosophy: It is a remarkable movement in modern philosophy which has taken shape since the late nineteenth century.

The phrase "Continental philosophy" *per se* denotes a post-Kantian movement of thought or tradition that was historically connected with, or historically started by, a group of French and German philosophers of the nineteenth and twentieth centuries. The canonical figures of this tradition include G. W. F. Hegel (1770–1831), Arthur Schopenhauer (1788–1860), Søren Kierkegaard (1813–1855), Friedrich Nietzsche (1844–1900), Edmund Husserl (1859–1938), Martin Heidegger (1889–1976), Maurice Merleau-Ponty (1907–61), Hans Georg Gadamer (1900–2002), Jean-Paul Sartre (1905–80), Paul Ricoeur (1913–2005), Michel Foucault (1926–1984), Jürgen Habermas (1929–), Jacques Derrida (1930–2004), and Richard Rorty (1931–2007). In comparison and contrast to an analytic approach understood in a broad sense, "Continental philosophy is sometimes distinguished by its style (more literary, less analytical, less reliance on formal logic), its concerns (more interested in actual political and cultural issues and, loosely speaking, the human situation and its "meaning"), and some of its substantive commitments (more self-conscious about the relation of philosophy to its historical situation)" (Brian Leiter). (It is noted that the geographical label is doubly misleading. For one thing, as is the case with the label "Western philosophy," philosophical ideas and methods involved in this philosophical movement are not intrinsically or conceptually associated only with the European continent; they have also been explored by philosophers in other philosophical traditions or geographical areas, including those in modern China. For another thing, those important contemporary analytic philosophers such as Gottlob Frege, Rudolf Carnap, Ludwig Wittgenstein, and Alfred Tarski finished their substantial works in continental Europe, but are not seen as "Continental" philosophers.)

Like the **analytic movement in modern Chinese philosophy**, the "Continental" philosophy study movement is also a significant movement in modern Chinese philosophy. Many scholars feel that the style and many ideas of "Continental" philosophy are kindred in spirit with those of many accounts in traditional Chinese philosophy. This partly explains why some Chinese philosophers have felt more at home when they read works in "Continental" philosophy than when they read works in Western analytic philosophy. Along with **Wang Guo-wei**'s division to the effect that "the lovely are not trustable while the trustable are not lovely," they have found many ideas in and style of "Continental" philosophy as lovely as many accounts in classical Chinese philosophy, in contrast to many doctrines in Western philosophy in the analytic tradition which would be rendered trustable but not lovely. Since the late nineteenth century, through several generations of modern Chinese philosophers' joint efforts, now almost all of the representative works of the major figures of "Continental" philosophy (especially Nietzsche, Sartre, Husserl, Heidegger, and Rorty) have been translated into Chinese.

Now there are two major fronts of the studies of "Continental" philosophy in modern Chinese philosophy. One is that of in-depth studies of some of those major figures or doctrines in "Continental" philosophy. The other is that of comparative studies of Chinese philosophy and "Continental" philosophy, especially those concerning Hegel, Heidegger, and Husserl, for the sake of **constructive engagement**. The latter constitutes an important contributing force to the **constructive engagement movement in modern Chinese philosophy**.

See **constructive engagement (methodology); constructive engagement movement in modern Chinese philosophy**
Further reading: Leiter 2006 (2.1); Mou 2009c (2.1); Zhang 2006 (2.1)

correlative thinking (correlative way of thinking): Although the phrase "correlative thinking" is often used to identify and characterize one representative way of thinking in classical Chinese philosophy which is closely related to the *yin-yang* way of thinking, the phrase has been used in different senses. As the literal sense ("mutually or reciprocally related") of "correlative" suggests, "correlative thinking" basically means a way of thinking that renders things, or distinct aspects of a thing, mutually related, interdependent, and complementary in a whole or (organic) unity, especially in their changing/becoming process.

When the phrase is used in a strictly methodological sense, it can (relatively narrowly) mean a "correlative" methodological perspective intended to point to and capture the changing/becoming aspect of a thing (and/or the changing/becoming process of things) which renders various manifestations of a thing (and/or those various things) mutually related and complementary. Or it can broadly mean a methodological approach that includes both the correlative methodological perspective in the above sense *and* a "correlative" methodological guiding principle: the latter renders distinct eligible methodological perspectives that point to various aspects of a thing or things mutually related and complementary for the sake of a comprehensive understanding of various aspects of a thing or the whole unity of various things. It is argued that *yin-yang* thinking as delivered in the classical *Yi-Jing* text is not merely a "correlative" or changing/becoming-concerned methodological perspective, but a "correlative" methodological approach understood in the above broad sense.

Sometimes the phrase is used not only in the above methodological sense but also in a more substantial sense to include a certain substantial cosmological view (cf. Hall and Ames), i.e., the *yin-yang/wu-xin* cosmology, which is sometimes labeled "correlative cosmology" (e.g., by Needham). In this case, the term "correlative thinking" often means both the changing/becoming-concerned methodological perspective and the correlative cosmology.

It is widely agreed that "correlative thinking" is, or can be, *referentially* used to denote a representative way of thinking in classical Chinese philosophy that is closely related to the *yin-yang* way of thinking. Yet it remains controversial how to identify and characterize such a way of thinking, how to look at its relation with other, seemingly competing ways of thinking (e.g., **analytic thinking**), and thus how to understand the content of the conception of correlative thinking (or of the term correlative thinking). One can address the following questions among others: Is it adequate to characterize correlative thinking in terms of "pre-logical" thinking in contrast to logical thinking (as Graham did)? Are correlative thinking and analytic thinking absolutely opposed to, and incompatible with, each other?

See **analytic thinking; being versus becoming; *wu-xin*; *Yi-Jing*; *yin-yang* way of thinking**

Further reading: Graham 1992 (2.1); Ames and Hall 1995 (2.1); Needham 1956 (2.5.3)

cosmology: There has been a long-term concern with cosmology in the Chinese tradition of thought. Cosmology explores the universe, especially its origin and structure, as a totality of all phenomena. There are two distinct kinds of cosmology: one is philosophically-oriented; the other is religiously/mystically-oriented. Philosophically-oriented cosmology is a subdivision of **metaphysics** and explores the origin and structure of the universe through **rational**-critical inquiry (rational metaphysical speculation and empirical or scientific evidence) and within a more or less coherent framework. Its method of rational-critical inquiry is distinguished from the mystically-oriented cosmological account of the origin and structure of the universe.

In classical Chinese philosophy, **the *yin-yang* metaphysical vision** as suggested in the *Yi-Jing* and the **Daoist** metaphysical account as suggested in the *Dao-De-Jing* are prominent, philosophically-oriented cosmological accounts. There were also some mystically-oriented cosmological interpretations in the Chinese tradition.

See *Dao-De-Jing*; Daoism; metaphysics; ontology; philosophy; rationality/rational; *wu-xin*; *Yi-Jing*; *yin-yang* metaphysical vision

Further reading: Cheng 1989 (2.5.3)

D

Da-Xue (*Ta Hsüeh*) 大學 (*Great Learning*): The *Da-Xue* is one of the *Four Books* (*Si-Shu*) (the other three are *Lun-Yü*, the *Mencius* and the *Zhong-Yong* [*Doctrine of the Mean*]), which Zhu Xi (1130–1200) in the *Song* Dynasty identified as the four most important Confucian classics.

See *Si-Shu*

Dai, Zhen (**Tai Chen**) 戴震 (style name "Dong-yuan" 東原: 1723–77) was born in Anhui Province, China, and is considered to be the most critical-minded Confucian of the early *Qing* Dynasty (1616–1838). Dai Zhen emphasized the philosophical interest in textual criticism of the Confucian texts, rather than historical interest alone. He criticized the *Song-Ming* **Neo-Confucian** view of *li* 理 by emphasizing the interdependence and interpenetration between *li* and concrete things. He also stressed coordination between human nature, emotion, and desire, instead of having them opposed to each other. Dai Zhen's representative works are the *Yuan-Shan* (*An Inquiry into Goodness*, 1766) and the *Meng-Zi-Zi-Yi-Shu-Zheng* (A *Study of the Philosophical Terms in the Mencius*, 1777).

See **Neo-Confucianism; *Qing* Confucianism**

Further reading: Cheng (Chung-yi) 2009 (1.10.2); Cheng (Chung-ying) 2003 (1.10.2)

dao 道 (**Way or the way things are; ultimate reality or the ultimate**): One primary, and non-mystical, understanding of *dao* in classical Chinese philosophy is that the *dao* is the way things are, no matter how a thinker or a school of thought understands the way things are and how he or she elaborates this understanding. The notion of *dao* is a fundamental, across-the-board reflective category in classical Chinese philosophy; a variety of schools of thought take the pursuit of the *dao* as a fundamental task or mission in their understanding and capturing of the way things are.

One classical, and representative, reflective understanding of *dao* is given in the Daoist classical text, **Lao Zi's *Dao-De-Jing***, where the *dao* is understood primarily as the metaphysical *dao* that exists throughout the universe. The **metaphysical** *dao* can be briefly characterized as follows. The *dao* as root is fundamental (the *Dao-De-Jing*, Chs. 1, 6, 21, 25, 34, 42); the *dao* as origin is universal in the sense that it is the origin of all things (Chs. 1, 25, 34, 40, 42); the *dao* is the one, and one unifying force that runs through the whole universe, in the above two senses; the *dao* as power is inherent in nature (in each thing of the universe) rather than transcendent beyond and above nature (Ch. 42); the *dao* as source is inexhaustible (Chs. 4, 6); the *dao* as whole is nature (in the above senses combined); the *dao* as the way of nature is the way of *yin-yang* complementary interaction to reach a harmonious balance (Chs. 2, 42, 77); the *dao* as the way of existence in time is eternal (Chs. 4, 6); the *dao* as the way of existence evolves and keeps changing dynamically (Ch. 1); the *dao* as the way of dynamic development is spontaneous and natural (because the *dao is* nature) (Chs. 25, 34). The metaphysical *dao* is thus not something like the Platonic Form, beyond and above, but consists of and in particular things in the universe, i.e., *wan-wu* (萬物 ten thousand things); when the *dao* is possessed or manifested by individual things, it becomes its manifested character, i.e., what *de* (德) means in its broad sense in the *Dao-De-Jing*. In sum, the *dao* is the ultimate source, unifying power, and fundamental principle of nature and the universe; it manifests itself through particular individual things.

As highlighted in the opening passage of the *Dao-De-Jing*, on the one hand, the *dao* is not absolutely beyond language delivery; rather, the *dao* can be talked about and captured in language, as Lao Zi's own linguistic practice in the *Dao-De-Jing* shows. On the other hand, the *dao* that has been characterized in finite descriptions is not identical with, or does not exhaust, the eternal *dao*.

One extension of the metaphysical *dao* in society is a person's performance following the way of the metaphysical *dao* (performance *dao* for short). Human virtue (i.e., what *de* 德 means in its narrow sense in the *Dao-De-Jing*), is considered to be the manifestation of the metaphysical *dao* in persons regarding morality. It is *de* as human virtue in this sense that endows human beings with the power that distinguishes them from other things. The *dao* in human society is also understood as the way that things in general attain a goal, concretely as a road or a path construed normatively or as a recommendation or guide, in the spirit of ***wu-wei***. Ways can be thus added to each other so we have ways of a person, a family, a community, and a species.

A person's pursuit of (or her performance following) the *dao* does not necessarily imply conforming to a predetermined path; the point is that any path that the *dao*-pursuing agent is currently paving is expected to be in accordance with, or capture, the way things are in nature. Daoism takes pursuing, modeling on, and performing the *dao* as the fundamental mission of the human being in their reflective inquiry. As Lao Zi emphatically points out: "The human being models him/herself upon earth; earth models itself upon heaven; heaven models itself upon the *dao*; the *dao* models itself upon what is natural" (Ch. 25).

See ***Dao-De-Jing***; **Daoism**; *de*; **Lao, Zi**; **metaphysics**; ***wu-wei***

Further reading: Cheng 2003 (1.5.2); Hansen 2003 (1.5.2); Liu 2009 (1.5.2); Mou 2003 (1.5.2); Smallyan 1977 (1.5.2)

Dao-De-Jing (***Tao Te Ching***) 道德經: It is one of the most important texts of Daoism and of Chinese philosophy. As far as its emphasis is concerned, the text as a single volume of 81 chapters can be divided into two parts. The first part comprises Chapters 1 – 37 and is the "*dao* 道" half of the text (the *dao* as the general metaphysical *dao*); the second part consists of Chapters 38 – 81, the "*de* 德" half of the text (the *de* as human virtue, or the manifestation of the *dao* in human beings that endow them with power). The text as a whole came to be known as 'the *Dao-De-Jing*' ('The Classic of *Dao* and *De*'). Though the identity of the author(s) of the text is disputed, its legendary author is Lao Zi; the text is thus also entitled 'the *Lao-Zi*' (the *Lao-Tzu*). The short, poetic *Dao-De-Jing* is the most frequently translated classical work of Chinese thought.

See also **dao**; *Daoism*; **de**; *Lao, Zi*

Further reading: Liu 2003a, 2009 (1.5.2); Moeller 2006 (1.5.2); Waley 1958 (1.5.2)

Daoism / philosophical Daoism / Daoist (*Dao-Jia* 道家): The term Daoism is a blanket term used to cover two kinds or species of Daoism: philosophical Daoism (usually called *Dao-Jia* 道家 in Chinese), and religious Daoism (usually called *Dao-Jiao* 道教 in Chinese), although both claim the same two texts, the **Dao-De-Jing** and the **Zhuang-Zi**, as their textual sources. Philosophical Daoism can be roughly classified into three related parts or stages of development: (1) **Classical Daoism**, whose central figures are **Lao Zi** and **Zhuang Zi** as proxy figures of the two Daoist classics, also called Lao-Zhuang Philosophy; (2) **Neo-Daoism**, consisting of thoughts delivered in the commentaries by philosophers such as **Wang Bi** and **Guo Xiang** on the *Dao-De-Jing* and the *Zhuang-Zi* during the *Wei-Jin* Dynasties; (3) contemporary studies of classical Daoism and Neo-Daoism in the twentieth and twenty-first centuries primarily for the sake of philosophical interpretation and/or **constructive engagement** in philosophy. Besides the *Dao-De-Jing* and the *Zhuang-Zi*, classical texts such as the *Lie-Zi*, the *Yi-Jing*, or the *Huang-Nan-Zi* were included in the Daoist classical texts by some *Han* Dynasty historians and some thinkers in Neo-Daoism like Wang Bi.

The central concern of philosophical Daoism is to explore *dao*, its identity, nature, and function (its '*dao* concern'). One primary goal of philosophical Daoism is to pursue (understand and capture) *dao* ('*dao* pursuit). The *dao* concern and *dao* pursuit of *philosophical* Daoism are not mystical undertakings, both for the sake of the open, critical character of philosophical Daoism and in view of the folk or pre-philosophical understanding of the identity of *dao* (i.e., the way things are) on which the reflective, naturalistic understanding of *dao* is based. Insofar as our pre-philosophical and reflective understanding of **truth** lies in (the truth-bearer's) capturing the way things are, *dao* concern is essentially a kind of truth concern, although *dao* concern is delivered in the Daoist conceptual and explanatory resources and involves distinct approaches in the common philosophical enterprise.

See classical Daoism; *dao*; *Dao-De-Jing*; Lao, Zi; Neo-Daoism; **truth**; **virtue (Daoist approach to virtue and moral cultivation)**; *wu-wei*; Zhuang, Zi; *Zhuang-Zi*

Further reading: Hansen 2006 (1.5.2); Liu 2009 (1.5.2); Moeller 2004 (1.5.2); Shen 2003 (1.5.2)

Dao-Tong 道統: The term *Dao-Tong* means the orthodox line of transmission of the Confucian Way as specified by **Zhu Xi**. The prominent figures in this line include those pre-Confucius legendary figures who were favourably referred to in the central texts of **classical Confucianism** and those Confucian thinkers whose views were celebrated by **Neo-Confucianism**. It is the Confucian tradition as specified from the point of view of Neo-Confucianism.

See **classical Confucianism; Neo-Confucianism; Zhu, Xi**

Dao-Xue 道學 (**Learning of *Dao***): The term *Dao-Xue* is used by scholars such as Fung Yu-lan to refer to **Neo-Confucianism**.

See **Neo-Confucianism**

de 德 (**virtue; manifestations of the *dao***): (1) Generally speaking, in the Chinese tradition the term *de* means human moral **virtue**. (2) In **Daoism,** and especially in the ***Dao-De-Jing*,** the term *de* is used in its related, broad and narrow senses: in its broad sense, it means manifestations of the (metaphysical) ***dao***, or individualized *dao*s, in particular things of the universe; in its narrow sense, it means the manifestation of the (metaphysical) *dao* in human beings regarding morality, human virtue, which endows human beings with the power that distinguishes them from other things.

See *dao*; *Dao-De-Jing*; Daoism; virtue
Further reading: Ivanhoe 1999 (1.5.2)

determinism: Determinism manifests itself in the classical Chinese tradition of thought typically in a certain form of fatalism. Thus challenges to determinism in classical Chinese philosophy were made primarily by refuting fatalism (e.g., in a **Mohist** way) or maintaining a certain kind of **self-freedom** (e.g., in a **Daoist** way).

Determinism is the view that all events, including human actions, are unavoidable and predetermined by their antecedent causes. Historically speaking, in ancient times, what was typically at issue was fatalism, or the belief that whatever happens is unavoidable, no matter how they happen to come about (by their causes or by anything else). In this way, determinism and fatalism are related but are not identical. Determinism is one form of fatalism in the sense that whatever happens is unavoidable by the (causal) conditions preceding it. However, another version of fatalism can result from other beliefs, say, from some theological ideas that God is all-powerful and has preordained everything that happens. It is interesting to note that, though fatalism in ancient times was a typical form of determinism and may have resulted at least partly from a lack of scientific knowledge, the modern forms of determinism as proposed by seventeenth- and eighteenth-century European philosophers tended to be the outcome of an alleged full knowledge of the world in terms of Newtonian physics.

See **Daoism; Mohism; self-freedom**

dialectical materialism and its development in China: Dialectical materialism is a general theory of **Marxist philosophy**. The extension or application of its general principles to looking at the history of human society and thought results in **historical materialism**. Generally speaking, dialectical materialism combines **materialism** with the Hegelian conception of dialectic. The former is considered to provide the foundation, while the latter supplies the three basic principles or laws governing how matters develop in a dialectical way: (1) the law of the transformation of quantity into quality, and vice versa; (2) the law of the interpenetration of opposites; and (3) the law of the negation of the negation. A key conception used in Hegel's dialectical method is *sublation* (German *Aufhebung*) to characterize how to move from the opposition between two contraries (thesis and antithesis) to a synthesis of the two. The synthesis preserves and incorporates what is reasonable and valuable in the two contraries to arrive into a new and higher perspective and discard what is not.

The further development of dialectical materialism as a philosophical theory constitutes one of the major movements of thought in modern Chinese philosophy since the beginning of the twentieth century. These ideas concerning the interaction of contraries are considered to be kindred in spirit with central ideas of the Chinese *yin-yang* **way of thinking** in significant ways. When Marxist philosophy in the form of dialectical materialism was introduced in China, its basic ideas were not totally strange or alien to many Chinese intellectuals. What is more philosophically interesting and significant is the creative development of dialectical materialism in China, represented by and well illustrated in **Mao Ze-dong**'s two philosophical essays, *On Contradition* and *On Practice*.

See **Ai, Si-gi; historical materialism; Mao, Ze-dong; Marxist approach to knowledge in modern Chinese philosophy; Marxist philosophy;** *yin-yang* **way of thinking**

Further reading: Dirlik 1997 (1.12.2); Knight 1990, 2005 (1.12.2); Tian 2005, 2009 (1.12.2)

Dong, Zhong-shu (Tung Chung-shu) 董仲舒(*c*. 179–104 BCE) is one key figure who established politicized Confucianism as the official ideology of the Chinese imperial state (from the *Han* Dynasty through to the fall of the *Qing* Dynasty in 1911), which developed from **classical** (philosophical) **Confucianism** (especially from **Xun Zi**'s ideas) in the light of social and political considerations. Philosophically, Dong's major contribution lies in integrating *yin-yang/wu-xing* **cosmology** into the Confucian ethical system, though such a cosmology preceded him. His major work is *Chun-Qiu-Fan-Lu* 春秋繁露 (*Luxuriant Dew of the Spring and Autumn Annals*), though subsequent scholars have suspected that the book was actually written by multiple authors.

See **classical Confucianism; Confucianism; cosmology;** *wu-xing*; *yin-yang*

Further reading: Ames 2003 (1.6.2); Hsiao 1979 (2.5.4)

dualism: Dualism is a view that asserts two fundamentally different (and separable) types of things in some domains. Some influential theories in the Western philosophical tradition take dualistic approaches to examine the nature of fundamental things: form versus matter, mind versus body, heart versus mind. Some representative accounts in Chinese philosophy take *non-dualistic* approaches. For example, the *yin-yang* **metaphysical vision** as delivered in the *Yi-Jing* renders ontologically interdependent, interpenetrating, and complementary two fundamental things: changing/becoming and unchanging/being. Also in the Confucian tradition, heart and mind are considered to be intrinsically related and metaphysically inseparable; therefore, an adequate English translation of the Chinese term, *xin*, in the Confucian context is considered to be 'heart-and-mind' and not 'heart' alone, though the latter gives the literal sense of the Chinese term.

See *xin*; *yin-yang* **metaphysical vision**

E

egoism: As early as the Warring States Period (480–222 BCE), a version of ethical egoism was advocated by **Yangism**. Ethical egoism, in general, is a doctrine in **conduct ethics** that considers the pursuit of self-interest as right: each for herself, or, more formally, one's action is morally right if and only if that action maximizes one's personal good as an end. But ethical egoism does not amount to egotism, or advocating selfishness: while the latter celebrates being selfish with no regard to others' well-being and interests, ethical egoism maintains that each (one specific person or anyone else) should maximize her own interest.

See **conduct ethics; ethics; Yangism**

enlightenment (in Buddhism) see *nirvana* 涅槃

enlightenment movement in modern Chinese philosophy: The enlightenment movement is the first prominent movement of thought in modern Chinese philosophy and began around the end of the first Opium War (1839–42), after which China became a semi-colonized country. The movement can be viewed as the Chinese intellectuals' response to crisis in the country in the face of invasion and oppression by many Western countries (later joined by Japan). They explored the reason why the West had become powerful while China, with its once glorious civilization, had become so weak. They were determined to enlighten the Chinese people by introducing Western thought, including Western philosophy, via translations of many Western classics and critically re-evaluating the Chinese tradition. Among others, **Hu Shi, Liang Qi-chao, Wang Guo-wei, Yan Fu,** and **Zhang Dong-sun** were the most distinguished Chinese enlightenment thinkers. Their work brought to China not only Western philosophical thought but also Western theories of liberty, equality and democracy and scientific method. The enlightenment movement prepared China for both the 1911 revolution, which overthrew China's last emperor, and for the May Fourth Movement in 1919, which firmly advocated science and democracy, and critically examined traditional Chinese culture. This profoundly influenced the Chinese people in critically looking at the ideological foundations of traditional Chinese society and shaped ideology in the modern period. The significance of the enlightenment movement in the history of Chinese philosophy does not lie in these Chinese thinkers' originality in working out philosophical ideas, but rather the enlightenment role that they creatively played: Western philosophical ideas were thus introduced to and associated with the Chinese situation and integrated into the Chinese philosophical tradition.*

See **Hu, Shi; Liang, Qi-chao; Wang, Guo-wei; Yan, Fu; Zhang, Dong-sun**

Further reading: Jiang 2009 (1.11.2)*

epistemology: Epistemology is a major subject in philosophy. It investigates the identity and nature of knowledge and the conditions under which we can know something. It is also called "theory of **knowledge**." Its typical concerns include the following questions: What is knowledge? Is knowledge possible? What constitutes the justification condition for knowledge?

There are rich resources in Chinese philosophy concerning epistemology which deserve further exploration and elaboration. Among others, philosophically interesting approaches include, but are not limited to: the **Mohist** approach to cognitive inference; **Confucius'** becoming aspect-concerned methodological perspective; **Zhuang Zi**'s thoughts on the identity of knowledge, the distinct status of knowing organs, and the relation between true knowledge and the true agent; **Wang Shou-ren**'s doctrine of the unity of knowledge and action; and **Mao Ze-dong**'s Marxist approach as given in his *On Practice*.

See **Confucius; knowledge; Marxist approach to knowledge in modern Chinese philosophy; Mohist;** *zhi-xing-he-yi* **(unity of knowledge and action); Wang, Shou-ren; Zhuang, Zi**

Further reading: Geaney 2002 (2.5.3); Hans and Gregor 1993 (2.5.3); Zhang 2002, Part Three (2.5.3)

er-di [*lun*] 二諦[論] **(double truth account)**: The doctrine of double truth (*er-ti* 二諦) was proposed by **Ji Zang**, a significant figure of **Chinese Buddhism** who elaborated and systematized the *Mahayana* doctrine of **Buddhism**. The major ideas of his double truth account are these. There are two kinds of truth – truth in the common sense and truth in the higher sense – occurring on each of three levels; what is the truth in the higher sense, at a lower level becomes merely truth in the common sense at the higher level. At the first level, common people take all things as real being and know nothing about their non-being, while the Buddhas would say that all things are in fact non-being and empty. At the second level, saying that all things are being is one-sided, but saying that all things are non-being is equally one-sided. At this level, the Buddhas would say that what is being is simultaneously what is non-being. At the third level, saying that the middle truth consists in what is not one-sided means making (fixed) distinctions, and so this is merely a common-sense truth. The higher truth at this level (i.e., the highest truth) consists in realizing that all distinctions are themselves one-sided (the middle path is neither one-sided nor not one-sided) and in achieving *nirvana*; the highest truth cannot be delivered via language that is full of distinctions, but needs to be contemplated in silence.

See **Buddhism; Chinese Buddhism; Ji, Zang;** *Mahayana* **Buddhism;** *nirvana*; *yan-yi-zhi-bian*

ethics: Ethics is a major reflective concern in classical Chinese philosophy. **Confucianism,** one of the two major influential movements of thought in classical Chinese philosophy, is a heavily ethics-concerned movement of thought, especially in its pre-*Han* period. Generally speaking, ethics is the study of morality and endeavors to investigate fundamental value through identifying and elaborating (1) good human character, and (2) moral rules or principles that distinguish right from wrong human conduct and thus regulate human conduct. Ethics is concerned with moral evaluation and prescription, which distinguish them from purely descriptive and factual statements about the world, and is thus normative in character. There are two central concerns in ethics: (1) Why should I be moral (act morally or be a moral person) – for its own sake (acting morally or being a moral person) or for its external consequence (self-serving or others-serving consequences)? (2) How should I live? There are two basic kinds of ethics that respond to the issue with their distinct but related focuses. One is **conduct ethics**, which focuses on the action dimension of human goodness (What should I *do*? How should I perform that kind of moral action?) and its ethical evaluation. The other is **virtue ethics**, which focuses on the character dimension of human goodness (What kind of person should I *be*?, How should I become that kind of person?) and its ethical evaluation.

See **conduct ethics; Confucianism; morality; virtue ethics**

evocative argumentation: Various forms of evocative argumentation were often adopted in classical Chinese philosophy. Evocative argumentation is a kind of argumentation that evokes (produces, suggests, or triggers) some subsequent thought or conclusion primarily in contrast to **logical argumentation** (i.e., evocative argumentation evokes its conclusions neither deductively nor inductively). Among various forms of evocative argumentation, there are **argument by (relevant) analogy**, argument by appealing to a certain fundamental human value, and argument by appealing to (credible) authority (on the issue under examination). It is sometimes called "rhetoric argumentation," "preferential argumentation," or "prohairetic argumentation."

See **argument by analogy; argumentation; deductive argument; logical argumentation**

Further reading: Mou 2009b (2.1); Rescher 1994 (2.1)

F

Fa-Jia 法家 see **Legalism**

Fa Zang (Fa-tsang) 法藏 (643–712) established a systematic doctrine (and thus is the actual founder) of *Hua-Yan*

Buddhism, one of the major schools in Chinese Buddhism, based on an extensive Chinese interpretation of the *Flower Garland Sutra*, a classical text of *Mahayana* **Buddhism**. Fa Zang's representative works include the *Jin-Shi-Zi-Zhang* (*Treatise on the Golden Lion*) and *Hua-Yan-Jing-Yi-Hai-Mai-Meng* (*Hundred Gates to the Sea of Ideas of the Flower Garland Sutra*).

See **Buddhism**; *Hua-Yan* **Buddhism**; *Mahayana* **Buddhism**

Fan, Zhen 范縝 (450–515) was one of the most influential thinkers in the **Confucian** tradition who argued against religious **Buddhism**. As religious Buddhism based its account of *karma* **and** *samsara* on the belief that the spiritual deity can exist independently of the physical body, Fan argued that the spiritual is an attribute and function of the physical and that the former cannot exist independently of the latter. His representative writing is *Shen-Mie-Lun* (*On Extinction of Spiritual Deity*).

See **Buddhism**; **Buddhist** *karma* **and** *samsara*; **Confucianism**

Fang, Dong-mei (**Thomé H. Fang**) 方東美 (1899–1977) is considered by some as one of the significant figures in **Contemporary Neo-Confucianism**. Nevertheless, he did not think of **Confucianism** as the only legitimate philosophy to be celebrated but also emphasized the importance of **Daoism** and *Mahayana* **Buddhism**, rendering the three interacting and complementary in the Chinese philosophical tradition. His representative works include *Chinese Philosophy: Its Spirit and its Development* (1981), and *Sheng-Ming-Li-Xiang-Yu-Wen-Hua-Lie-Xin* (*Ideal of Life and Cultural Types*, 1992).

See **Contemporary Neo-Confucianism**; **Daoism**; *Mahayana* **Buddhism**

fatalism see **determinism; Mohism; self-freedom**

filial piety see *xiao* (*hsiao*) 孝

freedom see **self-freedom**

Fung, Yu-lan (Feng You-lan) 馮友蘭 (1895–1990) was an outstanding and influential Chinese philosopher of the twentieth century. Fung had solid knowledge and training in both classical Chinese philosophy and Western philosophy. As early as the first half of the twentieth century, Fung consciously applied **analytic methodology** (largely conceptual analysis) in his studies of the history of **Chinese philosophy** and created his own metaphysical system in his book *Xin-Li-Xue* (*New Learning of Principle*, 1939), the purpose of which was to creatively combine ideas from Platonic neo-**realism, Daoism,** and *Chan* **Buddhism** in view of the *li-xue* tradition in **Neo-Confucianism.** His major works include *Zhong-Guo-Zhe-Xue-Shi* (*History of Chinese Philosophy* 2 vols., 1930, 1934; English translations 1953), *A Short History of Chinese Philosophy* (1948), and *Zhong-Guo-Zhe-Xue-Shi-Xin-Bian* (*New Edition of a History of Chinese Philosophy*, 6 vols., 1964–89).

See **analytic methodology; Chinese philosophy;** *li-xue*; **philosophy and philosophy in China**

Further reading: Cua 2003 (2.1); Fung 1948, 1953 (2.4)

G

ge-wu-zhi-zhi 格物致知 (**investigating things and extending knowledge**): The reflective uses of *ge-wu* and *zhi-zhi* appeared in the *Da-Xue*, one of the major Confucian classics, to indicate the first two of the four steps in moral self-cultivation: *ge-wu* (格物: investigating things), *zhi-zhi* (致知: extending knowledge), *cheng-yi* (誠意: making one's thoughts sincere), and *zheng-xin* (正心: rectifying the heart-mind). As the literal senses of the two phrases were open to distinct interpretations, **Zhu Xi** and **Wang Shou-ren** put forward their radically different interpretations, respectively representing the *li-xue* tradition and the *xin-xue* tradition within *Song-Ming* **Neo-Confucianism**. According to Zhu Xi, everything consists of *li* 理 (the abstract pattern or order underlying everything) and *qi* 氣 (concrete material force); *li* in human beings constitutes the normative guidance of human conduct; in the ideal state with pure *qi*, one's heart-mind would have perfect insight into *li*. However, because the endowment of *qi* (in most of us) is impure, one's insight into *li* can be obscured and thus make one fail to be fully ethical. In this way, self-cultivation is to restore the heart-mind's original ideal state through *ge-wu* (arriving at the *li* in things and affairs by extensively studying the classics and historical records) and *zhi-zhi* (expanding and deepening one's knowledge of *li* as the underlying pattern). In contrast, according to Wang, the heart-mind in its original state is already disposed to respond appropriately to particular situations (such a disposition was referred to by Wang as *liang-zhi* 良知, a kind of innate knowledge) without guidance from a separate understanding of *li*. Wang's point is not to deny there are thoughts about what is proper, but to emphasize that such a thought as *li* is an inseparable part of the heart-mind's disposition to respond appropriately and does not guide it. This embodies Wang's thesis of *zhi-xing-he-yi* (unity of knowledge and action) which renders inseparable proper conduct and thoughts about what is proper. Wang thus concluded it that "heart-mind is *li*" (*xin-ji-li* 心即理): *li* resides in the heart-mind instead of being acquired from outside. Wang did not deny that the state of the heart-mind can be obscured by selfish desires and also believed that self-cultivation is to reattain the heart-mind's original state. However, unlike Zhu's "restoring" approach, Wang emphasized discovering *liang-zi*/innate knowledge, which already resides in one's heart-mind through *ge-wu* (correcting or overcoming selfish desires) and *zhi-zhi* (letting one's innate knowledge reach out). No matter how they themselves saw it, Zhu and Wang's disagreement can be viewed as a difference in emphasis rather than a total opposition: *ge-wu* as arriving at the *li* in affairs without and *ge-wu* as correcting selfish desires within can be complementary and are both necessary to **self-cultivation.***

See ***Da-Xue***; **li** 理; ***li-xue***; **self-cultivation**; **Wang, Shou-ren**; ***xin-xue***; ***zhi-xing-he-yi***; **Zhu, Xi**

Further reading: Liu 2009 (1.9.2); Shun 2003 (1.9.2)*

global philosophy see **world philosophy**

Golden Rule: The Golden Rule, when considered as a methodological guide to how one should treat others, is often explicitly expressed in terms of the principle of reversibility as follows: "(Do not) do unto others as you would (not) desire others to do unto yourself." Nevertheless, the Golden Rule is essentially not an abstract, conventionally formulated rule but a presentation of collective moral wisdom. Its concrete versions in many cultural and philosophical traditions are nurtured by the insightful perspectives and explanatory resources historically developed in these traditions. Among others, two prominent and influential versions are the Christian version as given in the New Testament (especially see Matthew 7:12, 22:36–40; Luke 6:27–36) and **Confucius**' version as given in the *Lun-Yü* (especially see 4.15, 6.28, 12.2, 15.23). Although both base how to adequately apply such a methodological principle like reversibility on interpersonal love and care, ultimately they have their distinct moral foundations: the Christian version is based on the second commandment (love your neighbor) and eventually on the first commandment (love God), while Confucius' version is built on the most fundamental virtue, *ren* 仁, which is more profound than what its manifestation in treating others (interpersonal love and care) embraces.

Confucius' version of the Golden Rule (CGR for short) is presented in the *Lun-Yü* not as a rule-oriented, abstract principle but as a virtue-oriented moral guidance consisting of two central concepts, *shu* 恕 and *zhong* 忠, and three interdependent and complementary dimensions. (1) The methodological dimension of the CGR (i.e., the methodological aspect of *shu*) consists of the principle of reversibility ["(Do not) do unto others what you would (not) desire *others* to do unto yourself"] and the principle of extensibility ["(Do not) do unto others what you would (not) desire *yourself* to do unto yourself"]. (2) The internal starting-point dimension (i.e., the substantial aspect of *shu*) consists of the internal fundamental virtue *ren*, which provides an initial moral sensibility for putting the methodological dimension of the CGR into play. (3) The external starting-point dimension of the CGR (i.e., *zhong*) is the moral agent's sincere and devoted moral commitment to the responsibilities and duties specified by *li* 禮, regardless of the social status of the moral recipient; *zhong*, on the one hand, provides the external starting point for applying the principles of reversibility and extensibility by regulating the moral agent's desire through an external social institution, and, on the other hand, *zhong* itself ultimately is to be regulated and guided by *ren*, to which the substantial aspect of shu points and which serves as the internal starting-point for adequately applying the principles of reversibility and extensibility.

See **Confucianism; Confucius;** *li* 禮; *Lun-Yü; ren; shu; zhong*

Further reading: Allinson 1992 (1.2.2); Chan 2000 (1.2.2); Ivanhoe 1990 (1.2.2); Mou 2004 (1.2.2); Wang 1999 (1.2.2)

Gong-sun, Long (Kung-sun Lung) 公孫龍 (284–259 BCE) was a logician in ancient China and a representative figure of the **School of Names** (*Ming-Jia*). What distinguishes Gong-sun Long's work is his in-depth investigation into the relation between names and reality through conceptual analysis and rational argumentation. His thoughts are delivered in the *Gong-Sun-Long-Zi*. Three brief essays in the text, "On the White Horse," "On Referring to Things," and "On Hardness and Whiteness," are considered most important to an understanding of his thoughts. In contrast to **Hui Shi** (another important figure in the School of Names), Gong-sun Long emphasized the distinct aspects of things, though he did not ignore common aspects.

See **reference; School of Names; "White-Horse-Not-Horse" Thesis**

Further reading: Cheng 1983 (1.4.2); Fung 2009 (1.4.2); Graham 1986b (1.4.2); Hansen 1983 (1.4.2)

Graham, Angus Charles (1919–91) was born in Wales, and was Professor of Classical Chinese at the School of Oriental and African Studies, the University of London. He was a world authority on Chinese philosophy and

Chinese textual criticism in the twentieth century. His representative works include *Studies in Chinese Philosophy and Philosophical Literature* (1986; 1990), *Disputers of Tao: Philosophical Argument in Ancient China* (1989) and *Unreason within Reason* (1992).

gua 卦: In the **Yi-Jing** system, *gua* means an ideographic symbol, either as a trigram such as ☲ or as a hexagram such as ䷀, which consists of the divided and/or undivided lines, called *yao* or *yao* line: the divided line '--', called *yin yao* (line), and undivided lines '— ', called *yang-yao* (line). The *yin-yao* and *yang-yao* combined comprise eight trigrams, each of which consists of three *yao* lines, each of which is either *yin-yao* or *yang-yao*. Together with their original interpretations as indicated below, they are called *ba-gua* (eight-trigrams).

Trigrams	Names	Implied process Or Property	Sample of denotations
☰	*Qian*	Strength	Heaven
☷	*Kun*	Yielding	Earth
☳	*Zhen*	Activity	Thunder
☴	*Xun*	Bending	Wind
☵	*Kan*	Pit	Water
☲	*Li*	Brightness	Fire
☶	*Gen*	Stop	Mountain
☱	*Dui*	Pleasure	Marches

Any two of the eight trigrams combined result in one hexagram, which consists of six *yao* lines, each of which is either *yin-yao* or *yang-yao*. Thus there are a total of sixty-four hexagrams like ䷀. In the context of the hexagram (or trigram), once *yang-yao* and *yin-yao* are combined into a whole to represent a changing process (or a natural thing), *yang-yao* or *yin-yao* denotes a (kind of) *yang*-dominant or *yin*-dominant changing stage of that thing or process rather than *yang* force or *yin* force alone. However, when standing alone, the *yin-yao* line and *yang-yao* line are to stand respectively for the two mutually opposed but complementary forces in the universe, *yin* and *yang*. That is, each changing stage for which a *yang-yao* (or *yin-yao*) stands in the hexagram is the result of the interaction of the two basic forces, *yang* and *yin*. Moreover, each of the hexagrams is related to the others, especially the immediately preceding and subsequent ones. In this way, in the context of *all* the hexagrams, it would never be the case that the *yang* force or *yin* force is always in a dominant position; a *yang*-dominant or *yin*-dominant stage or process can change into a *yin*-dominant or *yang*-dominant stage or process. As a whole, neither *yin* nor *yang* can claim absolute priority over the other; they are equal with regard to metaphysical status: they are interdependent, interactive, and complementary.

See *Yi-Jing*

Guan-Zi (Kuan Tzu) 管子 (*The Book of Master Guan*): An encyclopedic collection of early Chinese materials from various sources (**Confucianism, Daoism, Legalism**, etc.) by Liu Xiang (77–6 BCE) written around 26 BCE, although it bears the name of Guan Zhong (prime minister of the State of *Qi*).

Guo, Xiang (Kuo Hsiang) 郭象 (d. 312) is one of the leading figures (second only to **Wang Bi**) of **Neo-Daoism** during the *Wei-Jin* Dynasty. He is considered to be by far the most important interpreter of the *Zhuang-Zi* who endeavored to reconcile metaphysical insight in seeking freedom and transcendence with moral and socio-political engagement. When addressing the central Neo-Doaist concern with how to understand a fundamental character of the *dao*, i.e., *wu* (non-being, nothingness) and its relation to *you* (being), Guo was opposed to Wang Bi: while Wang claimed that all beings originate from *wu*, Guo maintained that *wu* could not be the gateway to anything, but makes sense only in relation to *you* and that *you* must be self-engendered and eternal. Guo's major writing is the *Zhuang-Zi-Zhu* (*Zhuang-Zi Commentary*).*

See **Daoism; Neo-Daoism; Wang, Bi;** *you* versus *wu*; *Zhuang-Zi*

Further reading: Chan 2009 (1.7.2)*

H

Han, Fei (Han Fei Zi / Han Fei Tzu) 韓非 (280–233 BCE) was a Chinese intellectual and writer, one time favorite of the First Emperor of the *Qin* Dynasty, although he was later executed by the emperor. Like Li Si, the First Minister who devised the dynastic system, Han Fei was a student of **Xun Zi**. Han Fei's writings constitute the key source of the system later dubbed *Fa-Jia* (**Legalism**) in the *Han* Dynasty. His views are presented in the book bearing his name, *the Han-Fei-Zi.*

See **Legalism; Xun, Zi**

Further reading: Graham 1989, III.3 (2.4); Hansen 1992. Ch. 10 (1.2.2)

harmony see *he* 和

he 和 (諧) (harmony/harmonious; peace; concord): *He* is one of the central ideas in the Chinese philosophical tradition, which both embodies the ancient Chinese thinkers' (descriptive) understanding of the fundamental structure of the universe (including human society) and delivers their (prescriptive) projection of the ideal state of human society (harmonious brotherhood). This idea is intrinsically related to the other two basic ideas in the Chinese tradition: the *yin-yang* **way of thinking** as suggested in the *Yi-Jing*; and the classical thesis of *tian-ren-he-yi* (the unity of heaven and the human). The idea of *he* denies neither distinctions nor the interaction of contraries but points to their harmonious balance when they are complementary in character, as stressed by the *yin-yang* way of thinking. The thesis of *tian-ren-he-yi* provides the metaphysical foundation of *he* by highlighting the metaphysical unity and unification of heaven and the human.

There are two related emphases of the reflective idea of *he*: one is on the harmonious unification between human beings and their natural environment; the other is on the harmonious brotherhood and friendship among all members of human society while differentiating between individuals. The former is elaborated by **Lao Zi** in the *Dao-De-Jing* as he highlighted the ultimate unifying power of the *dao* among the human, earth, and heaven (see Ch. 25). The latter was well delivered by **Confucius** in the *Lun-Yü* via such simple but insightful statements as: "Morally superier persons (*jun-zi*) harmonize while having their distinctions [distinct identities, approaches, etc.]" (13.23), "When *li* 禮 is practiced, harmony is most valuable" (1.12), and "All within the four seas [throughout the world] are brothers" (12.5).

See **Confucius**; *Dao-De-Jing*; **Lao, Zi**; *Lun-Yü*; *tian-ren-he-yi*; *Yi-Jing*; *yin-yang* **way of thinking**

Further reading: Guo 2000 (1.1.2); Li 2006 (1.2.2)

He, Lin賀麟 (1902–92) was one of the pioneers and leading scholars in the **"Continental" philosophy study movement in modern Chinese philosophy**. One of He's significant contributions to the Chinese philosophical circle was the systematic introduction and interpretation of the philosophy of G. W. F. Hegel (1770–1831). He also carried out a comparative examination of Hegel's philosophy and some classical Chinese philosophers' doctrines (such as Zhu Xi's and Wang Fu-zhi's) and created his own system, which culminated in a Hegelian synthesis of ideas from Kantian philosophy and *Lu-Wang-xin-xue* in his *Jin-Dai-Wei-Xin-Lun-Jian-Shi* (*A Concise Interpretation of Modern Idealism*, 1942).

See **"Continental" philosophy study movement in modern Chinese philosophy**; *xin-xue*

heart-mind see *xin* (*hsin*) 心

heaven see *tian* 天

historical materialism: At the same time as **dialectical materialism** has been explored in modern Chinese philosophy, its corresponding theory, historical materialism, has also been extensively examined. This occurred especially during the second half of the twentieth century by the Chinese philosophical circle in mainland China. Historical materialism is the classical Marxist philosophical view, or theoretical framework, of the historical development of human society and thought. As such, it is distinguished from dialectical materialism. Dialectical materialism is the general theory of **Marxist philosophy** and has historical materialism as its extension, which focuses on the history of human society. According to historical materialism, changes in the economic foundation and productive forces of a society bring about social conflict or even class struggle, and the specific forms of social organization (or social superstructure) reflect the underlying structure of the economic base and means of production.

See **dialectical materialism and its development in China; Marxist philosophy**

holism: Holism stresses the priority of a whole over its parts. Chinese philosophy is considered to be a holistically-oriented philosophical tradition, though this claim by no means suggests that any individual Chinese thinkers must be holistically-oriented in philosophical inquiries. The holistic orientation is also shown in other ideological or cultural phenomena of Chinese civilization, such as certain distinct syntactic and semantic features of the Chinese language.

See **Chinese language and its related folk way of thinking; correlative thinking;** *wu-xin***;** *yin-yang*

Hong, Qian (Hung Tscha) 洪謙 (1909–92) was a leading figure who pioneered the development of the **analytic movement in modern Chinese philosophy,** especially during the first half of the twentieth century. He became a member of the Vienna Circle when he pursued his Ph.D. under the guidance of Friedrich A. M. Schlick (1882–1936) at the University of Vienna. After returning to China in the 1940s, Hong published his original work on the philosophy of the Vienna Circle in Chinese and made one earlier comparative-engagement endeavor to the debate between his logical positivist view and **Fung Yu-lan**'s neo-realist understanding of the status and role of **metaphysics.**

See **analytic movement in modern Chinese philosophy**

Hu, Shi (Hu Shih) 胡適 (1891–1962) pioneered work in identifying and characterizing ancient Chinese philosophy in a critical and systematic way in his *Zhong-Guo-Zhe-Xue-Shi-Da-Gang* (*An Outline of the History of Chinese Philosophy*, 1919) and *The Development of the*

Logical Method in Ancient China (dissertation, 1922). He was the most important advocate of John Dewey's **pragmatist** philosophy and among the most influential intellectuals in China during the first half of the twentieth century.

See **enlightment movement in modern Chinese philosophy; pragmatism**

Further reading: Jiang 2008 (1.11)

Hua-Yan **Buddhism** (*Hua-Yan-Zong*)華嚴宗: *Hua-Yan* Buddhism is one of the major schools in **Chinese Buddhism**. It is also called the "Flower Garland" school of Buddhism because it is based on the extensive Chinese interpretation of the *Flower Garland Sutra* 華嚴經, a classic text of **Mahayana** Buddhism. It was established during the period at the end of the *Sui* Dynasty and the beginning of the *Tang* Dynasty. Its earlier founders include Du Shun (杜順 557–640), who established *Hua-Yan* studies as a distinct field, and **Fa Zang**, who established a systematic *Hua-Yan* doctrine.

Hua-Yan Buddhism, together with *Tian-Tai* Buddhism, provided the metaphysical foundation for Chinese Buddhism. Its central idea is the doctrine of the mutual containment and interpenetration of all phenomena via its conceptions of the universal causation of the realm of *dharmas* (法界緣起) and of the perfect harmony of *dharmas* (法界圓融). According to this doctrine, all things are coexistent, interdependent, interrelated, interpenetrating, mutually inclusive, and mutually implied. In other words, one thing contains all things in existence, while all things contain one. Though both the *Tian-Tai* School and *Hua-Yan* School emphasized the interrelationship of all phenomena in the universe, *Hua-Yan* Buddhism emphasized not merely the interdependence of all things but also their mutual containment.

Hua-Yan Buddism had a profound impact on **Neo-Confucianism** during the *Song* and *Ming* Dynasties via the organic character of its doctrine of one containing all and all containing one, though the latter further holds that the universe is constantly renewed.

See **Buddhism; Chinese Buddhism; Fa Zang;** *Mahayana* **Buddhism; Neo-Confucianism;** *Tian-Tai* **Buddhism**

Further reading: Chang (Garma) 1971 (1.8.2); Cook 1977 (1.8.2); Gimello 1983 (1.8.2); Lai 1980 (1.8.2)

Huai-Nan-Zi (*Huai-nan Tzu*) 淮南子 is a Chinese philosophical classic of the *Han* Dynasty (around the second century BCE) which blends the ideas of **Daoism, Confucianism, legalism,** the *yin-yang* account, and the *wu-xing* account. The text was written by a group of scholars under the patronage of Liu An, the King of Huainan (r. 164–122 BCE), and consists of twenty-one chapters, resulting from the debates between Liu and guests at his court.

Huang, Zong-xi (**Huang Tsung-hsi**) 黃宗羲 (style name "Tai-chong" 太沖; honorific name "Li-zhou" 黎洲: 1610–95) is considered to be the last in the line of **Neo-Confucianism**. His representative works are *Ming-Yi-Dai-Fang-Lu* (*Waiting for the Dawn*), which stresses the need for political reform and constitutional law, and *Ming-Ru-Xue-An* (*The Records of Ming Confucianism*), which gives a systematic survey of all of the important Confucian schools of thought during the *Ming* Dynasty.

See **Neo-Confucianism**

Hui, Neng 慧能 (638–713) was one of the most important figures (the Sixth Patriarch) of *Chan* **Buddhism**. He advocated an immediate and direct approach to **Buddhist** enlightenment and became the founder of Southern *Chan* Buddhism, also called the "Sudden Enlightenment"

School of *Chan* Buddhism. The primary work attributed to Hui Neng is *Liu-Zu-Tan-Jing* (*The Platform Sutra of the Sixth Patriarch*), which covers the basic teachings of *Chan* Buddhism, though it is controversial how the work is related to Hui Neng.

See **Buddhism**; *Chan* **Buddhism**

Hui, Shi (Hui Shih) 惠施 (350–260 BCE) was an ancient logician in China and a major figure of the **School of Names** (*Ming-Jia*). He had a major influence on **Zhuang Zi**. We know of his ideas mainly from the *Zhuang-Zi*, particularly Chapter 33, *Tian-Xia*, where Hui Shi's philosophical thoughts are delivered in his ten, seemingly paradoxical propositions. Generally speaking, Hui Shi emphasized common aspects, the connections and unification of things, and the relativity of their distinctions, though he also paid attention to distinct aspects. Hui Shi as a "logician" was primarily concerned with the metaphysical foundation of logical discourse rather than with its purely formal character.

See **Hui Shi's Ten Propositions; School of Names;** *Zhuang-Zi*

Hui Shi's Ten Propositions: Hui Shi's philosophical thoughts are primarily delivered in his ten, seemingly paradoxical propositions (Chapter 33, *Tian-Xia*, of the *Zhuang-Zi*) as follows.

(1) "The greatest dimension [of the universe] has nothing beyond itself and is thus called 'the great unit', while the smallest dimension [of the universe] has nothing within itself and is thus called 'the small unit'."

(2) "That which has no thickness cannot be increased in thickness, and yet in extent it covers one thousand *li* [miles]."

(3) "The heaven is as low as the earth; mountains are on the same level as marshes."

(4) "The moment the sun reaches the zenith at noon, it is declining; the moment the creature is born, it is dying."

(5) "A great similarity differs from a little similarity; this is called 'the little similarity-and-difference'. All things are both similar/identical to one another and different from one another; this is called 'the great similarity/identity-and-difference'."

(6) "The South has no limit and has a limit."

(7) "One goes to the State of *Yüe* today and arrives there yesterday."

(8) "Connected rings can be in separation."

(9) "I know where the center of the world is: it is in the north of the State of *Yan* and the south of the State of *Yüe*."

(10) "Extend love to all things; the universe is the one unity."

Hui Shi emphasizes the common aspects, connections, and unification of things, as in (1) and (10), and the relativity of their distinctions, as in (2), (3), (4), (6), (7), and (9). He also pays attention to distinct aspects, in (5) and (8).

See **Hui, Shi; School of Names;** *Zhuang-Zi*

Further reading: Fung 2009 (1.4.2); Graham 1989 (1.4.2)

human (moral) nature: The Chinese thinkers in the **Confucian** tradition have been seriously and significantly concerned with the issue of original human (moral) nature. This is because of its involvement in how to carry out moral **self-cultivation** to fulfill the Confucian mission and whether **virtue** has its due "metaphysical" foundation in original human nature. There are three representative views on this issue and thus three distinct models of moral cultivation in the Confucian tradition.

One is the view of **Mencius** who argued that human nature is originally good. His major points are these: (1) four kinds of moral potentials exist within every human being; (2) the four moral potentials are visible and active like the sprouts (*duan* 端); (3) innate moral sensibility/feeling makes one able to do good; (4) every one is able to become a moral sage; (5) innate moral sensibilities are merely moral sprouts: although they are visible and active; they are tender and fragile, so, if you neglect them, you will lose them; (6) what is ignoble or evil results from: (a) nourishing the smaller parts (minor desires) in one's nature and failing to nourish the greater parts (major desires); (b) failing to avoid evil external influences – in other words, failing to take care of the tender and fragile moral sprouts or "greater qualities." Mencius thus suggested his *development* model of moral cultivation: moral cultivation lies primarily in developing one's already-possessed initial or innate moral sensibility.

Second is **Xun Zi** who argued that human nature is originally evil and that goodness is the result of conscious effort. Xun Zi emphasized that by "human nature" he means "the [finished] product of Nature" or something natural that "does not require any work to be produced" rather than a predisposition (like a shoot that is yet to be developed). Firmly sharing the Confucian belief that anyone can become a Confucian *jun-zi* via moral self-cultivation, Xun Zi thus proposed his *re-formation* model of moral cultivation: moral cultivation lies primarily in re-forming and transforming one's evil nature via conscious and disciplined moral cultivation.

Third, **Zhu Xi**'s view is somewhat different but incorporates elements from both Mensius and Xun Zi. He held that the human being originally has good nature (the *li* 理 as principle or pattern) which is typically obscured by selfish inclinations (parts of *qi* within us). Zhu Xi therefore proposed a discovery model of moral cultivation: one needs to make a serious and conscious effort to discover one's already-possessed *li* nature by seeing through *qi* of varying degrees of turbidity (i.e., reforming one's selfish, disordered inclinations). This model thus adopts aspects of both the development and re-formation models.

Philosophical **Daoism** has its own distinct understanding of how to look at the issue of human (moral) nature. Unlike the Confucian approach, **Lao Zi** never explicitly claimed that human nature is born good or bad. Rather he referred people to the natural (and thus "virtuous") state of infants. Lao Zi's point is this: when claiming that human nature is originally *good* or *bad*, one may have a pre-set pattern of what is good or bad. This is used as a criterion of moral worth to assess the original nature of human beings. When one conceptualizes certain natural traits into a moral appraisal system, one is at risk of formulating them into an imposed doctrine and forgetting the genuine *dao*. He thus warns us: "When the great *dao* declines, the doctrine of humanity and righteousness arose. When formulated knowledge and wisdom appeared, there emerged great hypocrisy" (Ch. 18).

See **Confucianism; Lao, Zi; Mencius; self-cultivation; virtue; Xun, Zi; Zhu, Xi**

Further reading: Cua 2005a (1.2.2); Ivanhoe 2000 (1.2.2); Lau 2000 (1.2.2); Mahood 1974 (1.2.2)

humanism: Humanism, generally speaking, is the tendency to emphasize human beings and their status, importance, powers, achievements, interests, or authority in contrast to those non-personal or supra-personal entities or powers that are supposed to be opposite to human beings. **Confucian** humanism emphasizes the moral and social dimensions of humanism: (1) to search for ideal moral personality through moral **self-cultivation**; (2) to strive for harmony (**he**) in the human world; (3) to seek heaven (universe) and humanity in harmony on the basis of the unity of heaven and the human (*tian-ren-he-yi*).

See **Confucianism**; *he*; **self-cultivation**; *tian-ren-he-yi*

humanity see *ren* 仁

I

idealism: Some strands and thoughts in classical Chinese philosophy (for example, the line of *xin-xue* within **Neo-Confucianism**) are idealist in character, though the forms they take are distinct from those in the Western tradition. Generally speaking, idealism is any view that holds that reality is fundamentally mental in nature or mental idea-dependent. It is opposed to **materialism, naturalism,** and **realism** which are concerned with the external world. Depending on how "mental (idea)" is understood, there are various forms of idealism. Subjective idealism holds that to exist is to be perceived ("mental idea" here means subjective or personal perception), while objective idealism claims that all existence is a form of one objective or absolute mind.

See **materialism; naturalism; Neo-Confucianism; realism;** *xin-xue*

ideographic language: An ideographic language like Chinese is a written system that consists of ideographic or pictographic written forms; these visually represent the objects that they are intended to pick out via ideographic association or pictographic resemblance. Ideographs are distinguished in Chinese as characters that combine other elements to remind users of its intended use. An ideographic language like Chinese allows a written form to be associated with a variety of sounds of spoken languages and hence serves as a common means of communication.

Arguably, the syntactic and semantic structure of the Chinese ideographic language somehow bears on how Chinese folk ideology evolved and then influences the ways in which certain philosophical questions are posed and certain reflective (say, ontological) insights are formed. One might argue that this influence is bi-directional instead of one-directional. On the one hand, the way in which the Chinese language originally formed was influenced by the way people thought at that time. On the other hand, when linguistic practice became relatively stable and had been followed and passed on generation to the next, it influenced the way Chinese language speakers thought to some extent. One suspects that the syntactic–**semantic** structures and uses of distinct kinds of languages (e.g., an ideographic language like Chinese and a phonetic language like Greek or English) might play a role to a greater or less degree in pushing philosophical theorization in distinct directions on some of the reflective issues in philosophy.

See **Chinese language and its related folk way of thinking; Chinese language and reflective way of thinking in Chinese philosophy; semantic/semantics**

Further reading: Cheng 1987 (2.5.2); Graham 1989 (2.5.2); Hansen 1983 (2.5.2); Mou 1999 (2.5.2)

inner sageliness and outer kingliness see *nei-sheng-wai-wang* 內聖外王

intuition: Many thinkers in classical Chinese philosophy pay special attention to the role played by intuition in their reflective explorations. However, the identity, status, and function of intuition vary in different contexts. For example, **Mencius** and his supporters in the **Confucian** tradition emphasized the important role played by people's intuitive, initial moral sensibility which comes from their original good human nature; **Wang Shou-ren** emphasized the role played by *liang-zhi* (a kind of intuitive innate knowledge) in *ge-wu-zhi-zhi*. Generally speaking, intuition is a kind of non-inferential, immediate awareness, which can be either inter-subjectively shared by normal human beings in a community (e.g., some shared logical or mathematical intuitions; some intuitive, initial moral sensibility, if any), or possessed by some as a result of certain kinds of long-term (intellectual or moral) cultivations (e.g., some scientific intuitions; some cultivated moral intuitions), or attained by pre-theoretic (or pre-philosophical) uses (if any) of the notions and their linguistic expressions (e.g., pre-theoretic, intuitive understanding of **truth**).

See *liang-zhi*; **Mencius**; **truth**; **Wang, Shou-ren**

J

Ji, Zang (Chi-tsang) 吉藏 (549–623) was a significant figure in **Chinese Buddhism**. He elaborated and systematized the doctrine of **Three-Treatise Buddhism**, a school in *Mahayana* **Buddhism**, in the Chinese context. He is also known for his double-truth account (*er-di-lun* 二諦論). His work bridged **Daoism** and **Buddhism** and contributed to the emergence of *Chan* **Buddhism**.

See **Buddhism**; *Chan* **Buddhism**; *er-di-lun*; *Mahayana* **Buddhism**; **Three-Treatise Buddhism**

Jin, Yue-lin 金岳霖 (1895–1984) was one of the pioneers and leading scholars in the **analytic movement in modern**

Chinese philosophy. In addition to his significant contributions to the systematic introduction of deductive logic to the Chinese philosophical circle in his book *Luo-Ji* (*Logic*, 1936), Jin published systematic works in **metaphysics** and **epistemology** in his *Lun-Dao* (*On Dao*, 1940), which blended ideas from **Daoism**, Cheng-Zhu-*li-xue* and contemporary philosophy, and *Zhi-Shi-Lun* (*Theory of Knowlegde*, 1983).

See **analytic movement in modern Chinese philosophy**

jun-zi 君子 (**morally superior person**): The term *jun-zi* means a person of nobility. Before **Confucius**, what had been considered the defining feature of nobility was one's blood connection with the ruler (the literal sense of *jun*), say his son(s) or daughter(s) (the literal sense of *jun-zi*). Confucius revolutionized the defining feature of nobility: it has nothing to do with one's kinship relation to the ruler but lies in one's moral character. A *jun-zi* is a morally superior person, or gentleman, who (fully) achieves the fundamental virtue (i.e., *ren*), through moral **self-cultivation**. Confucius held that the ultimate concern which a person should have, and the primary worthwhile thing a person can do, is to strive to become such a morally superior person.

See **Confucius**; *ren*; **self-cultivation**

justice: One of the major concerns in classical Chinese philosophy is with human morality, which is related to its concern with the issue of justice, especially in the **Confucian** tradition. Generally speaking, justice is the moral value of social institutions or of persons' inclinations to appropriate (say, fair or harmonious) cooperation and treatment of others. Justice may be divided into retributive justice (the punishment of criminals, restitution for harm) and distributive justice (access to the resources necessary for a good life). For example, in contrast to justice as fairness among equals, the Confucian approach treats justice as harmony among unequal members of the social community; the Confucian notion of justice is understood on the basis of the Confucian fundamental virtue *ren* and the Confucian notion of love with distinction.

See **Confucianism; harmony; *ren***
Further reading: Cline 2007 (1.2); Fan 2003 (1.2)

K

Kang, You-wei (K'ang Yu-wei) 康有為 (style name "Guang-sha" 廣廈; alternative name "Chang-su" 長素:1858–1927) was a leading **Confucian** reformer in modern Chinese social and political philosophy and critically re-evaluated the Confucian tradition for the sake of political reform. His two major works, *Xin-Xue-Wei-Jing-Kao* (*A Study of the Forged Classics of the [Wang Mang] Xin Period*, 1896) and *Kong-Zi-Gai-Zhi-Kao* (*Confucius as a Reformer*, 1897), provided important theoretical groundwork for the Hundred-Day Reform (*Bai-Ri-Wei-Xin* 百日維新) in 1898, in which he and his student **Liang Qi-chao** actively participated; his utopian work *Da-Tong-Shu* (*The Book on the Great Unity*, 1880–1902) set out a plan for an ideal society through blending ideas from many sources (such as **Confucian**, Christian, **Buddhist**).

See **Enlightenment Movement in modern Chinese philosophy; Liang, Qi-chao**

knowledge: There are rich resources in classical Chinese philosophy concerning reflective studies of knowledge (for example, in the works of **Zhuang Zi** and **Wang**

Shou-ren). Knowledge (*zhi* 知 or *zhi-shi* 知識 in Chinese) is considered to be the principal epistemic attainment. Although what counts as knowledge is at issue in **epistemology**, for heuristic purposes, and given a broad understanding of what counts as knowledge, it is helpful initially to identify distinctions between types of knowledge. Although philosophical controversy has arisen over some of those distinctions *per se*, they can serve as useful initial reference points regarding types of knowledge for the sake of further examination.

There is a distinction between propositional knowledge (also referred to as "knowing that" or knowledge that something is so), which is traditionally explained as justified true belief, and non-propositional knowledge. Non-propositional knowledge includes practical knowledge (also referred to as "knowing how" or knowledge of how to do something) and knowledge by acquaintance (also referred to as knowledge by direct awareness). An example of practical knowledge is one's knowledge of how to ride a bicycle; and an example of knowledge by acquaintance is one's knowledge of one's parents by direct awareness. There is a wide span between purely propositional knowledge and purely practical knowledge: much knowledge has elements of both propositional knowledge and practical knowledge. As far as (purely or impurely) propositional knowledge is concerned, there is a distinction between empirical (*a posteriori*) propositional knowledge (e.g., one's knowledge that snow is white) and non-empirical (*a priori*) propositional knowledge (e.g., one's knowledge that 2 + 2 = 4).

In classical Chinese philosophy, Zhuang Zi, a brilliant figure in philosophical **Daoism**, made his insightful points concerning various issues of knowledge as follows (see Inner Chapter 2 of the *Zhuang-Zi*). First, there is a variety of eligible knowing organs of the human being whose epistemic status is rendered eventually equal; this is in contrast to the position that the inter-subjective rational mind is the only eligible knowing organ. Second, there is a variety of knowable, knowing-worthy aspects of the object of study to be known, instead of considering a certain aspect (say, the definite aspect) of the object of study as the only worthy aspect to be known. Third, there are various species of eligible knowing agents, instead of considering the human knowing agent as the only eligible knowing agent.

There are rich reflective resources concerning practical knowledge in Chinese philosophy (such as **Wang Shouren**'s thesis of *zhi-xing-he-yi* and Mao Ze-dong's **Marxist approach to knowledge in modern Chinese philosophy**). By definition, practical knowledge aims at, and/or requires, practice. Practical knowledge, generally speaking, consists of two related contents: (1) its cognitive content which can result from learning and be articulated in terms of propositional knowledge (resulting from knowing that); (2) its actuating import which is intrinsically related to (either results in or result from) practice. Practical knowledge consists of two kinds of knowledge with regard to the relation between the knowing component and the action component in the whole process of practical knowledge: (1) prospective knowledge, which is acquired before action; (2) retrospective knowledge, which is acquired after action. Knowledge is more or less practical knowledge when it is located within a wide spectrum between purely knowing that and purely knowing how.

See **epistemology**; **Marxist approach to knowledge in modern Chinese philosophy**; *zhi-xing-he-yi*; **Zhuang, Zi**; *Zhuang-Zi*

Further reading: Geaney 2002 (2.5.3); Hans and Gregor 1993 (2.5.3); Zhang 2002, Part Three (2.5.3)

L

Lao Zi (Lao Tzu) 老子 (his legendary family name is "Li" 李; given name "Er" 耳; style name "Dan" 聃: before the fourth century BCE?): The identity of Lao Zi is controversial. According to one legendary account, Lao Zi was born in the State of *Chu* (roughly Hunan Province now); Confucius once consulted Lao Zi about rites. Traditionally, Lao Zi is associated with the authorship of the *Dao-De-Jing* (thus also entitled "the *Lao-Zi*"); he is credited as the founder of **Daoism** and is one of the two central figures of **Classical Daoism** (the other figure is **Zhuang Zi**). Although it is controversial to what extent the *Dao-De-Jing* captures the real sayings of the historical Lao Zi, Lao Zi can be seen as a proxy figure who speaks for the ideas delivered in the text. This is made possible and reasonable if our purpose is to understand the teachings in the *Dao-De-Jing* as a whole and appreciate how they can contribute to our treatment of fundamental concerns in philosophical inquiry.

See *dao*; *Dao-De-Jing*; Daoism; self-cultivation; *you* versus *wu*

Further reading: Liu 2009 (1.5.2); Shen 2003 (1.5.2)

Legalism / Legalists (*Fa-Jia* 法家): Legalism is the ideology of a particular group of intellectuals and statesmen (the legalists) during the Warring States Period (480–222 BCE) and *Qin* Dynasty (221–206 BCE) which emphasized the indispensable role played by *fa* (法 standards and laws) in governing states. In Legalism, these standards/laws include weights, measures, the width of chariots, etc. and derivatively includes penal codes as public, statutory punishments mechanically geared to named wrongs. One earlier leading figure of Legalism is **Shang**

Yang, who was responsible for the design of the imperial State of *Qin*, which eventually unified China (221 BCE).

Although Legalism is sometimes contrasted to **Confucianism** in terms of "governing by law" versus "governing by virtue," Legalism was more an art of rulership than a distinct philosophical doctrine; the Legalists were "more Machiavellian pragmatists than political philosophers" (Ames). Philosophically speaking, Legalism can be seen as emphasizing the law-governing dimension of the extension of Confucianism to statecraft, one dimension that is considered to be complementary with another dimension, i.e., governing by **virtue.** Many of the Legalists had a close, ideological relationship with pre-*Han* Confucians; for example, **Han Fei,** a leading Legalist, was a student of **Xun Zi,** one of the most important **classical Confucians.**

See **classical Confucianism; Confucianism; Han, Fei; Shang, Yang; Xun Zi**

Further reading: Ames 1993 (2.5.4); Graham 1989, Part III, Ch. 3 (2.4); Hansen 1994 (2.5.4); Hsiao 1979 (2.5.4)

li 禮 **(rules of propriety; rites):** The term *li* 禮 indicates rites, propriety, ceremony and, in some accounts, conventions in general, including mores. In **Confucius'** teachings, although *ren* is the most fundamental **virtue** (the basis of humanity and the ultimate guide to human action), Confucius recognizes that more concrete, particular, and immediate guides to action are required in everyday life. Those concrete guides Confucius found in the rules of propriety (*li*), which cover various, socially established rules governing social, moral, and religious practices (ranging from rituals, customary codes, ceremony regulations to moral rules). Confucius thinks that practicing *li* is an important, even indispensable, way to cultivate and realize the potential of **humanity:** (1) the virtue potential has to be revealed, strengthened, and cultivated through actual human actions which need those ready-made, socially established concrete guides to regulate; (2) *li* has its social and public character and emphasizes the openness of the participants to each other; this kind of open, shared participation in life with others can evoke and foster the development of *ren*. As far as the regulative relation between *ren* and *li* is concerned, *ren* is the ground of adequate *li*; what makes *li* an adequate standard of conduct is the fact that it is in accord with *ren*; customs, rituals, regulations, and rules eventually should be regulated by *ren* (cf., 3.3, 5.18). In **Mencius'** teachings, *li* as a rite is identified with various, socially established rules of conduct, and is also considered to be an ethical attribute that involves a general disposition to follow *li* as rites and a mastery of the details of *li*, enabling one to follow *li* with ease.

See **Confucius; Golden Rule; *ren*; self-cultivation; *yi***

Further reading: Cua 2005b (1.2.2); Lai 2006 (1.2.2); Shun 2002 (1.2.2)

li 理 (**principle, pattern, reason, or rationale**): The term *li* expresses one of the most important concepts in Chinese philosophy and the central concept in *Song-Ming* **Neo-Confucianism**. Literally, *li* means principle, pattern, reason, or rationale. It had yet to be a prominent concept in the pre-*Han* classical Chinese philosophy. Nevertheless, during the *Wei-Jing* Dynasty, **Wang Bi** began characterizing the *dao* in terms of *li* in his commentaries on **Lao Zi's** *Dao-De-Jing*: wherever Lao Zi talked about destiny and fate (*ming* 命), Wang would substitute *li* (principle of nature). Furthermore, in the *Song* and *Ming* Dynasties, the concept of *li* became so central in *Song-Ming* Neo-Confucianism that the latter has been labeled *Song-Ming li-xue* (宋明理學 *Song-Ming* study of *li*) in the broad sense of *li-xue*. All Neo-Confucian philosophers considered *li* to be the ultimate metaphysical principle of the universe and **xin** (心 mind-heart) as the agent with the ability to regulate one's behavior in accordance with *li* inherent in *xin*. Nevertheless, within Neo-Confucianism, there are two major distinct approaches to *li* and its relation to *xin* (mind-heart): one is **Cheng Yi** and **Zhu Xi**'s approach, which is called *Cheng-Zhu-li-xue* (程朱理學: Cheng Yi and Zhu Xi's study of principle); the other is **Lu Jiu-yuan** and **Wang Shou-ren**'s approach, which is called *Lu-Wang-xin-xue* (陸王心學 Lu Jiu-yuan and Wang Shou-ren's study of mind-heart).

See **Cheng, Yi**; *ge-wu-zhi-zhi*; *li-xue*; *li-yi-fen-shu*; **Lu, Jiu-yuan; Neo-Confucianism; Wang, Shou-ren; *xin*; *xin-xue*; Zhu, Xi;**

Further reading: Fung 1934 (1.9.2); Liu 2009 (1.9.2)

li-xue 理學 (**study of principle**): The term *li-xue* can be used in a broad sense to mean *Song-Ming li-xue* (i.e., *Song-Ming* **Neo-Confucianism**), as all Neo-Confucian philosophers took *li* 理 to be the ultimate metaphysical principle and their works center on studies of *li*. It can be also used in a narrow sense to mean *Cheng-Zhu-li-xue* (程朱理學: Cheng Yi and Zhu Xi's study of principle), which was represented by **Cheng Yi**'s teachings and **Zhu Xi**'s teachings concerning *li* and its relation to **xin** (心 mind-heart), in contrast to *Lu-Wang-xin-xue*. According to Zhu Xi's **dualistic metaphysics** of *li* and *qi*, *li* as the ultimate principle of the universe is static, eternal, universal, and transcendent, while *qi* as material force is dynamic, transient, particular, and immanent. As far as their metaphysical constitutions are concerned, *li* and *qi* are neither mixed nor distinct from each other; but *li* inheres in *qi* to manifest itself in the world. One's *xin* is made of the subtlest kind of *qi*, which has the ability to regulate one's behavior in accordance with *li* inherent in *xin*; but for most of us *qi* of which *xin* is made is impure and *li* inherent in *xin* can be obscured. One needs to restore *li* in *xin* by *ge-wu-zhi-zhi* (i.e., investigating things and affairs within and without, including studying the classics, and expanding one's knowledge of *li*).

See **Cheng, Yi;** *ge-wu-zhi-zhi;* *li* 理; **Neo-Confucianism;** *qi;* *xin;* *xin-xue;* **Zhu, Xi**

Further reading: Chan 1973 (1.9); Fung 1934, 1948 (1.9); Liu 1998, 2009 (1.9)

li-yi-fen-shu 理一分殊 (one principle with many manifestations): The slogan *li-yi-feng-shu* was first suggested by **Cheng Yi**, a **Neo-Confucian** thinker, and stresses that the universal moral principle manifests itself in many distinctive moral duties and responsibilities and in distinctive particular moral agents. However, it is **Zhu Xi** who explicitly gave a systematic elaboration of the general metaphysical import of the dictum, although it is **Zhang Zai** who first suggested such a metaphysical import. Zhu Xi explains how the fundamental One, or *li* 理 as the ultimate origin and source (*tai-ji*), is inseparable from, but manifests itself in, the myriad particular material things that come from some basic material fluid, *qi*, and result from the interaction of *yin* and *yang*.

See **Cheng, Yi;** *li* 理; **Neo-Confucianism;** *qi;* *tai-ji;* *yin-yang;* **Zhang, Zai; Zhu, Xi**

Further reading: Liu 2003 (1.9)

Liang, Qi-chao (Liang Ch'i-ch'ao) 梁啟超 (style name "Zhuo-ru" 卓如: 1873–1929) was a leading reformist of the **Confucian** tradition in the late *Qing* Dynasty and a distinguished thinker in the **enlightenment movement in modern Chinese philosophy**. Liang, together with his mentor **Kan You-wei**, actively participated in the Hundred-Day Reform of 1898. He put forward his doctrine of new citizenship (*xin-ming-lun* 新民論), which emphasized the indispensable role played by two complementary kinds of virtue, both of which a modern citizen is expected to possess: virtue for the public good (*gong-de* 公德), to whose cultivation the Western tradition can contribute much; and personal virtue (*si-de* 私德), to whose cultivation the Chinese tradition can contribute much. His representative work is *Yin-Bing-Shi-He-Ji* (*Collected Works of Yin-Bing-Shi*, 1936).

See **enlightenment movement in modern Chinese philosophy; Kang, You-wei**

Further reading: Jiang 2008 (1.11.2)

Liang, Shu-ming 梁漱溟 (style name "Shou-ming" 壽銘: 1893–1988) was one of the important figures of **contemporary Neo-Confucianism**. His philosophical thought was a modern development of the *xin-xue* tradition within *Song-Ming* Neo-Confucianism, which incorporated ideas from **Consciousness-Only Buddhism** and Western philosophy (especially Henri Bergson's and Arthur Schopenhauer's thoughts which identify the universe as 'live' and in a continuous state of flux and evolution). His representative work is *Dong-Xi-Wen-Hua-Ji-Qi-Zhe-Xue* (*Eastern and Western Cultures and Their Philosophies*, 1921).

See **Contemporary Neo-Confucianism**

liang-zhi 良知 (**innate knowledge**): **Wang Shou-ren** used the notion of *liang-zhi* to characterize the particular transparent quality of a basic kind of knowledge, which is an innate knowledge and was considered by him as the foundation of knowledge. In comparison and contrast, the notion of *liang-zhi* seems to be partially similar to what René Descartes used the term "clear and distinct ideas" to signify: the latter denotes ideas that have a particular transparent quality so that we cannot imagine them to be false but accept them as indubitable.

See **knowledge**; **Wang, Shou-ren**; *xin-xue*; *zhi-xing-he-yi*

Lie-Zi (*Lieh-tzu*) 列子: The text under the title *Lie-Zi* is classified as one of the **classical Daoist** texts. Though it has traditionally been ascribed to an ancient thinker whose name is Lie Zi, we know little about him and the identity of the actual author remains distputed. It has been argued that the contents and style of this text are broadly similar to **Zhuang Zi**'s and that the ancient text compiled in Lie Zi's name was composed in the late fourth century.

See **classical Daoism**; **Daoism**; **Zhuang, Zi**

logical argumentation: Together with **evocative argumentation**, logical argumentation plays an important role in philosophical inquiries of classical Chinese philosophy. It is not merely explicitly and directly addressed in the texts of ancient thinkers like **Mo Zi** and **Gong-sun Long** but also implicitly and indirectly resorted to in classical texts like Confucius' *Lun-Yü* and *Zhuang-Zi*.

A logical argument is a set of statements in which one or more of the statements, the premise(s), purport to provide a reason or evidence for the truth of another statement, the conclusion, either deductively or inductively way. When it does, we say that the premises entail or support the conclusion, or that the conclusion "follows from" the premises. We traditionally divide logical arguments into deductive and inductive arguments. Sometimes logical argumentation means only deductive reasoning. The two basic principles of deductive reasoning are the principle of non-contradiction and the law of identity. The principle of non-contradiction states that (in regard to certain relevant identities of the items under examination) it is not the case that both *p* and not *p* (where *p* is any proposition). The law of identity states that, for everything *x* (in regard to the aspect of *x* that keeps the identity of *x* under examination), *x* is identical with itself. We distinguish between good and bad deductive arguments. The criteria for good arguments concerning deductive reasoning are two: validity and soundness. A valid argument is a deductive argument with a form such that it is structurally impossible for its premises to be true and its conclusion false. A sound argument is a valid argument with true premises.

As for the relationship between logical argumentation and the other major type of argumentation, evocative argumentation, it is argued that the two types of argumentation cannot be totally immune from, but are complementary to, each other.

See **argumentation; evocative argumentation**

Further reading: Mou 2009b (2.1); Rescher 1994 (2.1)

Lu, Jiu-yuan (Lu Chiu-yüan) 陸九淵 (style name "Zi-jing" 子靜; honorific name "Xiang-shan" (Hsiang-shan) 象山: 1139–93) was an important Confucian thinker of the Southern *Song* (1127–1279) who initiated the movement of *xin-xue* (learning of mind-heart) was continued by **Wang Shou-ren**, and thus also known as Lu-Wang *xin-xue*. The movement of *xin-xue* as an alternative movement within **Neo-Confucianism** criticized **Cheng Yi** and **Zhu Xi**'s movement of *li-xue* (learning of principle). Lu was more interested in social, political, and moral issues and emphasized the need to take personal responsibility for social moral actions. His works were collected into *Xiang-Shan-Xian-Sheng-Quan-Ji* (*The Collected Works of Lu Xianshan*, 1212).

See **Neo-Confucianism; Wang, Shou-ren;** *xin-xue*

Further reading: Liu 2009 (1.9.2)

Lun-Yü 論語 (the *Analects*): The *Lun-Yü*, a collection of sayings and conversations between **Confucius** and his disciples, was compiled by Confucius' followers between about 500 BC and 249 BC. It is traditionally considered to be the most reliable source of Confucius' teachings. Although the extent to which this classical text captures the original sayings of the historical Confucius is controversial, for the purpose of understanding the ideas in the *Lun-Yü* as a whole and to appreciate how they can contribute to our treatment of fundamental concerns in philosophical inquiry, Confucius in the *Lun-Yü* can be taken as a proxy figure who speaks for the ideas delivered by this classical text of **Confucianism**.

See **Confucianism; Confucius; interpretation**

Further reading: Brooks and Brooks 1998 (1.2.2); Ivanhoe 2002 (1.2.2); Sahleen 2002 (1.2.2); Slingerland 2000, 2009 (1.2.2); Van Norden 2002 (1.2.2)

M

Madhyamika Buddhism see **Three-Treatise (Middle-Way) Buddhism**

Mahayana (the Great Vehicle) Buddhism大乘: *Mahayana* Buddhism is one of two basic types of **Buddhism**. Its views are these: (1) All individuals are riding together in a large vehicle toward salvation; to help save others by means of compassion is its ideal. Mahayana Buddhism is thus also called "Great Vehicle" Buddhism, in contrast to the other basic type of Buddhism, *Hinayana* Buddhism, which emphasizes that each individual rides his own "Small Vehicle" to save himself ("Small Vehicle" Buddhism). (2) It sees that the great majority of people are too weak and frail to face a life fraught

with suffering and misery without turning to some transcendental source of help, love, and mercy; it assures
the masses that the **Buddha** offers faith and hope to the
weak and timid; so prayer and worship play an important role. (3) Buddha nature is always present in every
sentient being; every living being is a potential Buddha;
samsara (mundane existence as the chain of birth and
death) and *nirvana* are not separate realms but one and
the same reality seen from different points of view.
When ignorance is overcome, this same world will be
experienced as *nirvana*; one then realizes that one has
always been in *nirvana*, only one was not aware of it
owing to the veil of ignorance (*avidya*). (4) We cannot
directly perceive the ultimate reality but only the phenomenal world as captured through our senses and
intellect; the ultimate reality is emptiness (*sunyata*) in
the sense that it is non-dual, nameless, formless, uncre-
ated, and ineffable; it can only be apprehended in a
non-sensual, non-intellectual intuition (*prajna*).

There are two major schools in *Mahayana* Buddhism:
the *Madhyamika* **School** and the **Consciousness-Only
School** (also called the *Yogacara* school). The former is
more influential. Both were introduced into China during
the late *Sui* Dynasty and were actively interpreted and
studied for several centuries but then declined around
ninth century. Their influence on Chinese philosophy was
exerted primarily through the general Buddhist ideas they
delivered and the former's partial derivative (*Chan*
Buddhism) rather than by their distinct interpretations of
them.

See **Buddhism; Buddhist** *karma* **and** *samsara*;
Consciousness-Only Buddhism; *Madhyamika* **Buddhism;**
nirvana

Further reading: Gimello 1976 (1.8.2); Lai 2009
(1.8.2); Williams 1989 (1.8.2)

Mao, Ze-dong (Mao Tse-dung) 毛澤東 (1893–1976) was a Marxist philosopher who tried to synthesize Marxist **dialectical materialism** and traditional **Chinese philosophy**. It is widely acknowledged that Mao made a significant contribution to the development of **Marxist philosophy**, including Marxist epistemology, via his two representative philosophical writings: *Shi-Jian-Lun* (*On Practice*, 1937) and *Mao-Dun-Lun* (*On Contradiction*, 1937). It is considered by many that, besides spelling out his account of the relation between **knowledge**/theory and practice, Mao's *On Practice* gives a clear and neat presentation of Marxism's basic position on knowledge.

See **dialectical materialism and its development in China; historical materialism; Marxist philosophy**

Further reading: Dirlik 1997 (1.12.2); Knight 1990 (1.12.2); Schram 1989 (1.12.2); Tian 2009 (1.12.2)

Marxist philosophy: The development of Marxist philosophy in China in the twentieth century is a remarkable facet of modern Chinese philosophy. Marxist philosophy is one of the three major components of Marxism originally put forward by Karl Marx (1818–83), the German philosopher and the founder of revolutionary communism, and Friedrich Engels (1820–95), Marx's collaborator. (The other two components are Marxist conceptions of political economics and of scientific socialism.) Marxist philosophy consists of **dialectical materialism** and **historical materialism**: the latter is viewed as an extension of the former and looks at the nature and historical development of human society. It is noted that what Marx and Engels explicitly and systematically developed is historical materialism. A systematic elaboration of Marxist positions on metaphysics, epistemology, etc. (i.e., what is called dialectical materialism) has been largely developed by subsequent Marxist philosophers, including Chinese Marxist philosophers like **Mao Ze-dong**. The development of Marxist philosophy in China was largely implemented through the **development of dialectical materialism in China** and came to fruition in Mao Ze-dong's philosophical thought including his **Marxist approach to knowledge** in China.

See **dialectical materialism and its development in China; historical materialism; Mao, Ze-dong; Marxist approach to knowledge in modern Chinese philosophy**

Further reading: Dirlik 1997 (1.12.2); Fogel 1987 (1.12.2); Knight 2005 (1.12.2); Tian 2009 (1.12.2)

materialism / materialist: Various forms of materialism have developed in classical and modern Chinese philosophy. Generally speaking, materialism as a philosophical view holds that the world is entirely composed of matter. It is opposed to both **idealism**, which holds that reality is fundamentally mental in nature, and to mind–body **dualism**. (Materialism as a philosophical view is not related to the view that advocates the excessive desire for goods and wealth.) In classical Chinese philosophy, some philosophers like **Zhang Zai** and **Wang Fu-zhi** had strong materialist orientations in their philosophies. In **Marxist philosophy**, materialism combines with the Hegelian dialectical method resulting in **dialectical materialism**. Dialectical materialism has developed in modern Chinese philosophy through the Marxist movement in China and the creative efforts of Chinese Marxist philosopher like **Mao Ze-dong**.

See **dialectical materialism; idealism; Mao, Ze-dong; Marxist philosophy; Wang, Fu-zhi; Zhang, Zai**

Marxist approach to knowledge in modern Chinese philosophy: The Marxist approach to knowledge in the Chinese tradition is well presented in **Mao Ze-dong**'s *On Practice*.

Mao's Marxist approach to knowledge can be characterized in terms of a dialectical materialist theory of the
unity of knowing and doing, or of theory and practice.

As this terminology suggests, there are three related
dimensions to this approach: the materialist dimension,
the dialectical dimension, and the unity-of-knowing-
and-doing dimension. These three dimensions are intrinsically related to three general background points of
Marxism, as follows: (1) The materialist point: the
Marxist regards human beings' productive activity as
the most fundamental practical activity and as the deter-
minant of all other activities; through productive activity and social practice human beings also gradually
acquire knowledge in varying degrees about certain
human interrelations. (2) The dialectical methodological
point in terms of the Hegelian dialectical model: as Mao
put it: "Practice, knowledge, more practice, more knowledge; the cyclical repetition of this pattern to infinity,
and with each cycle, the elevation of the content of practice and knowledge to a higher level." (3) The Marxist
point concerning the nature and function of philosophical theory (including theory of knowledge): the mission
of philosophers lies not merely in understanding and
explaining the world, but in changing, transforming,
and remolding it. In this way, Mao's Marxist approach
to knowledge can be presented in terms of the following
cycle: (1) Practice→knowledge (explaining the world):
practice→perceptual knowledge→rational knowledge
(from one's experience, contact with the external world
and practice of changing reality, one initially achieves
perceptual knowledge; via thinking, a further leap to
rational knowledge); (2) knowledge→more practice
(more important: changing the world): rational
knowledge→targeted practice/practice of changing the
world; (3) more practice→more knowledge. Through

this practice, theory and knowledge are tested and developed. When changing the objective world, one's subjective world is also changed. As internal contradictions and struggles continue and as practice develops, a new cycle begins.

Mao's approach, with its emphasis on the unity of theory and practice, is kindred in spirit to some extent with **Wang Shou-ren**'s account of the unity of knowledge and practice (*zhi-xing-he-yi*). More generally, Mao's approach, with its emphasis on sensitivity to situation and practice, shows an affinity with the becoming-aspect-concerned orientation in the Chinese tradition. On the other hand, it is clear that Mao's approach is distinguished from traditional approaches in the Chinese tradition by its intrinsic connotation of the basic points of Marxism. To this extent, Mao's Marxist approach to knowledge as presented in *On Practice* combines distinct insights and resources from both the Western and Chinese traditions and illustrates one way of how some ideas or orientations from different traditions can be incorporated into an organic whole in a reflectively interesting way.

See **being versus becoming; dialectical materialism and its development in China; epistemology; knowledge; Mao, Ze-dong; Marxist philosophy;** *zhi-xing-he-yi*

Further reading: Schram 1989 (1.12.2); Tian 2009 (1.12.2)

Mencius (Meng Zi, Meng Tzu) 孟子 (given name "Ke" 軻; style name "Zi-Yü" 子輿: 371–289 BCE) is considered as second only to **Confucius** in importance in the **Confucian** tradition due to his sophisticated elaboration and further development of many major points of Confucius' *Lun-Yü* and also to his influence on **Neo-Confucianism**. The collection of Mencius' sayings and dialogues with others is known as the *Mencius*. Among others, Mencius' views on moral **self-cultivation** and **human (moral) nature** are most significant and influential. Mencius highlighted four fundamental moral attributes as four aspects of the ethical ideal and relates them to *xin* (heart-mind), the site of both affective and cognitive activities: (1) *ren* (humanity): a moral disposition in heart-mind, an affective concern for others, both not wanting to harm others and not being able to bear the suffering of others, (2) *yi* 義 (righteousness): a moral attribute that emphasizes strictness with oneself, a commitment to adhere to certain ethical standards that involve both not acquiring things by improper means and not accepting others' improper treatment of oneself; (3) *li* 禮 (observance of rites): an ethical disposition to follow *li* as rites and a mastery of the details of *li*, enabling one to follow *li* with ease; and (4) *zhi* 智 (wisdom): an ethical attribute that means the ability to ascertain what is proper in accordance with the circumstances. Mencius elaborated the relationship between these fundamental virtues and human (moral) nature through his doctrine of human nature and his development model of moral self-cultivation: (1) the incipient disposition of the four fundamental moral attributes like sprouts are already possessed by each heart-mind; (2) human nature is thus originally good; (3) the ethical ideal is to fully develop four moral sprouts already in one's heart-mind; (4) one's moral self-cultivation lies primarily in *developing* one's innately possessed initial moral sensibility to achieve full virtue; and (5) in one's moral self-cultivation, one also needs to extend one's moral sprouts in one's outward actions to the social environment as a moral obligation. There are rich resources of moral psychology in Mencius' teachings, of which modern scholars have made significant elaborations and development.

See **classical Confucianism; Confucianism; human (moral) nature;** *Mencius;* **self-cultivation; virtue**
Further reading: Cheng 2003 (1.2.2); Chong 2009 (1.2.2); Ivanhoe 2000 (1.2.2); Shun 1997 (1.2.2); Wong 1991 (1.2.2)

Mencius **(Meng-Zi)** 孟子 (*The Book of Mencius*): The *Mencius* is a collection of Mencius' sayings and dialogues, and is one of the orthodox *Four Books* (*Si-Shu*) of **classical Confucianism.**
See **classical Confucianism; Mencius;** *Si-Shu*

metaphysics 形而上學 (*xin-er-shang-xue*): Metaphysics is a major area of philosophy which inquires into the most basic and general issues concerning the nature, constitution, and fundamental character of reality or the world (sometimes the study of the *ultimate* or deepest aspects of reality). Metaphysics inquires especially into those questions concerning reality that are either currently or intrinsically beyond the purview of scientific methods.
Metaphysical study in Chinese philosophy has a long tradition. In the **Dao-De-Jing** (Ch. 42), one finds this **Daoist** insightful aphorism regarding the ultimate origin and fundamental structure of the universe:

> The *dao* generates the one.
> The one generates the two [*yin* and *yang*].
> The two generate the three [*yin, yang,* and *qi* (氣)].
> The three generate ten thousand things.
> All things carry *yin* and embrace *yang*,
> Through *yin-yang* interaction and blending with *qi* they reach harmony.

The *dao* is global and general in character rather than limited to local particulars: the *dao* underlies and generates ten thousand things rather than being restricted to the manifest shapes of what is generated. Thus, in another classical text, the *Yi-Zhuang* (see *Xi-Ci*, Ch. 12), the *dao* is characterized as *xing-er-shang-zhe* 形而上者, (what underlies the manifest shapes of [ten thousand] things): "what is above, or underlies, physical form is called '*Dao*'; what exist in the shape of physical form are called '*qi*' (器, vessels and implements)." The study of the *dao* in its primary sense is thus called *xing-er-shang-xue*, meaning the study of what underlies the physical shape of ten thousand things. One can also find a strong metaphysical orientation in *Song-Ming* **Neo-Confucianism**.

In the Western tradition, this kind of reflective investigation is called "metaphysics," and the term can be traced back to the Greek philosopher Aristotle. Aristotle placed his writings on these sorts of questions after his writings on physics, and the writings were thus called "metaphysics" which derives from the Greek *meta ta physica*, literally "after the physics." It is no wonder that the ancient phrase *xing-er-shang-xue* was used as the Chinese counterpart of the term "metaphysics" when the latter was translated into Chinese: both are kindred in spirit or even come close to being identical in meaning.

See **being versus becoming**; **cosmology**; *Dao-De-Jing*; **Daoism**; *li* 理; **Neo-Confucianism**; **nominalism**; **ontology**; *qi*; **self-constitution**; **self-freedom**; **universals**; *wu-xing*; *xu*; *Yi-Zhuan*; *yin-yang* **metaphysical vision**; *you* versus *wu*

Further reading: Cheng 1989 (2.5.3); Graham 1989 (2.5.3); Zhang 2002 (2.5.3)

methodology (method): Methodology, in both contemporary study of classical Chinese philosophy and in meta philosophical examination of its nature and status, has become prominent and significant, especially when comparative engagement between distinct approaches from Chinese and other traditions are made. The reasons include these: (1) Distinct approaches from different traditions are typically marked by distinct methodologies. So, to understand the former's relation, one needs to understand the latter's relation. (2) Methodological reflection on a substantial approach enhances one's understanding of the approach in a broader context and helps one pinpoint its validity and limitations. (3) Exploration of philosophical methodology helps one differentiate distinct dimensions or levels of the structure of a methodological approach, which otherwise would be easily conflated; this aids a greater understanding of the approach's contents.

Indeed, terms such as "method," "methodology," or "methodological approach" are ambiguous and vague; they are often used to mean a number of things in philosophical inquiries and need clarification and differentiation. Given that the term "methodological approach" means a way of responding to how to approach an object of study, the term might be used to mean one of the following (or more than one simultaneously): (1) a methodological perspective (or a perspective method); (2) a methodological instrument (or an instrumental method); (3) a methodological guiding principle (or a guiding-principle method). It is especially important and effective to understand the distinction between them and their relationship in the studies of Chinese and comparative philosophy for the purpose of exploring how distinct (methodological) approaches in different traditions can learn from each other and jointly contribute to the common philosophical enterprise.

Roughly speaking, a methodological perspective (or a methodological perspective simplex) is a way to approach an object of study that is intended to point to a certain aspect of the object and capture or explain that aspect in terms of its characteristics. It has the minimal metaphysical commitment that there *is* that aspect of the object or that the aspect is genuinely (instead of being merely supposed to be) possessed by the object. There is a distinction between eligible and ineligible methodological perspectives concerning an object of study. If the aspect to which a methodological perspective is intended to point is genuinely possessed by the object of study, it is considered *eligible* with regard to that object. Otherwise, the methodological perspective is considered *ineligible* with regard to that object. For example, given that an object of study genuinely possesses its **being**-aspect and **becoming**-aspect, one can take a being-aspect-concerned (or becoming-aspect-concerned) perspective to capture the being-aspect (or becoming-aspect) of the object of study.

A methodological instrument is a way by which to implement (or give tools to realize) a certain methodological perspective (often implicitly). In philosophy, such methodological instruments include a variety of argumentations and inferences, together with their associated explanatory and conceptual resources, for the explicit or direct purpose of justification and exposition (deductive argument, argument by analogy, etc.) or giving clear and cogent analysis.

A methodological guiding principle is a way concerning how to guide the use and evaluation of a certain methodological perspective (or group of perspectives), or a certain methodological instrument to implement the methodological perspective, with regard to an object of study. It is presupposed by the agent who takes that perspective (or one or more among the group of the perspectives) and its related instrument; and its role is to guide and regulate how the perspective or instrument should be evaluated (its status and its due relation with other perspectives or instruments) and used (how to choose among the group of perspectives or instruments), and how the purpose and focus that the perspective serves should be set. There is a distinction between adequate and inadequate methodological guiding principles concerning a certain methodological perspective with regard to an object of study.

Generally speaking, the merit, status, and function of a methodological perspective *per se* can be evaluated independently of the methodological guiding principle that the agent might assume in her actual application of the perspective. One's reflective practice *per se* of taking a certain methodological perspective as one's current working perspective amounts to neither losing sight of other genuine aspects of the object nor rejecting other eligible perspectives in one's background thinking, nor presupposing an inadequate methodological guiding principle that would render ineligible other eligible methodological perspectives (if any). However, whether taking a certain methodological perspective is regulated by an adequate or inadequate guiding principle does matter. When one's application of an eligible methodological perspective as part of one's reflective practice is guided by an adequate guiding principle and contributes to adequate understanding of the object of study, one's application of that perspective is philosophically constructive.

To help the reader capture more easily this abstract presentation of the nature and status of the three methodological ways and their distinction, the following 'method-house' metaphor can be used to illustrate the points. Suppose that a person intends to approach her destination, say, a house (the object of study), which has several entrances – say, a front door, side door, and skylight (a variety of aspects, dimensions, or layers of the object of study). She then takes a certain path (a certain methodological perspective) to enter the house, believing that the path leads to the entrance on one side (say, the front door) or the entrance on the other side (say, the side door) of the house. If the path really leads to a certain entrance to the house, the path is called "eligible"; otherwise it is called "ineligible" (thus the distinction between eligible and ineligible methodological perspectives). When she takes a certain path to enter the house, she holds a certain instrument in her hand (a methodological instrument) to clear her path, say, a scythe if the path is overgrown or a shovel if the path is heavily covered with snow. She also has a certain idea in her mind (a methodological guiding principle) that explains why she has taken that path instead of another, and guides her to have an understanding (adequate or inadequate) of the relation of that path to other paths (other methodological perspectives). Surely such a guiding idea can be adequate or inadequate (adequate or inadequate methodological guiding principle): for example, if she recognizes and renders other eligible paths also eligible and thus compatible with her current path, then her guiding idea is adequate. In contrast, if she fails to recognize this and thus renders her current path exclusively eligible (the only path leading to the house), then her guiding idea is inadequate, although her current path *per se* is eligible.

See **analysis; argumentation; constructive engagement; evocative argumentation; logical argumentation; synthesis**

Further reading: Davidson 2001 (2.1); Graham 1985 (2.1); Hansen 1992 (2.1); Liu 2001 (2.1); Mou 2001b, 2009b (2.1); Neville 2001 (2.1); Rescher 2001 (2.1); Shun 2001 (2.1); Wang 1988 (2.1); Yu and Bunnin 2001 (2.1)

Ming-Jia 名家 see **School of Names**

Mo-Jia 墨家 see **Mohism**

Mo, Zi (Mo Tzu) 墨子 (given name "Di" 翟: 470–391 BCE) was the founder of **Mohism** (*Mo-Jia*). His teachings are presented in the *Mo-Zi*. His work is the first that is presented in argumentative form in classical Chinese philosophy and develops serious criticisms of **classical Confucianism.**

See *Mo-Zi*; **Mohism**

Further reading: Wong 2003 (1.3.2)

Mo-Zi (Mo Tzu) 墨子: The *Mo-Zi* is the classical text of Mohism. Its 45 chapters come in two major parts: (1) Chapters 1–39 constitute the textual sources for early Mohism; (2) Chapters 40–45 constitute the textual sources for later Mohism, among which Chapters 40–43 are called the Mohist Canon.

See **Mo, Zi; Mohism**

Mohism / Mohist (*Mo-Jia* 墨家): Mohism or Mohist philosophy, generally speaking, can be characterized in terms of one methodological orientation and two major theses in contrast to the Confucian approach. Methodologically speaking, Mohists were concerned with *bian* (arguing out alternatives by distinguishing) and the standards by which to distinguish *shi-fei* (right and wrong alternatives). Its founder, **Mo Zi**, put forward his account of Three Tests for Any Doctrine, his "three-standard" methodological strategy (*san-biao-fa* 三表法). (1) Any doctrine needs to undergo three tests: (a) the *ancient authority test*: it must have its basis (to examine whether it would have agreement with the practice of the sage kings above); (b) the *direct experience test*: there must be evidence for it (to examine it by inquiries into the actual experience of the ordinary people below); (c) the *utilitarian test*: it must have practical application (to examine whether it coincides with the *benefit* of the ordinary people of the state). (2) Among the three tests, the utilitarian test provides a principle with which to judge all traditional morality and outweigh any ancient authority.

The foregoing primary utilitarian test suggests one substantial thesis concerning morality that criticized the traditional **Confucian morality**, i.e., the utilitarian principle to the effect that one should maximize the goodness (utility) of consequences of our actions for all people affected. Although both **Confucius** and Mo Zi discussed *ren* (humanity) and *yi* 義 (righteousness), with Confucius, there was a fundamental difference between *jun-zi* (the morally superior person) and *xiao-ren* (the morally inferior person): the former is after *yi* while the latter after *li* 利 (benefits/profits). In contrast, according to Mo Zi, all ethical virtues are eventually to be understood in terms of their beneficial results.

Another related major thesis of Mohism is its idea of universal care for everyone (*jian-ai* 兼愛). In contrast to the Confucian emphasis on one's love with a distinction in view of relations of kinship with oneself, Mohists emphasized that one needs to show impartial concern for everyone, irrespective of their kinship with oneself. Also in contrast to the Confucian approach, Mohists advocated universal care because of its beneficial effect rather than basing it upon any inherent goodness in human beings or of the act.

Mo Zi and his followers justified their moral thoughts by resorting to *tian* (天, heaven) as natural authority via the concept of *tian-zhi* (天志, heaven's intention): *tian* is like a wisest moral agent whose intention provides a reliable, objective ultimate criterion of morality. They also refuted **fatalism** in terms of the three-standard methodological strategy and maintained a certain form of **self-freedom**.

See **Mo Zi**; **morality**; *ren*; *tian*; **utilitarianism**; *yi* 義

Further reading: Fraser 2002, 2009 (1.3.2); Graham 1989 Part II Ch.2 (2.4), 2003 (1.3.2); Hansen 2003 (1.3.2); Lum 1977 (1.3.2); Wong 2003 (1.3.2)

moral cultivation see **self-cultivation**

moral discretion see *quan* 權

morality: One of the major issues in classical Chinese philosophy is its perennial concern with human morality and its (self) **cultivation,** which has been well illustrated in the reflective pursuits of the two most important movements of thought in classical Chinese philosophy: **Confucianism** and (philosophical) **Daoism.**

Morality is a fundamental, normative value of human (external) conduct and (internal) character with regard to rightness and goodness. Its reflective examination in philosophy is moral philosophy or **ethics.** It is fundamental because it directly involves the fundamental identity of human beings, because it concerns those dimensions of human character and conduct that are of serious consequence to human welfare and well-being, and because the rules and principles capturing this value are considered eventually to regulate and override other social prescriptions and rules (rules of etiquette, professional codes, or legislative laws). It is normative because such value intrinsically implies certain standards (moral standards) by which each member of human society should live; this is independent of whether or not each member of human society actually behaves that way and whether or not each member of human society is actually that kind of person. In short, it is prescriptive, rather than descriptive, in character.

See **Confucianism; Daoism; ethics; self-cultivation**

Mou, Zong-san (Mou Tsung-san) 牟宗三 (1909–95) is considered to be a very original, and perhaps the most influential thinker, in **Contemporary Neo-Confucianism**. He was the student of **Xiong Shi-li**, the founder of Contemporary Neo-Confucianism, but developed his own philosophical system. He took a comparative approach to his study of Chinese philosophy and developing his own system, especially in view of Kant's theoretical framework. He was among the first modern Chinese philosophers who effectively applied conceptual analysis to examining the ideas and insights of traditional Chinese philosophy. His representative works include *Zhi-De-Zhi-Jue-Yu-zhong-Guo-Zhi-Xue* (*Intellectual Intuition and Chinese Philosophy*, 1974) and *Yuan-Shan-Lun* (*On the Summum Bonum*, 1985), which set out his philosophical system.

See **Confucianism; contemporary Neo-Confucianism**
Further reading: Liu 2003 (1.13.2); Tan 2009 (1.13.2)

mystical/mysticism: Some portions and strands of classical Chinese thought have been considered to be mystical in character or to manifest mysticism. Nevertheless, two questions remain: (1) whether, and to what extent, such a characterization is adequate with regard to these portions and strands; (2) what the due relationship between Chinese philosophy and such portions and strands in Chinese thought is.

The defining character of mystical experience, mystical objects, and mystical beliefs (if any) is considered to be their defying inter-communicable expression in language, incommensurate with language, and hence unprovable or inexplicable in terms of inter-subjectively accessible resources (either linguistic or conceptual/explanatory). Mysticism attempts to gain, or is a way of gaining, knowledge or understanding of a certain subject matter, or union with divine nature (e.g., God) by means of ecstatic contemplation via mystical experience, mystical objects, or mystical beliefs.

It is arguably right that, insofar as one defining character of **philosophy** (**philosophical inquiry**) lies in its fundamental critical character, which in turn requires the linguistically inter-communicable and inter-accessible character of philosophical ideas, a *philosophical* inquiry might begin with, but cannot eventually rest content with, something mystical; this would render the inquiry closed to criticism and intelligible reflective examination.

See **Chinese philosophy; philosophy**

N

nature/natural: In Chinese thought, generally, the natural is contrasted with the social or conventional. Nature is associated with *tian* or the constant movement of the heavenly bodies. In human actions, a natural action implies an easy flow, a smooth fit with reality, and a sense of tranquility/satisfaction in execution or performance, as what **Daoism** delivers via its conception of *wu-wei*. In Daoism, both nature and natural actions are considered to be *zi-ran* 自然 (self-so; natural)

　　See **Daoism;** *tian*; *wu-wei*

　　Further reading: Ames 1998 (1.5.2); Lai 2007 (1.5.2); Slingerland 2003 (1.5.2); Wang 2003 (1.5.2)

naturalism: A view that explains all things in the world eventually in terms of nature or all natural things in the universe. **Lao Zi**'s metaphysical view as delivered in the *Dao-De-Jing* is considered to be one version of naturalism, though it is quite distinct from some contemporary versions of naturalism that give explanations by the methods characteristic of the natural sciences.

See *Dao-De-Jing*; idealism; Lao, Zi; metaphysics; realism

nei-sheng-wai-wang 內聖外王 (inner sageliness and outer kingliness): A slogan in the **Confucian** tradition which highlights the two intrinsically related aspects of the Confucian mission: on the one hand, one should strive to become a *jun-zi*, a morally superior person; on the other hand, one need actively participate in social transformation to help others and the whole of society improve in accordance with *ren* and *li* 禮.
See **Classical Confucianism; Confucianism;** *jun-zi*; *li* 禮; *ren*

Neo-Confucianism (*Song-Ming* **Confucianism**) 宋明儒學: Neo-Confucianism is a movement within the **Confucian** tradition and is the second major stage of its development, roughly during the *Song* Dynasty (960–1279), *Yuan* Dynasty (1206–1368), and *Ming* Dynasty (1368–1644) so also called "*Song-(Yuan)-Ming*" Confucianism. The Confucian scholars in the *Song* Dynasty took up the challenge from **Daoism** (in the form of **Neo-Daoism** which became popular in the *Wei-Jin* Dynasties) and from **Buddhism**, which became prominent in the *Sui* and *Tang* Dynasties, and started the trend of Neo-Confucianism with sophisticated philosophical theories.

The major thinkers in Neo-Confucianism include **Shao Yong, Zhou Dun-yi, Cheng Hao, Zhang Zai, Cheng Yi, Zhu Xi, Lu Jiu-yuan, Wang Shou-ren**, and **Huang Zong-xi** (though Huang lived in the early *Qing* Dynasty). Along with one basic line throughout the Confucian tradition, Neo-Confucianism is also concerned with how one strives to become a *jun-zi* through moral **self-cultivation**. Nevertheless, in contrast to the **classical Confucian** philosophers, one shared line among the Neo-Confucian philosophers is their subscription to the principle of the interconnection between the way of heaven and human nature/destiny (*tian-dao-xing-ming-xiang-guan-tong* 天道性命相貫通), in response to the challenges from Buddhism and Daoism. However, there are two distinct major trends or schools of thought among the Neo-Confucian philosophers: *Cheng-Zhu-li-xue* (Cheng Yi and Zhu Xi's learning of principle) and *Lu-Wang-xin-xue* (Lu Jiu-yuan and Wang Shou-ren's learning of mind-heart). Huang Zong-xi, a philosopher in the earlier *Qing* Dynasty, also belonged to the latter trend of Neo-Confucianism.*

See **Cheng, Hao; Cheng, Yi; Confucianism; Huang, Zong-xi;** *jun-zi*; *li-xue*; **Lu, Jiu-yuan; self-cultivation; Shao Yong; Wang, Shou-ren;** *xin-xue*; **Zhou, Dun-yi; Zhu, Xi**

Further reading: de Bary 1975 (1.9.2); Liu 1998, 2009 (1.9.2)*

Neo-Daoism: Neo-Daoism refers to a significant **Daoist** movement of thought in Chinese philosophy, between the third and sixth centuries (roughly during the *Wei-Jin* Dynasties), which is also labeled *xuan-xue* (玄學 the learning of the profound *dao*). Responding to the political chaos and corruption of the late *Han* Dynasty and the partial failure of **Confucian** orthodoxy as the state ideology and for the sake of exploring an ideological alternative, the movement set out to elaborate further the profound meaning of the classical **Daoist** heritage, primarily through commentaries on the three Daoist classical texts, the *Yi-Jing*, the *Dao-De-Jing*, and the *Zhuang-Zi*, which were later collectively labeled the *San-Xue* (三玄 *the Three Profound Treatises*). The representative thinkers of the movement include He Yan (*c.* 207–49), Xun Can (*c.* 212–40), **Xi Kang** (*c.* 223–62), **Wang Bi** (226–49), Ouyang Jian (late third century), and **Guo Xiang** (died 312).

Neo-Daoism is primarily concerned with interpretation and understanding, as Neo-Daoist thinkers carried out philosophical inquiries primarily through their commentaries on the Daoist classics in critical response to commentary methods of the *Han* Confucian learning. The concern resulted in the debate on the relation between speech and meaning (言意之辯 *yan-yi-zhi-bian*). Although a minority of Neo-Daoists, like Ouyang Jian, argued for the thesis of *yan-jin-yi* (言盡意 meaning-delivery within speech capacity), most of Neo-Daoists denied it: for example, Xi Kan maintained *yan-bu-jin-yi* (言不盡意 meaning delivery beyond speech capacity); Wang Bi advocated *de-yi-wang-xiang* (得意忘象 forgetting speech once meaning is achieved). Another basic issue that Neo-Daoists addressed is how to understand one fundamental character of the *dao*, i.e., *wu* (non-being, nothingness) and its relation to *you* (being). Wang Bi argued that *wu* was the "original reality," while *you* was a variety of functions of *wu*, while Guo Xiang maintained that *wu* could not be the gateway to anything but makes sense only relative to *you* (only *not* this being or *not* that being) and that *you* must be self-engendered and eternal.*

See **classical Daoism; Daoism; Guo, Xiang; Wang, Bi; Xi, Kan;** *yan-yi-zhi-bian*; **you** versus **wu**

Further reading: Chan 2009 (1.7.2)*

New Confucianism see **Contemporary Neo-Confucianism**

nirvana 涅盤 (enlightenment / emancipation): This is a **Buddhist** notion of enlightenment. The word *nirvana* literally means "blowing out", as of a lamp, or "extinction". According to Buddhism, one attains *nirvana* when the ultimate state of enlightenment (i.e., Buddhahood) is achieved and when one escapes from **samsara** – the eternal cycle of rebirth. Buddhism further stresses *nirvana* in terms of *tathata* (suchness) and *sunyana* (nothingness or emptiness). Suchness is the authentic state of one's mind which captures things as they are beyond all predications such as existence or non-existence and one or many. It transcends the ordinary senses, ideas, and definitions. It is thus called *sunyata*, which means emptiness, for it is empty of all the alleged permanent/fixed attributes that were imposed via predications. *Sunyana* cannot be understood by ordinary intellectual process but only through *prajna*, a kind of transcendental wisdom or a special kind of intuitive knowledge.

See **Buddha; Buddhism; Buddhist *karma* and *samsara*; prajna**

Further reading: Gregory 1987 (1.8.2); King 1991 (1.8.2)

nominalism: It has been argued that there is a strong nominalist orientation in the texts of some of the ancient thinkers (such as **Gong-sun Long**) of classical Chinese philosophy which actually refutes Platonic realism concerning universals or pre-empties the Platonic one–many problem, although this view remains controversial. Nominalism is the view that **universals**, the things shared by individual particular things, do not really exist in the external world except as shared concepts in the human mind or as (common/abstract) names in language. A modest version of nominalism maintains that universals do not really exist in the external world but do exist as abstract concepts in the human mind; this kind of nominalism is also called "conceptualism." In contrast, a strong version of nominalism insists that universals exist neither in the external world nor in our mind but only as names in our language.

See **Gong-sun, Long; universals**

Further reading: Cheng 2007 (1.4.2); Fung (Yu-lan) 1952 (1.4.2); Fung (Yiu-ming) 2007 (1.4.2); Hansen 1983 (1.4.2); Mou 2007 (1.4.2)

one principle with its many manifestations see *li-yi-fen-shu*
理一分殊

ontology: Ontology is a central branch of **metaphysics** which
inquires into what exists and the nature, structure and
fundamental principles of things that exist in the universe. Chinese philosophy has its rich resources in ontology, from the *yin-yang* **metaphysical vision** and the
Daoist *dao-de*-complementarity metaphysical vision to
the Neo-Confucian *li-yi-fen-shu* metaphysical view.
    See **cosmology;** *dao;* *li-yi-fen-shu;* **metaphysics;** *yin-
yang* **metaphysical vision**

P

perspectivism: Various kinds of perspectivism have been
suggested in the Chinese tradition as well as in the
Western tradition. "Perspectivism" is a blanket term
used (ambiguously) to refer to a number of different
kinds of metaphilosophical attitudes, methodological
guiding principles, or even more systematic methodological frameworks concerning how to look at the nature
and status of a variety of perspectives taken to approach
an object of study.
    There are two basic types of perspectivism, a subjective
one and an objective one. When the term "perspectivism"
is used to mean the former, it is sometimes used as
another label for, or characterized in terms of, a radical,
"anything goes" version of conceptual relativism. Given
an object of study together with its possessed aspects or
attributes, subjective perspectivism renders relevant and
eligible any (methodological or substantial) perspective

CHINESE PHILOSOPHY A–Z   113

so long as that perspective is projected from the subjective agent (or a group of agents), whether or not the perspective really points to (some aspect of) the object; in other words, the validity of a perspective is merely relative to the conceptual scheme of the subjective agent (the group of agents) and sufficient for its relevance and eligibility. Subjective perspectivism is thus taken as a major argument against external **realism** and for **idealism**.

In contrast, objective perspectivism bases the relevance and eligibility of a perspective (given an object of study) on whether the perspective points to some aspect that is objectively (instead of merely believed to be) possessed by the object of study. From the point of view of objective perspectivism, given an object of study and given that the identity of its genuine aspect (including those that result from its development), it is not the case that any perspective goes, but only those eligible perspectives that point to genuine aspects of the object can go.

Zhuang Zi's methodological framework, as suggested especially in Inner Chapter 2, *Qi-Wu-Lun*, of the *Zhuang-Zi*, is considered a kind of perspectivism. How to interpret Zhuang Zi's version of perspectivism is controversial: some view it as a kind of subjective perspectivism or a radical, "anything goes" version of conceptual relativism, while others argue that it is a kind of objective perspectivism.

See **philosophical methodology; pluralism; relativism; Zhuang, Zi;** *Zhuang-Zi*

Further reading: Kjellberg and Ivanhoe 1996 (1.5.2); Mou 2008b (2.1)

philosophy / philosophical inquiry (*zhe-xue* 哲學) **and philosophy in China**: This is a kind of reflective inquiry, labeled "philosophy" in English and *philosophia* (literally "love of knowledge/wisdom") in Greek, while 哲學, with its transliteration *zhe-xue*, in Chinese (originally meaning "learning of knowledge/wisdom"). It has several characteristic features which collectively distinguish it from other kinds of learning or studies. (1) Philosophical inquiry asks fundamental questions, with various fundamental concerns, about the world and the human being; (2) philosophical inquiry is critical in the sense that it does not blindly accept anything but bases it on justification and has it subject to criticism; and (3) philosophical inquiry establishes its conclusions intrinsically through argumentation, justification, and explanation. In view of these fundamental characteristics, Chinese philosophy is kindred in spirit to other philosophical traditions, although it has distinct ways to deliver them. It is partly true that, historically speaking, there is no separation among literature, history, and philosophy in ancient Chinese thought. It is also partly true that there seems to be no separation between philosophy and religion in ancient Chinese thought. Nevertheless, this amounts to saying neither that there is no significant conceptual distinctions between those inquiries nor that we cannot reflectively and effectively focus on one dimension of the whole in the subsequent reflective examination (say, its philosophical dimension). We *can* do that, depending on the primary purpose of a project in reflective examination. For example, if one's primary purpose is to examine how an idea or approach in one tradition could contribute to a philosophical issue, together with some other approach (either from the same tradition or from another tradition), instead of just giving a historical description, then one is entitled to focus only on the philosophical dimension or even only on some aspect(s) of the philosophical dimension most relevant to the current concern.

Although philosophy and religion have fundamental concerns in common, and although a historical movement of thought can contain both elements, philosophy is distinguished from religion in two closely related ways. (1) Philosophical inquiry is critical in nature in the sense that it does not *blindly* claim or accept anything and nothing is *absolutely* excluded from a philosophical inquirer's gaze. This includes a philosopher's attitude toward her own claims. Though she can very firmly maintain her current position (not blindly but on the basis of argumentation, understood broadly), a philosopher is expected to be open-minded and have her position open to criticism and possible revision or change, rather than rendering it absolutely immune from criticism. (2) Philosophical inquiry establishes its conclusions *intrinsically and primarily through **argumentation**, *justification, and explanation* rather than being based on faith.

See **argumentation**; **Chinese philosophy**; **philosophical methodology**

Further reading: Cua 2003 (2.1); Fung 1948, 1953 (2.4); Mou 2009b (2.1); Ragland and Heidt 2001 (2.1)

prajna: *Prajna* is used in **Buddhism** to refer to a kind of intuitive knowledge-achieving capacity and process to reach an integral and holistic understanding of reality and thus *nirvana*. *Prajna* is considered to be radically different from ordinary reasoning; it is considered to constitute the true source of all genuine knowledge; it is not inter-subjectively furnished but can result from cultivation and meditation.

See **Buddhism**; *nirvana*

pluralism: In modern Chinese philosophy, many studies that carry out comparative approaches adopt certain forms of pluralism when looking at the relation between distinct approaches under comparative examination. For example, many projects in the **constructive engagement**

movement in modern Chinese philosophy are pluralistically-oriented. Pluralism is the view that there is a plurality of sound answers, alternative points of view, or distinct approaches to questions about a given subject matter or object of study. The alternative points of view or distinct approaches are not necessarily incompatible but complementary, especially when they set out to capture distinct aspects or dimensions of the subject matter or the object of study. Attention needs to be paid to the distinctions and connections between (various versions of) pluralism, **perspectivism**, and **relativism**.

See **constructive engagement movement in modern Chinese philosophy; perspectivism; relativism**

pragmatic / pragmatism / pragmatics: Some strands and thoughts in classical Chinese philosophy are considered to be pragmatic in character. A *pragmatic* approach in philosophy, generally speaking, includes (though does not merely mean) a methodological perspective that is intended to capture, emphasize, or be sensitive to situated uses of involved conceptual and explanatory resources in contexts, their users' relevant intentions in the uses, and/or the consequence or utility of such practices. For example, a *pragmatic* perspective concerning the function of the notion of truth can hold that one function of (the notion of), and/or one epistemic means by which to identify, the truth of a statement lies in the utility of accepting it. Such a methodological perspective can be associated with various (adequate or inadequate) methodological guiding principles with regard to how to look at the relation of the pragmatic perspective to other methodological perspectives concerning an object of study (e.g., a correspondence perspective or a coherence perspective on the issue of truth). Stronger than merely a pragmatic perspective, *pragmatism* can be characterized in terms of a pragmatic perspective plus a (pragmatist) guiding principle that renders the pragmatic perspective exclusive or superior to other perspectives (if any) concerning an object of study. For example, rejecting a "correspondence" understanding of the nature of truth, a *pragmatist* account of truth can hold that the very nature of the truth of a statement lies in the utility of accepting it. In linguistics, in contrast to **semantics**, *pragmatics* is the study of situated uses of language which involve particular speech contexts and a language user's intentions; in the philosophy of language, there is a distinction between semantic and pragmatic approaches, which are closely related to semantics and pragmatics respectively.

Though distinct, **Confucius'** approach to moral **self-cultivation** in the *Lun-Yü* and **Lao Zi**'s approach in the *Dao-De-Jing* show a pragmatic character (see Further reading).

See **self-cultivation; semantic/semantics; truth**

Further reading: Ames and Hall 1987 (1.2.2); Mou 2002 (1.5.2); Xiao 2006 (1.2.2)

principle see *li* 理

Pure-Land Buddhism (*Jing-Tu-Zong***)** 淨土宗 is a form of Chinese Buddhism that was often found within *Mahayana* **Buddhist** practice; it did not become an independent sect until it reached Japan. In contrast to *Chan* **Buddhism, Three-Treatise Buddhism,** and **Consciousness-Only Buddhism** of **Chinese Buddhism,** Pure-Land Buddhism was more practically concerned than theoretically concerned, and more religious 'faith'-oriented than philosophically-oriented. Instead of meditative efforts toward enlightenment, Pure-Land Buddhism teaches that, through devotional faith, one can be reborn in the Pure Land in which enlightenment is guaranteed.

See **Buddhism; Chinese Buddhism;** *Mahayana* **Buddhism;** *nirvana*
Further reading: Tanaka 1990 (1.8)

Q

qi (*ch'i*) 氣: The term *qi* in classical Chinese philosophy means a kind of vital breath-like matter-energy which is the most fundamental stuff of everything. *Qi* can be light (spirits) or dense (material things). In **Neo-Confucianism**, there is a rich literature on *qi* and its relation to *li* 理 and ethics.
　　See **Neo-Confucianism;** *li* 理; *li-xue*; **Zhang, Zai**

qing (*ch'ing*) 情 (**affections, emotions**) **and** *li* 理 (**principle, rationale**): One significant concern in Chinese philosophy is with the relationship between *qing* (as in human emotions, affections, or feelings) and *li* (either as a principle in the objective universe or as a principle in the subjective mind that is to capture the objective *li* via cognitive rationality). A prominent orientation with regard to the concern in Chinese philosophy is to treat them as "metaphysically" interdependent, interconnected, or even interpenetrating and "functionally" complementary, kindred in spirit with the *yin-yang* **way of thinking.** There are some popular Chinese sayings that reflect such a coordinated, complementary consideration of both *qing* and *li*, such as *he-qing-he-li* (合情合理 in accordance with both *qing* and *li*), *tong-qing-da-li* (通情達理 considerate in view of both *qing* and *li*), and *bu-he-qing-li* (不合情理 not in accordance with *qing* and *li*). Given the traditional distinction between heart and mind as discrete locations respectively of emotions and rationality, an adequate translation of the Chinese character *xin* (心, literally heart) that reflects such an orientation is "heart-mind," rather than "heart." This highlights the point that the affections/emotions and cognitive rationality do not metaphysically or physically reside in separate locations, but are intertwined, interpenetrating, and interdependent.

See *li* 理; *xin*; *yin-yang* way of thinking

Qing Confucianism: *Qing* Confucianism is a specific movement within the **Confucian** tradition during the early *Qing* Dynasty (the period between its early years and the Opium Wars, roughly 1616–1838) which criticized orientations in *Song-Ming* **Neo-Confucianism** and had its own distinctive emphases. It is not a mere collection of those Confucians who lived in the early *Qing* Dynasty. For example, **Huang Zong-xi** was a Confucian in the *Qing* Dynasty but is considered to belong to the Neo-Confucian tradition instead of the movement of *Qing* Confucianism. Two prominent representatives of *Qing* Confucianism are **Yan Yuan** (1635–1704) and **Dai Zhen** (1723–77). The historical background to the emergency of *Qing* Confucianism is the downfall of the *Ming* Dynasty and its related political and social crisis: most Confucians of the early *Qing* viewed this as a sign of the ideological crisis of *Song-Ming* Neo-Confucianism (This crisis concerned the perceived failure to pay due attention to the practical role of Confucianism in setting the world in good order and the over-emphasis on metaphysical speculation.) In contrast to the Neo-Confucian subscription to the principle of *tian-dao-xing-ming-xiang-guan-tong* (天道性命相貫通, the interconnection between the Way of Heaven and human nature and destiny), the thinkers of *Qing* Confucianism such as Yan Yuan and Dai Zhen switched to a largely naturalistic outlook, either redefining the value and function of Confucianism in view of its role in setting the world to right (e.g., in Yan Yuan's case) or emphasizing the interdependence and interpenetration between *li* 理 (as principle) and concrete things, and between human nature and human desire (e.g., in Dai Zen's case).*

See **Confucianism; Dai, Zhen;** *li* 理; **Neo-Confucianism; Yan, Yuan**

Further reading: Liu 2009 (1.9.2); Cheng 2009 (1.10.2)*

quan (*ch'üan*) 權 (**moral discretion**): *Quan* is an important notion in the Confucian tradition of *dao* (***Dao-Tong***), meaning moral discretion or the weighing up of competing options sensitive to a current circumstance. The notion is to be understood in view of the distinction between *jing* 經 (the standard) and *quan*, while this distinction is related to the Confucian concern with the relationship between *chang* 常 (the constant) and *bian* 變 (the changing). **Zhu Xi** highlights their relation in this way: "*Jing* pertains to the constant aspect of *dao*, and *quan* to the changing aspect of dao" (*Zhu-Zi-Yu-Lei*, 6.1A). The exercise of *quan* is to be guided by *yi* 義 (righteousness) and *li* 理 (principle/reason).

See **Confucianism;** *Dao-Tong*; **Zhu, Xi**

Further reading: Cua 2003 (1) (1.9.2)

R

rationality / rational: In the Chinese philosophical tradition, rationality as the capacity of the human mind-heart (or *xin* 心, the human heart-mind) to reason or engage in **argumentation**, is understood in broad terms. It is neither limited to an intersubjective capacity of doing logical argumentation (such as deductive reasoning) nor excludes emotional elements (especially when the subject of the capacity is the human heart-mind, as some thinkers in Chinese philosophy have emphasized).

See **argumention/argument**; *xin*

realism: Realism is one of the important conceptual resources in characterizing and interpreting the nature and features of several metaphysical accounts suggested in classical Chinese philosophy. Realism is any doctrine that affirms the real existence of some kind of thing(s) in an area of discourse. This can include the external world, universals, other minds, moral properties, aesthetic properties, etc. For example, realism regarding universals holds that universals really exist beyond the human concept and language. Realism regarding the external world holds that the existence of the external world is independent of mind, in contrast to **idealism**.

See **idealism; materialism; naturalism**

reason see **rationality**

rectification of names see *zheng-ming*

reference (the issue of reference): One significant question that some thinkers in classical Chinese philosophy explored with regard to the issue of reference is whether, and in what way, the referring agent contributes to the identity of a thing when referring to the thing. Though having distinctive backgrounds and concerns, **Gong-sun Long**, a **Mohist**, and **Zhuang Zi** are considered similar in their approach to this issue: a referring agent's referring action, which involves her purpose and focus, assigns a certain identity to the thing referred to, or specifies some aspect(s) of the referent as its identity (or multiple identities). In being sensitive to one's purpose and focus, one is entitled to make a perspective shift in one's referring practice to focus on some other aspect of the referent as its identity. This kind of approach can be called the "purpose-perspective-sensitivity approach."

In his essay *Zhi-Wu-Lun* (On Referring to Things), Gong-sun Long emphasizes: "No things [that are identified or named as things] are not what are referred to [by linguistic names] . . . If there is no referring in the world, nothing can be called a 'thing'. If without referring [names], can anything in the world be called 'what is referring to'?" Gong-sun Long's point here is that the relevant contributing elements involved in the subject's act of referring via a name (such as what the subject's purpose is, which aspect of the referent the subject intends to seek or focus on, etc.) make their intrinsic contributions to the identity of the referent of the name. This point is also explicitly and emphatically addressed in his essay *Bai-Ma-Lun* (On the White Horse): "What makes a white horse a horse is their same [common] aspect given that is what is sought. If what is sought is the common aspect, a white horse would not be distinct from (*bu-yi*) a horse [in regard to the common aspect]. If what is sought is not some distinct but the same aspect, then why is it that yellow and black horses satisfy what is sought in one case but not in the other? It is evident that the two cases are distinct" (my translation). This crucial passage gives the fundamental rationale behind a number of Gong-sun Long's arguments for the thesis "[the] white horse [is] not [the] horse." The statement "The white horse is not the horse" is just another way to say in everyday language "The white horse has its distinct aspect which the horse does not [necessarily] have," while the statement "The white horse is the horse" is just another way to say in everyday language "The white horse has its common aspect which the horse [necessarily] does have." Each of the two can be true, depending on which aspect of the white horse the referring subject is focusing on and is thus refering to with regard to the identity of the white horse. In so doing, he alerts us to avoiding the danger of over-assimilating distinctions, especially when the distinctive aspects need to be emphatically focused on.

Zhuang Zi proceeds essentially in the same direction on this issue (see the *Zhuang-Zi*, Inner Chapter 3, *Yong-Sheng-Zhu*). Given an ox as a whole already there, what is its identity? How should one refer to it in terms of language? How should one identify it? As something whose identity is exclusively determined by its "essence," or as flesh and bones? It seems to Zhuang Zi that, based on one's specific purpose, one can legitimately refer to an ox as made up of flesh and bones. One can say that, from the Zhuang Zi style view of the philosophy of language, the relation between language and an object in the world is not one-to-one but many-to-one: there are multiple referring expressions that refer to various genuine aspects of the same object. Depending on one's purpose, one is entitled to take a certain perspective to focus on one aspect of the object and thus identify the object as what the referring expression capturing that aspect would tell. What is important is that these distinctive referring expressions refer to different aspects of the same object, the ox as a whole, which are metaphysically complementary to each other.

See **Gong-sun Long; Mohism; Zhuang, Zi**

Further reading: Li 2003 (1.5.2); Mou 2006 (2.5.2); 2007 (1.4.2)

ren (*jen*) 仁 (**humanity, human-heartedness**): The **Confucian** conception of *ren* was proposed by **Confucius** in the *Lun-Yü* and has occupied a central position in Confucian philosophy. It means *the* defining virtue of *jun-zi* (morally superior persons), which was characterized and emphasized in Confucius' thought as the most fundamental virtue among others. The term "*ren*" has been translated into English in a number of ways: *benevolence, man to manness, perfect virtue, human-heartedness, humanity,* etc. However, Confucius himself did not intend to give a single definition of *ren* but gave various characterizations sensitive to specific situations and contexts. Generally (but roughly), speaking, *ren* as the fundamental virtue is a fundamental moral sensibility which consists in appreciation of and reverence for fundamental human value; one's *ren* virtue manifests itself as interpersonal love and care when treating others. In the Confucian tradition, *ren* as interpersonal love and care, on the one hand, is love for all humans; on the other hand, it is love with distinction, or graded love (*ai-you-cha-deng* 愛有差等), in view of relations of kinship with oneself, in contrast to universal love/care for everyone (*jian-ai* 兼愛) as advocated by **Mohism**.

To achieve full *ren* virtue, one needs to make serious efforts to cultivate one's moral character. Confucius suggests some characteristic ways to carry out moral **self-cultivation**: "To master oneself and return to *li* 禮 are [joint ways to achieve] *ren*" (12.1); "A person of *ren*, wishing to establish his own character, also establishes the character of others, and wishing to be prominent himself, also helps others to be prominent. To be able to judge others by what is near to ourselves may be called the method of realizing *ren*" (6.28). Once one has captured the spirit of *ren*, one can find out what one should do in a given situation. Because each concrete situation is distinctive from any other, one needs to customize one's characterization of *ren* to certain concrete situations. If Confucius did not make any attempt to give a single definition of *ren*, it is not because he did not have a coherent and systematic understanding of it but because the complete meaning of *ren* is beyond a single formulated definition due to its fundamental character.

See **Confucius**; ***jun-zi***; ***li*** 禮; **self-cultivation**

Further reading: Chan 1955 (1.2.2); Shen 2003 (1.2.2); Shun 2002 (1.2.2)

righteousness see ***yi*** 義

Ru-Jia 儒家 see **Confucianism**

S

sage / sage king: The term "sage" in Chinese thought, and especially in the Confucian tradition, refers to an ideal wise or moral person. The phrase "sage king" means a collection of idealized wise and moral founders of Chinese society, including particularly pre-*Zhou* legendary leaders like Yao 堯, Shun 舜, and Yu 禹, but sometimes including the *Zhou* founders, King Wen 文王 and King Wu 武王.

See **classical Confucianism; Confucianism**

School of Names (*Ming-Jia* 名家): The School of Names is concerned with the general issue of the relation between names and actuality. Its members are also known as dialecticians or sophists because of their emphasis on rational argumentations and their focus on the deep structures of concepts. They carried out the study of how language works. Two major figures in this school are **Gong-sun Long** and **Hui Shi**. Generally speaking, Gong-sun Long emphasized the distinct aspects of things, though he did not ignore their common aspects, as his **"White-Horse-Not-Horse" thesis** shows. In contrast, Hui Shi stressed common aspects, connections, and the unification of things and the relativity of their distinctions, though he also paid attention to their distinct aspects, as some of his **Ten Propositions** shows.

See **Gong-sun Long; Hui, Shi; Hui Shi's Ten Propositions; "White-Horse-Not-Horse" thesis**

Further reading: Fung (Yiu-ming) 2009 (1.4.2); Fung (Yu-lan) 1952 Ch. 9 (2.4); Graham 1989 Part I, Ch. 5(2.4)

self-constitution, at the individual level: As human beings we characteristically reflect on our nature and our place in the world by asking: Who am I? What constitutes myself? Given that a human being lives in human society, how do we understand the social and individual character of the self? As far as the constitution of self (of the human agent) at the individual level is concerned, there are several representative but seemingly competing approaches. Plato (428–348 BCE) dealt with the issue in terms of his classical analysis of the "soul": the soul (permanently) has three separate parts, the rational (reason), the spirited or passionate (emotions), and the appetites (desires); all of them as parts of human nature are constantly present and we can be consciously aware of them; to establish a harmonious balance within the self and achieve what is proper to our nature, we need to be fully rational and use rationality to govern our emotions and desires.

A **Buddhist** approach to this is based on its core idea regarding the fundamental nature of the world, i.e., its thesis of the three signs of being. Among the three signs of being, the first one, that nothing is permanent, is considered the most fundamental, while another sign of being, that there is no self, is an extension of the foregoing sign of being. Given that the self (*atman*) as traditionally rendered is permanent and eternal, Buddhism argues that the eternal fixed self simply does not exist (*anatman*) because all (conditioned) things are impermanent. **Xuan Zang**, a Chinese Buddhist master of the **Consciousness-Only Buddhism**, gives his elaboration of the Buddhist thesis of non-self: the self is nothing but the evolution and transformation of inner consciousness. Buddhist thought in this regard is similar to that of David Hume (1711–76) in the British empiricist tradition, though they serve very different aims. Hume argued that it is impossible for us to stand outside our sense experience to know ourselves as enduring substantial selves and that a self is no more than a bundle of perceptions that are in constant flux.

Whereas both Plato's and Buddhist analyses start with apparent or conscious phenomena concerning the constitution of the self, Sigmund Freud (1856–1939) turned his focus to the unconscious domain of the self, later termed the *id*, which is essentially irrational (cannot be explained rationally) and which is inaccessible except via dreams, unintentional errors, etc. It seemed to Freud that this unconscious domain exerts a significant influence on the waking conscious self, the ego. The *id* contributes to many of the conflicts within the ego through its interaction with a special part of ego, the superego, which contains the conscience, the moral codes acquired from parents, society, and others who were influential in one's early childhood.

It might be the case that each of the foregoing accounts captures partial truth, or a certain dimension or layer, of the self-constitution and thus contributes to a complete understanding of various aspects of the self-constitution at the individual level.

See **Buddhism; Consciousness-Only Buddhism; self-constitution at the social level**

Further reading: Lai 2009 (1.8)

Self-constitution, at the social level: The issue concerning the constitution of the self at the individual level points to a related issue, that of the social versus individual character of the self. This is one of the central concerns of Chinese social and political philosophy.

Is the fundamental character of the self primarily individual or social, or in some way both? On the one hand, the independent and controlling rational part of the self in Plato's account and the distinctive *id* part of the self in Freud's account would render the self as having an individual, discrete, or autonomous character. Yet on the conditional and impermanent nature of the self in the Buddhist account and the superego part of the self in Freud's account, it seems that the self has a dependent or social character. As a matter of fact, the individualist consideration has been the mainstream orientation in the Western tradition. This extends from Socrates and Plato, who stuck to their principles against the popular opinions of their time, to modern capitalism which celebrates private ownership and individual initiative in the production process. But an individualist orientation has always had its challengers, especially when this orientation tends to overemphasize the individual character of the self and underestimate or even ignore the social character. G. W. F. Hegel (1770–1831) and Karl Marx (1818–83) are representative challengers from the nineteenth century who emphatically pointed to the historical and social character of the self.

As the sciences have made the progress, and as modern globalization has emerged since the nineteenth century, the social character of the self has become more and more apparent and significant. The pros and cons debate continued through the twentieth century. Martin Heidegger (1889–1976), a German existentialist, argued against the collective social identity of the self as one's own *Dasein* surrendered to the Others, or the *they-self*. As Heidegger sees it, the they-self is actually no one at all. He urges us to find our "authentic" self, i.e., "the Self which has been taken hold of in its own way." Heidegger's view can be viewed as a contemporary reaction against (actual or alleged) excessive socialization. Defending his predecessors and responding to new challenges from existentialism, Alasdair MacIntyre (1929–) emphasizes the social character of the self, arguing that "the story of my life is always embedded in the story of those communities from which I derive my identity." It seems that the fundamental character of the self can be neither an exclusively social one nor an exclusively individual one. Both those who emphasize the social character of the self, like MacIntyre, and those who stress the individual character of the self, like Heidegger, capture partial truth with regard to the fundamental character of the self. So what is really at issue is how one can achieve a balanced understanding and produce an account that does justice to both the social and individual character of the self. Also we require, practically speaking, guidance in maintaining a due balance between our personal growth and self-fulfillment on the one hand, and our own social relevance, responsibility, and obligations in the community and society, on the other.

Though it is agreed that the Chinese tradition has been largely persuaded by a **Confucian**-based relational and thus social understanding of the person, instead of by any notion of discrete individuality, how to interpret such a Confucian-based social understanding of the self with regard to the relation between individual interest and social interest is controversial. One influential interpretation takes it that the Confucian conception of the self is the ideal of the selfless person who is always willing to subordinate his own interests to the interest of a social group. This interpretation assumes that, in the Chinese context, community interest and self-interest are mutually exclusive. Another interpretation of the Confucian conception of the self renders community interest and self-interest as essentially interdependent and complementary instead of mutually exclusive. It is noted that the Confucian conception of the self is to some extent a prescriptive one seeking the *ideal* of (moral) self, and thus one can say that it is a moral approach concerning value rather than a metaphysical approach concerning fact, or what really is. Nevertheless, the Confucian conception of self as a whole does have a profound metaphysical foundation with regard to human nature and the human social character and is thus not purely prescriptive but understands value and fact as intrinsically related. In this way, the Confucian way of looking at the relation between individual interest and community interest might suggest a constructive understanding of how the individual character and social character of the self are profoundly or metaphysically related.

See **Confucianism; self-constitution at the individual level**

Further reading: Ames et al. 1994 (2.5.3); Munro 1969 (2.5.3)

self-cultivation (*xiu-shen* 修身): One's (moral) self-cultivation involves preparing, improving, and developing one's moral sensibility to become a morally superior person via various means, including careful attention, conscious study and training, or by more unconventional methods. All three major movements of thought in classical Chinese philosophy (**Confucianism,** philosophical **Daoism,** and **Chinese Buddhism**) emphasize moral self-cultivation in their distinct ways.

In the Confucian tradition, a primary concern is with how one strives to become a *jun-zi* (a morally superior person) through moral self-cultivation, as first set out by **Confucius.** Emphasizing the interplay between *ren* and *li*

禮 in contexts, Confucius took a situational, **pragmatic** approach in characterizing **virtues,** such as *ren* and *xiao,* and giving advice on self-cultivation. Some of the subsequent Confucian thinkers more explicitly suggested different models of self-cultivation. Based on distinct understandings of original human (metaphysical and/or moral) nature and its relation to moral cultivation, three representative models have been suggested: the **Mencius-**style *development* model, the **Xun Zi-**style re-formation model, and the **Zhu Xi-**style discovery model. According to the development model, one's moral self-cultivation lies primarily in *developing* one's innate initial moral sensibility to achieve full virtue, as one's original moral nature is good. According to the re-formation model, one's moral self-cultivation lies primarily in *re-forming* one's incipient 'bad' tendencies or dispositions and thus transforming one into a virtuous person. According to a discovery model (generally speaking, adopted by **Neo-Confucian** thinkers), everyone has innately whatever is needed to achieve full virtue, which is nevertheless hidden by one's selfish inclination; one's moral self-cultivation lies primarily in making efforts to discover this source of virtue within oneself through *ge-wu-zhi-zhi.*

In comparison and by contrast, **classical Daoism** put more emphasis on cultivating spontaneous virtue by following *wu-wei.* In the *Dao-De-Jing* (Ch. 38), **Lao Zi** drew a distinction between *shang-de* and *xia-de*: *shang-de* (上德 superior virtue) is the high level of spontaneous morality experienced within, which repeats the spontaneous nature of initial (infants') spontaneous morality but can result from conscious effort and disciplined morality; in contrast, *xia-de* (下德 inferior virtue) is the *excessive* development of deliberate, disciplined, designed, ruled-oriented morality which would often result in taking fixed and formulaic rules as the *final* and *absolute* moral authority, *unnecessary* self-unsatisfaction, *over*-conscientiousness, or hypocrisy. Emphasizing the ultimate goal of achieving *shang-de*, rejecting any fixed rule as the absolute moral authority, and stressing being sensitive to the need of situated natural processes through ***wu-wei***, Lao Zi drew our attention to two possible directions of post-deliberation development of moral self-cultivation: one is to negatively or excessively develop into *xia-de*; the other is to positively develop into *shang-de*.

In Chinese Buddhism, partially influenced by Daoism and in view of its ultimate goal to achieve ***nirvana***, **Chan Buddhism** emphasized cultivation without cultivation as the way toward becoming enlightened: nonparadoxically, it is to cultivate without deliberate effort and purposeful mind, i.e., to cultivate oneself naturally. This involves two significant distinctions: that between initial deliberate and conscious cultivation, and cultivation without deliberate and conscious efforts; and that between original naturalness as a gift of nature and cultivated naturalness as a product of the cultivation.

See *Chan* Buddhism; Chinese Buddhism; Confucianism; **Daoism**; *de*; *ge-wu-zhi-zhi*; **human (moral) nature***; **jun-zi**; *li* 禮; Neo-Confucianism; **pragmatic**; *ren*; **virtue**; *wu-wei*; *xiao; yi* 義

Further reading: (1) for the Confucian approach: Ames and Hall 1987 (1.2.2); Ivanhe 2000 (1.2.2); Shun 2003 (1.2.2); Van Norden (2003) (1.2.2); (2) for the Daoist approach: Mou 2002 (1.5.2); Slingerland 2003 (1.5.2); Smullyan 1977 (1.5.2); (3) for the Buddhist approach: Fung 1948 Ch. 22 (2.4); Gregory 1987 (1.8.2)

self-freedom: The issue of (self-) freedom has been significantly addressed in both the Chinese tradition and the

Western tradition in their distinctive and philosophically interesting ways.

Self-freedom is a **metaphysical** issue over whether the human agent has freedom (or *is* free) to make her own choices and thus carry out her own actions instead of being predetermined to do so. The issue as addressed here is metaphysical in kind, instead of ethical or attitudinal, because it involves function and agency as related to the metaphysical constitution of the self and the metaphysical connection of the self with the outside world, including the social environment. The issue is significant because it has important implications for our moral, personal, and social lives. For instance, whether one moral agent is supposed to be morally responsible for her action depends in part on whether she is free to carry out her actions. It would seem that one is not responsible for what one is forced to do or is unable to avoid, no matter how hard one tries.

Generally speaking, **determinism** renders all events unavoidable and predetermined by their causes. Historically speaking, in the ancient past, what was typically at issue was **fatalism** to the effect that whatever happened was unavoidable, no matter by what (by their causes or anything else). Determinism and fatalism are related but not the same. Though fatalism was a typical ancient form of determinism and may have resulted at least in part from a lack of scientific knowledge of the world, the modern forms of determinism as presented by seventeenth- and eighteenth-century philosophers tended to result from alleged full knowledge of the world in terms of Newtonian physics.

In Chinese philosophy, **Mo Zi** refuted fatalism in terms of his "three-standard" methodological strategy. It is instructive to see to what extent Mo Zi's refutation is philosophically interesting. Two things are certain in his refutation of fatalism: first, he set out to establish general standards by which any doctrine, including fatalism, should be tested; second, he based his judgment to a large extent on his intuitive or common-sense observations. This strategy is not idiosyncratic or obsolete; some contemporary philosophers use it in a constructive way.

One radical approach from the other side is (metaphysical) libertarianism, which claims that (hard) determinism is false and that human beings are free. According to Jean-Paul Sartre (1905–80), the self does not possess any pre-set essence or fixed nature but freely decides what to make of the self, and in this sense, her existence precedes her essence. Advocates of either hard determinism or libertarianism are called "incompatibilists" insofar as one thing is common to both sides: the human being's freedom is not compatible with a belief in causal determinism.

In contrast to incompatibilism, compatibilists think that causal determinism is true but we are nevertheless free. The compatibilist's approach typically involves reexamining the concept of freedom (or the characteristics of causal chains) and specifies it (them) in a way that is consistent with causal determinism (or freedom). Indeed, the term "free" or "freedom" is ambiguous. Although all accounts of freedom involve voluntariness with an absence of certain sorts of determination, they diverge at that point. There seems to be a number of different understandings of freedom, though they can be consistent, and thus some accounts of freedom include elements from more than one of them: (1) freedom of indifference to the effect that one is free if each choice one deliberates upon is an open alternative insofar as it is possible but not yet necessarily determined by antecedent conditions; (2) freedom of spontaneity to the effect that one is free if one acts as one desires or feels like in performing the action; (3) freedom as autonomy to the effect that one is free if one's choice is determined by one's character, one's certain understanding of higher values, or available reasons; (4) freedom of origination to the effect that one is self-determining and (at least sometimes) originates one's own behavior. One recent approach of this kind (Richard Taylor's) is based on the conception of freedom of origination: it is a person (as a whole) as a self-moving agent, but not merely part of her or something within her, that is the cause of her own activity; an agent, which is a substance and not an event, can nevertheless be the cause of an event.

Zhuang Zi's approach resists a hasty and rushed classification of his **Daoist** understanding of freedom into the above ready-made categories of "determinism," "libertarianism," or even "compatibilism" (as the latter is specified in terms of the first two). Daoists maintain that the universe has its own general and fundamental principle, the *dao*, which somehow, or naturally, unifies all things, including human beings and human society as part of the whole universe. However, the natural way of unifying all things and thus the natural connections among them is hardly an exclusively "causal" one – the Daoist approach in this regard is open-ended. Human freedom consists in one's (intuitively or reflectively) realizing and capturing the global *dao*, via its local manifestation (*de*) in oneself (one's distinctive natural ability) and in many particular things in the surrounding environment and through one's learning, deliberation, and cultivation. Thus it consists in being able "voluntarily" (thus "naturally" or "freely") to float with the *dao*. Zhuang Zi's conception of (relative) happiness renders one's understanding of the *dao* and one's freedom of spontaneity intrinsically related: one's (relative) happiness consists in one's doing what one is able to do *and* what one feels like doing. To be truly free is to capture the *dao* (both the *dao* in the surrounding environment and one's natural ability as individualized *dao* in oneself) and follow the *dao* naturally or in the way of ***wu-wei*** (doing those things that are not against the *dao* and fully and freely exercising one's natural ability). In this way, one's freedom is a dynamic process rather than a static, pre-furnished state.

See ***dao***; Daoism; determinism; fatalism; Mo, Zi; Mohism; ***wu-wei***; Zhuang, Zi

Further reading: Ames 1998 (1.5.2); Smullyan 1977 (1.5.2)

semantic / semantics: The issue of semantics in the Chinese language and its philosophical interpretation is controversial in the Chinese philosophy of language. Several reflective hypotheses have been suggested (see Further reading).

The term "semantic/semantics" in its standard sense means the study of the relation between linguistic expressions and the extra-linguistic objects for which they stand; such a relation is usually called a "semantic relation." The "semantic" concept of truth is named in this sense: i.e., an account that explains the truth (property) of linguistic sentences by specifying a kind of "about" relation between the sentences and the extra-linguistic objects which they are *about*. Also in this sense, the term is used in contrast to syntax and **pragmatics**.

See **Chinese language and reflective way of thinking in Chinese philosophy; pragmatic/pragmatics; truth**

Further reading: Ames and Hall 1987 (2.5.2); Cheng 1987 (2.5.2); Hansen 1983 (2.5.2); Harbsmeier 1989 (2.5.2); Mou 1999 (2.5.2)

Seng, Zhao (Seng-chao) 僧肇 (384–414) was the leading disciple of Kumarajina (鳩摩羅什 344–413); although the latter introduced to China the basic thought of **Three-Treatise Buddhism** established by Nagarjuna (龍樹 second century CE) via his doctrine of *Madhyamika*, Seng Zhao further elaborated and transmitted the doctrine in China. He is considered to be a bridge between **Buddhism** and **Daoism**. **Ji Zhang** further developed his ideas in this direction. His major writing is the *Zhao-Lun* (*The Book of Zhao*).

See **Buddhism; Ji, Zang; Three-Treatise Buddhism**

Shang, Yang 商鞅 (real name "Gong-sun Yang" 公孫鞅: died 338 BCE) was an early leading figure of **Legalism** and a Chinese statesman responsible for the design of the first imperial state, *Qin*, which eventually unified China (221 BCE). He relied on publicized and objective standards (*fa*, routinely translated as "laws") to rationalize trade and official regulations. He probably left no actual writings, though there is a work written in his name.

See **Legalism**

Shao, Yong (Shao Yung) 邵雍 (style name "Yao-fu" 堯夫: 1011–77) was a major thinker in the *Song* Dynasty (960–1279) and one of the founders of *Song-Ming* **Neo-Confucianism**. He developed a cosmological scheme based on the *Yi-Jing* text. His representative writings are the *Huang-Ji-Jing-Shi* (*Supreme Ultimate Ordering the Universe*) and the *Yi-Chuang-Ji-Rang-Ji* (*Yi River Teacher's Beating the Rang*).

See **Neo-Confucianism**

Shen, Dao (Shen Tao) 慎到 (*c.* 350–275 BCE) was a thinker in the Warring States Period who influenced both **Legalism** and **Daoism**. He emphasized power, circumstances, and natural tendency through his conception of *shi* 勢.

See **Daoism; Han, Fei; Legalism**

shi-fei 是非 (what is this versus not what is this; being this versus being not this; right/adequate versus wrong/inadquate): In classical Chinese philosophy, the concepts of *shi* and *fei* constitute a basic pair of evaluative categories extensively applicable in various reflective areas from **metaphysics** to **ethics**: fitting what is (this) versus not fitting what is (this), being this versus being not this, or (being) right/adequate versus (being) wrong/inadequate. The evaluative status and metaphysical implication of the two terms *shi* and *fei* in classical Chinese philosophy are closely related to the primary semantic features of the two terms used in ancient Chinese before the *Han* Dynasty.

In the ancient Chinese before the *Han* Dynasty, the term *shi* (是) served primarily as a demonstrative pronoun, meaning "this," with the following semantic features: (1) it is a referring term which semantically or directly refers to the thing as a whole that is singled out by *shi*; (2) *shi* has an indexical character (i.e., exactly which thing as a whole, or which specific identity of the thing, is singled out by *shi* is sensitive to the context in which *shi* is used). What *shi* refers to is *what is this*: the first semantic feature is highlighted by *what is* this (i.e., *shi* functions as direct-reference symbol to point to *what is* – the thing as a whole that exists; it shows its existential use – similar to the existential use of "to be" in English), while the second semantic feature is highlighted by what *is this* (i.e., *shi* functions as an indexical to demonstrate the identity of the thing referred to in the context; it show its predicative use, but distinguishes from the predicative use of "to be" – *shi* was not a mere copula that needs another word as its complement but was a self-complement as ". . .*is this*" shows). The term *fei* (非) is used primarily as a negative prefix, typically with a noun or an adverb, meaning "non," "not," or "the lack of"; when it is used with *shi*, it indicates the negation of the reference, what is this, of *shi*: it negates or denies either *what is* this [not "this" thing as a whole (but something else)] or what is *this* [not "this" specific identity or aspect of the thing (but some other specific identity or aspect of the thing)]. (Aristotle made the distinction between the existential and predicative uses of "to be", as illustrated respectively by the distinction between "The *dao* is" and "The *dao* is great". **Angus Graham** suggested that *shi-fei* corresponds to the predicative case, while *you-wu* to the existential case. Nevertheless, the foregoing analysis suggests that *shi* has a double existential-predicative usage and that *fei* thus has a two-way negation usage.)

The concepts of *shi* and *fei* in the context of classical Chinese can be viewed as reflective elaborations of the foregoing semantic features of the term *shi* and *fei* in language use before the *Han* Dynasty. This in turn might bear on the folk meaning and usage of the two terms as a combined noun phrase, "*shi-fei*", after the *Han* Dynasty. The concept of *shi* still means *what is this*, but its two folk semantic features were elaborated in this way: (1) its semantic referent is designated as a normative goal to pursue or as a normative criterion or standard to meet as Chinese philosophy has its long-term tradition of *qui-shi* 求是 (pursuing what is); (2) when being used in contrast to the concept of *fei*, the indexical character of *shi* is generalized into a reference to any *specific* identity of the normative standard in view of a certain *specific* discourse or context; in contrast, the concept of *fei* constitutes a negation or violation of the specific identity of the normative standard (and implicitly suggests some other specific identity of normative standard). Nevertheless, *shi* and *fei* are not necessarily incompatible: when *shi* and *fei* refer respectively to two distinct but complementary identities of the same thing (*what is this* versus *what is not this but that*), they can be complementary. In this way, in the **Mohist** discourse or context, there is the Mohist specific normative standard for what counts as *shi* (what is this) and *fei* (what is not this), while in the **Confucian** discourse context there is the Confucian specific normative standard for what is this. **Zhuang Zi** made a metaphilosophical examination of the evaluative status and metaphysical implication of *shi* and *fei* and emphasized the possibly complementary character of *shi-fei*.

It is noted that the issue of how to understand and characterize the concepts of *shi* and *fei* in classical Chinese philosophy is controversial. For some other accounts, see Further reading.

See **Confucianism; Mohism;** *you* **versus** *wu***; Zhuang, Zi**
Further reading: Graham 1989 (2.5.2); Hansen 1992 (2.5.2)

shu 恕: *Shu* as specified in **Confucius'** *Lun-Yü* is a virtue complex whose understanding constitutes a central concept of Confucius' version of the **Golden Rule** ("CGR"). The virtue *shu* comprises its methodological aspect and its substantial aspect. The methodological aspect of *shu* consists of such moral dispositions concerning how to treat others as *ji-suo-bu-ru wu-shi-yu-ren* 己所不欲，勿施于人 (15.23), *ji-yu-li-er-li-ren ji-yu-da-er-da-ren* 己欲立而立人，己欲達而達人 (6.28), etc.; their interpretative understandings can be presented in terms of the principle of reversibility ["(Do not) do unto others what you would (not) desire *others* to do unto yourself"] and the principle of extensibility ["(Do not) do unto others what you would (not) desire *yourself* to do unto yourself"]; these two guiding principles constitute the methodological dimension of the CGR. The substantial aspect of *shu* points to the internal fundamental virtue *ren*; its reflective understanding constitutes the internal starting-point dimension of the CGR, which provides an initial moral sensibility for bringing the methodological dimension of the CGR into play and is supposed to regulate the external starting dimension of the CGR, i.e., the reflective understanding of *zhong*.

See **Confucianism; Confucius; Golden Rule;** *Lun-Yü*; *ren*; *zhong*

Further reading: Chan 2000 (1.2.2); Ivanhoe 1990 (1.2.2); Mou 2004 (1.2.2); Wang 1999 (1.2.2)

Si-Shu 四書 (the *Four Books*): The *Si-Shu* (the *Four Books*) consist of the *Lun-Yü* (the *Analects*), the **Mencius** (The books of Mencius), the **Zhong-Yong** (*Doctrine of the Mean*), and the *Da-Xue* (*Great Learning*), which **Zhu Xi** (1130–1200) in the *Song* Dynasty identified as the four most important **Confucian** classics.

See *Da-Xue*; *Lun-Yü*; *Meng-Zi*; *Zhong-Yong*

sincerity see *cheng* 誠

skepticism: Skepticism is an account that denies, or puts it into doubt, that knowledge of some subject matter is possible, e.g., moral skepticism and scientific skepticism. The basis of the doubt may be the difficulty of proof or human fallibility, and the strength of the doubt may range from denial that there is a fact of the matter on which knowledge is based to worrying that the proofs are not as sound as they are believed to be.

One needs to be careful in characterizing some Chinese thinkers in terms of this label. For example, Zhuang Zi's approach is sometimes presented as a kind of skepticism; nevertheless, his style of skepticism needs to be understood in terms of his thought as a whole. Zhuang Zi did not deny the possibility of knowledge of the external world but put into doubt the absoluteness and one-sidedness involved in evaluating various aspects of the knowledge-achieving process. Among others, first, knowing and not-knowing are relative to the aspect of the object of study: (not) knowing *this* aspect of the object does not amount to (not) knowing *that* aspect; Zhuang Zi thus brings into doubt whether the agent who knows (does not know) *this* aspect does (not) knows *that* aspect. Second, knowing and not-knowing are relative to the knowing organs of the knowing agent: (not) knowing via one knowing organ does not amount to (not) knowing via another organ; Zhuang Zi thus brought into doubt whether the agent who knows (does not know) via one knowing organ does (not) knows via another organ.

See **Zhuang, Zi**

Further reading: Kjellberg and Ivanhoe 1996 (1.5.2); Mou 2008 (1.5.2)

Sun, Zi 孫子 (given name "Wu" 武: fourth century BCE): Sun Zi was a military strategist and is attributed with writing the classical Chinese treatise on military strategy, the *Sun-Zi* (*The Art of War*). Sun Zi emphasized that the way to achieve victory is to work in harmony with nature rather than resorting to brute force, and to outwit the enemy and win by wisdom without having to engage in a battle. Many ideas in the work are kindred in spirit with **Daoism**.

See **Daoism**

synthesis / synthetic: Similar to the concept of analysis, the concept of synthesis is an important conceptual resource in reflective interpretion of classical Chinese philosophy in the following three senses of the term: (1) The term "synthesis" in its technical sense means a specific instrumental method that combines separate things or ideas into a complete whole. The term can thus be used to indicate a general methodological guiding principle or attitude that looks at things holistically. Many traditional Chinese philosophers are considered to take that methodological stance. (2) A synthetic statement is contrasted to an "analytic" statement: a statement whose truth value does not derive solely from the meaning of the terms used or its logical structure, or a statement with (empirical) content. (3) In the Hegelian model in the Western tradition, it is a key notion used to highlight one mode of a dynamically balanced ending of one cycle of the interacting process of thesis–antithesis contraries via sublation (i.e., to keep what is valid and adequate in the contraries while discarding what is not). This can be compared and contrasted with the **yin-yang** model of interaction which illustrates the **yin-yang way of thinking** and presents another mode of the dynamically balanced ending of one cycle of the interacting process of *yin-yang* contraries via complementarity.

See **analysis/analytic; methodology**

T

tai-ji 太極 (the great ultimate): The term "*tai-ji*" means the ultimate source of the universe and the unity of all things in the universe. The term first appears in the *Yi-Zhuang* (Commentaries on the *Yi-Jing* text in the classical sense): ". . . in the *Yi* system, there is the Great Ultimate (*tai-ji*) which generates the Two Norms (*liang-ji*) [*yin* and *yang*]; the Two Norms generate the Four Images (*si-xiang*) [major *yin*, major *yang*, minor *yin*, and minor *yang*]; the Four Images generate the Eight Trigrams (*ba-gua*); the Eight Trigrams determine fortune and misfortune; fortune and misfortune produce the great enterprise" (*Xi-Ci-Zhuan*, Part 1). **Zhou Dun-yi** gave his **Neo-Confucian** elaboration of *tai-ji* which became the basis of **Neo-Confucian** metaphysics.

See *gua*; Neo-Confucianism; *Yi-Jing*; *yin-yang*; Zhou, Dun-yi

Tang, Jun-yi (T'ang Chün-i) 唐君毅 (1909–78) was one of the leading figures of **contemporary Neo-Confucianism** and presented a modern interpretation of **Neo-Confucianism**, especially its idealistic wing (i.e., *Lu-Wang-xin-xue*). Like other Neo-Confucians, Tang sought to establish a metaphysical foundation for ethics. In contrast to other contemporary Neo-Confucians, he paid more attention to cultural issues through a comparative examination of Western and Chinese philosophy for the sake of the modernization of Chinese culture. His works are collected in *Tang-Jun-Yi-Quan-Ji* (*The Completed Works of Tang Jun-yi*, 1986).

See **contemporary** Neo-Confucianism; Neo-Confucianism; *xin-xue*

Further reading: Chan 2002 (1.13.2); Tan 2008 (1.13.2).

Three-Treatise (Middle-Way) Buddhism (*San-Lun-Zong*) 三論宗: Three-Treatise Buddhism, called '*Madhyamika*' 中觀 in Sanskrit, is a major school in **Mahayaha Buddhism**. Nagarjuna (龍樹 second century CE) is generally regarded as the founder of this school. During the late *Jin* Dynasty Kumarajiva (鳩摩羅什 344–413) introduced the basic thought of this School to China through his translations of its three most important treatises; the School in China is thus called "the Three-Treatise School". **Seng Zhao**, Kumarajiva's disciple, continued to promote the school's doctrine in China. **Ji Zang** elaborated and systematized the doctrine in the Chinese context.

The central idea of this school is emptiness (*sunyata*) in the sense that all phenomena are empty of "self nature": they have no intrinsic and independent reality apart from the causes and conditions from which they arise. The only genuine reality is emptiness itself. So the school is also called "the School of Emptiness".

The school rejects two extreme approaches and holds the "middle way" between them: one extreme doctrine is absolute realism, which consists in the belief in unchanging being, while the other extreme position is nihilism, which renders all things non-existent. The school maintains that everything is a becoming and a process. The school is thus called "the School of the Middle Way"(*Zhung-Zong* 中宗).

The foregoing thoughts of Three-Treatise Buddhism are kindred in spirit in some rspects to Chinese philosophy, especially **Daoist** thought. As a matter of fact, in their own distinct ways, Seng Zhao and Ji Zang formed a bridge between Daoism and **Buddhism**, whose combination resulted in *Chan* **Buddhism**.

See **Buddhism**; *Chan* **Buddhism**; **Daoism**; **Ji, Zang**; *Mahayana* **Buddhism**; **Seng, Zhao**;

Further reading: Chan 1963, Chs. 21–2 (2.2); Chappell 1987 (1.8.2); Lai 2009 (1.8.2); Robinson 1967 (1.8.2)

tian (*t'ien*) 天 (**heaven; nature-sky-heaven**): The term *tian* signifies a basic conceptual category in Chinese philosophy and is one of the fundamental notions of Chinese mentality. It is the natural authority in many systems of Chinese thought, particularly **Confucianism, Mohism**, and **Yangism**. *Tian* predetermines or commands the emperor and thus sets the social order on its way. **Daoists** are sometimes taken to replace the authority of *tian* with that of the *dao*.

One basic literal sense of the term is "heaven",

signifying the creative origin of all; its earlier usage can be traced back to the records of the *Zhou* Dynasty in which *tian* was considered to provide the basis of the legitimacy of the emperors as rulers through *tian-ming* 天命 (mandate of heaven). The emperors were thus considered to be *tian-zi* 天子 (sons of heaven) and were supposed to embody heaven via their virtue of **ren** and **yi** 義 (or benevolence and justice as what *ren* and *yi* are revealed in treating others in society). During the Spring and Autumn Period, the concept of *tian* changed as *Zhou* royal authority collapsed; *tian* came to mean nature itself with its fate or mission rather than being related to *tian-zi* as the symbol of the benevolent and just creator. After that, generally speaking, the term was used to refer to natural authority in many systems of Chinese thought, particularly Confucianism and Mohism, though the concept of *tian* as natural authority was elaborated in distinct ways in these different systems or even in a complex array of distinct approaches in the same system. For example, **Confucius** took *tian* more as the natural foundation of moral mission via his concept of *tian-ming*: each human being has a natural capacity (original moral sensibility) to practice goodness; each human being needs to implement the mandate of heaven as his moral mission through **moral cultivation** for the sake of becoming a *jun-zi*. The Mohists took *tian* more as the agent-like natural authority via the concept of *tian-zhi* (天志, heaven's intention): *tian* is like the wisest moral agent whose intention provides a reliable, objective standard of morality.

The foregoing distinct but related meanings of the term *tian* in various systems of Chinese thought bear on the folk notion of *tian* in ordinary discourse. Two popular sayings in modern, everyday discourse reflect them to various extents. One is *mou-shi-zai-ren, cheng-shi-zai-tian* (谋事在人, 成事在天), meaning that the way to plan and contrive to do things lies in one's efforts, while whether one can succeed lies in heaven's own course. The other is *ting-tian-you-ming* (听天由命) meaning letting heaven decide how something will develop and follow fate (as decreed by heaven).

See **Confucianism; Daoism; Mohism;** *tian-ren-he-yi*

Further reading: Finazzo 1967 (1.2.2); Fu 2003 (1.2.2); Schwartz 1985, Ch. 2 (2.5.3)

tian-ming 天命 (**decrees or mandate of heaven**) see *tian*

tian-ren-he-yi 天人合一 (**unity of heaven and the human**): The basic point of the conception of *tian-ren-he-yi* as one general thesis in classical Chinese philosophy is to emphasize the unity (*he-yi* 合一) of heaven (*tian* 天), human being, and human society (*ren* 人) in the two related senses. In a general metaphysical sense, the human being and human society are considered to be parts of heaven as nature. In a moral sense, heaven has its moral mission as *tian-ming*, which is to be implemented through the human being's moral virtue and moral conduct. In a unified metaphysical and moral sense, heaven as endowed (original) human moral nature exists in all human beings.

See **Confucianism;** *he*; *tian*; *wu-xin*

Tian-Tai (*T'ien T'ai*) **Buddhism** 天台宗: *Tian-Tai* Buddhism is one of the major schools of **Mahayana Buddhism** in **Chinese Buddhism,** which was founded by Zhi Yi (智顗 Chih-I, 538–97) at Tiantai Mountain in Zhejiang Province during the *Sui* Dynasty. It is also called the "Lotus School" because it was established primarily based on the Lotus Sutra 《法華經》.

The central thought of *Tian-Tai* Buddhism consist of three ideas: (1) The perfect harmony of triple truth (三諦圓融) – (a) the truth of emptiness: all phenomena (*dharmas*) are empty of self-nature but depend on causes for their production; (b) the temporary truth: on the other hand, all phenomena are thus produced and do have a temporary and dependent existence; (c) the truth of means: all phenomena are both empty of existence and have temporary existence. The three truths are thus intrinsically related to each other; consequently, the three are one, while one is the three. (2) The true nature of all *dharmas* (phenomena) (諸法真性): the foregoing mutual identity of all *dharmas* is their true nature. (3) The three thousand worlds immanent in an instance of thought (一念三千): all phenomenal worlds are immanent in each other; all worlds are so mutually involved and identified that they are engaged in every moment of thought (this does not amount to saying that they are produced by any individual mind).

See **Buddhism; Chinese Buddhism;** *Mahayana* **Buddhism;**

Further reading: Chappell 1983 (1.8.2); Swanson 1989 (1.8.2)

transcendence / transcendental: The foundations of the works of some important ancient thinkers, such as **Zhuang Zi,** in classical Chinese philosophy are considered to be transcendental (sometimes the term "transcendent" being used with a nuance) in character. In philosophy, a transcendental view, topic, or question means something that goes beyond the scope of a certain finite area or the limit of a certain finite way of looking at things (either sense experience or a finite perspective or logic/mathematics, or . . .). So something characterized as "transcendental" is intended to explore, capture, or comprehend things at a higher level. A transcending subject can be a natural thing like *tian* (constant nature as the "author" of the moral standard, in the **Mohist** case) or *xin* (human heart-mind as a constant and stable source of moral insight, in **Mencius**' case), or some divine entity like God, or a well-cultivated, vision-holding human agent (in **Zhuang Zi**'s case) or the rational subject's inter-subjective **rationality** (in Kant's case). A transcendental character is sometimes associated with **dualism**; but it is not necessarily so, as arguably in some cases of Chinese philosophy.

See **dualism; Mencius; Mohism; rationality;** *tian*; *xin*; **Zhuang Zi**

Further reading: Ames and Hall 1995 (2.1); Graham 1989, Part II, Section 3 (2.4); Hansen 2001 (2.1); Mou 2008b (2.1); Roetz 1993 (1.2.2)

truth: The philosophical concern with truth has been signficantly addressed both in (some of the major movements of thought of) the Chinese tradition and in the Western tradition in their distinctive ways. As one prominent case in the Chinese tradition, the *dao* pursuit in the **classical** (philosophical) **Daoism** is essentially a Chinese way of delievering the pursuit of truth in a philosophically interesting way.

The term 'truth' as used in philosophy signifies either the property of truth (the property possessed by true beliefs or statements), or the notion of truth, or a collection of truths (i.e., true beliefs or statements), or some distinct function of the truth predicate, depending on contexts of reflective examination. The philosophical concern with truth ("the truth concern") has its distinct but related dimensions: among others, the metaphysical dimension concerning the nature of truth, the explanatory role dimension concerning the explanatory role of the notion of truth, the linguistic dimension concerning the linguistic functions of the truth predicate, and the epistemological dimension concerning the criterion of truth. (A classical distinction between truth nature and truth criterion is this: the former is examined by asking what constitutes truth, what truth consists in, or what it is for a truth-bearer to be true, while, given a certain understanding of truth nature, the latter is examined by asking what a criterion is or means by which to achieve probable truths.) There are four representative competing reflective approaches to the metaphysical dimension of the truth concern (reflective accounts *of truth*). The correspondence account (including the semantic account as its variant) claims that truth lies in (a truth-bearer's) capturing (via corresponding to) reality, or the way things are. The coherence account claims that truth lies in (a truth-bearer's) coherence with other truth-bearers. The pragmatic account claims that truth lies in a truth-bearer's utility for accepting it. More recently, the deflationist account (deflationism) renders all the aforementioned accounts substantive (in the sense that they inflate the due content of our notion of truth) and sets out to deflate various inflated contents back to its non-substantive content (some syntactic and pragmatic functions of the truth predicate).

The philosophical concern with truth involves, or starts with, a reflective contemplation of its subject by thinking about the relation between the pre-theoretic understanding of truth and its reflective counterpart. There are two basic attitudes in this connection: the non-revisionist and the revisionist towards a pre-theoretic understanding of truth (i.e., a *true* sentence or claim captures things as they are, or that truth consists in capturing the way things are). The non-revisionist attitude asserts that philosophy should not be revisionary of our intuitive understanding of truth unless there are very strong theoretical or practical reasons in favor of revision. In contrast, the revisionist attitude asserts that philosophy should revise (or even dramatically alter) our intuitive understanding of truth. For example, among the aforementioned accounts of truth, the correspondence account and the deflationist account (allegedly) take the non-revisionist attitude, while the pragmatic account and the coherence account take the revisionist attitude.

The non-revisionist attitude (via some sort of correspondence account) has been widely adopted among (a silent majority of) philosophers for the following reason. Our pre-theoretic, intuitive "way-things-are capturing" understanding of truth plays so central a role in our theorizing about the world that, if it is overthrown when there are no strong theoretical or practical reasons for doing so, there seems to be nothing to be gained by changing the ways we think about truth pre-philosophically and much to be lost. What the pre-theoretic "way-things-are capturing" understanding of truth and its reflective counterparts in philosophy catch is a most significant dual-directional relation between the subjective (the human being's beliefs, thoughts, statements, etc.) and the objective (the way things are, or reality) – the former capturing (or a sort of "corresponding/conforming to") the latter, the latter making the former true. Such a cross-categorical relation (or a semantic relation when the subjective is presented in terms of the linguistic item) is a fundamental relation which the human being needs to take seriously. (It is noted that the metaphysical commitment of the notion of truth *per se* about such a dual-directional relation is minimal: it is not about what reality is – the realist or anti-realist; a conflation is to treat the notion of truth as a certain metaphysical notion of what reality is.)

The foregoing explanation of the two basic attitudes is especially relevant to the examination of the philosophical concern with truth in Chinese philosophy: its identity, nature, and distinct features. Some scholars argue that there is no philosophical concern with truth as a (semantic) cross-categorical "way-things-are capturing" in classical Chinese philosophy. Others suggest that the significant notion of truth in classical Chinese philosophy is a pragmatic notion (or an existential notion of "truth-as-a property of persons", or a metaphysical notion of "truth-as-what really is"). They actually argue that there is no significant concern with *truth as capturing the way things are* in classical Chinese philosophy. This thesis is highly controversial. Given that the *dao* is fundamentally the way things are (as the philosophical Daoism understands it) and that the *dao* pursuit thus lies in capturing the way things are, the *dao* pursuit is essentially a Chinese way of delivering the truth pursuit in a philosophically interesting way. In this sense, and to this extent, the philosophical concern with truth (along the line with our pre-theoretic understanding of truth) is not extinct but constitutes one of the fundamental concerns in classical Chinese philosophy at least in one of its major components – philosophical Daoism.

See **Daoism; semantic**

Further reading: Hall 1997 (2.5.2); Hansen 1985 (2.5.2); Mou 2006 (1.5.2), 2009 (2.5.2); Smith 1980 (2.5.2)

U

ultimate concerns: Ultimate concerns are concerns with the most fundamental things of the world and human society, and are deeply cared about.

unity of heaven and the human see *tian-ren-he-yi*

unity of knowledge and action see *zhi-xing-he-yi*

universals: The **metaphysical** issue of universals has been addressed in the Chinese tradition, as well as in the Western tradition, in distinct ways. The term "universal" refers to a single universal entity (if any) that is common or (strictly) identical across, and can be instanced or manifested by, a number of particular things (individual concrete things with their own specific characteristics). The philosophical issue of universals is concerned with the metaphysical identity, status, and nature of universals, the metaphysical nature of particulars, and the relation between universals and particulars. From these concerns the following questions arise: Do universals really exist? If they do, which are primary, universals or particulars? How are they related? Furthermore, there is a Platonic one–many problem which has been explicitly addressed in the Western philosophical tradition: How we are to characterize the status of a single universal that is strictly identical across many particular things and how are we to explain the way in which these particulars share the universal? There are three major approaches to the issue: (1) **realism** concerning universals holds that universals really exist in the world beyond our thought and language; Platonic realism further maintains that universals do not exist in, but beyond and above, our sensible world; (2) radical **nominalism** admits the existence of universals only in language (i.e., only as nominal existence); (3) conceptualism (sometimes viewed as a modest version of nominalism) considers universals as only having existence as concepts in our thought as well as linguistic existence in our language.

Although such a debate was not carried out in the same manifest and explicit way in classical Chinese philosophy as in the ancient Western philosophy, the issue was addressed and handled in the texts of ancient Chinese thinkers like **Gong-sun Long** and **Lao Zi** in recessive and implicit ways. It is controversial how to interpret the implications of those ancient Chinese thinkers' approaches to the issue. In the case of Gong-sun

Long, there are several seemingly competing interpretations: a Platonic realist one, a radical nominalist one, and a conceptualist one.

See **Gong-sun, Long; Lao, Zi; nominalism; realism**

Further reading: Cheng 2007 (1.4.2); Fung (Yu-lan) 1952 (1.4.2); Fung (Yiu-ming) 2007 (1.4.2); Hansen 1983 (1.4.2); Mou 2007 (1.4.2).

utilitarianism: An early Chinese version of utilitarianism is the **Mohists'** ethical approach. Utilitarianism is a **consequential** ethical theory which defines right action in terms of maximizing some general good or utility (economic benefit, happiness, pleasure, or other beneficial results). The typical scope of concern is all humans or all sentient beings. Act utilitarianism calculates benefits for each individual act, while rule utilitarianism uses the formula to select among valid *rules* of morality.

See **consequentialism; Mohism/Mohists**

Further reading: Yan 1998 (2.5.4); Wong 1989 (1.3.2)

V

virtue: One of the major concerns in classical Chinese philosophy is the issue of moral **self-cultivation** – how to cultivate oneself to become a person of moral virtue (a *jun-zi* in the **Confucian** tradition). A virtue is a character trait which is to be valued and admired and whose possessor is thus rendered good or better, morally, intellectually, or in some other aspects. Moral virtue is the primary focus of **virtue ethics**.

See *de; jun-zi;* **morality; self-cultivation; virtue ethics**

virtue ethics: In the Chinese tradition, **virtue** ethics has been a dominant major concern in moral philosophy (especially in **Confucianism**). Virtue ethics is a kind of ethics that is concerned primarily with virtues by exploring the identity and nature of virtue, the relationship between various virtues, how to cultivate moral characters, etc. In contrast to **conduct ethics**, the basic questions in virtue ethics include: What kind of virtuous person should I be? and How should I become that kind of person? In the Chinese tradition, the reflective examination of virtues can be found as early as in **Confucius'** *Lun-Yü* and **Lao Zi's** *Dao-De-Jing* on moral **self-cultivation**. In the Western tradition, the study of virtue ethics can be traced back to Plato and Aristotle, though conduct ethics became a major undertaking in modern Western philosophy. Comparative examination of Chinese and Western virtue ethics traditions has been a significant issue in studies of Chinese and comparative philosophy.

See **conduct ethics; Confucianism; ethics;** *jun-zi*; *yi* 義; *ren*; **self-cultivation; virtue**

Further readings: Chong 2007 (1.2.2); Ivanhoe 2000 (1.2.2); Shun 1997 (1.2.2); Van Norden 2003 (1.2.2); Wong 2006 (2.5.4); Yu 2007 (1.2.2)

W

Wang, Bi (Wang Pi) 王弼 (style name "Fu-si" 輔嗣: 226–249) was the best-known leading figure of **Neo-Daoism** during the *Wei-Jin* Dynasty. His most important works are commentaries on the *Dao-De-Jing* and the *Yi-Jing*, which themselves have become classics in Chinese philosophy. Like other Neo-Daoist thinkers, Wang also endeavored to reconcile the metaphysical insight of **Daoism** in seeking freedom and transcendence with moral and socio-political engagement. Wang's creative interpretation of the *dao* in terms of *wu* (non-being, nothingness) started a new current of thought, labeled *xuan-xue* (玄學 the profound learning of the *dao*) and a debate over the relation of *you* versus *wu*. Wang argued that *wu* was the original reality while *you* was a variety of functions of *wu*, in contrast to Guo Xiang's position that *wu* makes sense only in relation to *you*.

See **dao**; ***Dao-De-Jing***; **Daoism**; **Neo-Daoism**; ***Yi-Jing***; *you* versus *wu*

Further readings: Chan 2008 (1.7.2)

Wang, Chong (Wang Ch'ung) 王充 (style name "Zhong-ren" 仲任: 27–97) was a **materialist** philosopher during the *Han* Dynasty. Wang is viewed as one of the most critical and original thinkers of his age. On the one hand, in his remarkable work *Lun-Heng* (論衡 *Critical Essays*), Wang insisted that the words of previous sages (such as **Confucius, Mencius,** and **Mo Zi**) as well as common superstitions should be treated critically instead of being blindly believed. On the other hand, he argued for his materialist monism of *qi*: all things throughout the universe originate from, and are various manifestations of, the fundamental material vital force *qi*. Wang also maintained a kind of **fatalism**. His view had a positive effect on the subsequent **Neo-Daoism** which presented a more naturalistic **metaphysics** against religious **Daoism**.

See **materialism**; *qi*

Further reading: Nylan 2003 (1.6.2)

Wang, Fu-zhi (Wang Fu-chih) 王夫之 (style name "Er-nong" 而農; alternative name 'Chuan-shan' 船山: 1619–92) was an important **Confucian** philosopher of the late *Ming* and early *Qing* Dynasties. Being influenced by **Zhang Zai,** Wang is well known for his **materialist** philosophy and for his criticism of idealist **Neo-Confucianism** or *xin-xue*. Wang maintained a kind of **materialist**

stance, arguing that *qi*, as the material vital force, is the only fundamental and independent existence, and that *li* 理, as the principle of *qi*, does not have independent existence. Wang's version of materialism is featured with its dialectical view of changing: the material universe is endlessly changing and self-movement results from the interaction of internal opposing forces. Wang's ideas in social and political philosophy contributed to his popularity in modern China: he argued that government should benefit the people instead of those in power, and that history is the continuous progress of human society. Wang's ideas in these connections inspired, and were admired by, late *Qing* reformist thinkers like Tang Si-tong (譚嗣同: 1865–98) and **Liang Qi-chao**. Wang's works were later compiled in the *Chuan-Shan-Yi-Shu* (*Surviving Works of Wang Fu-zhi*).

See **Confucianism;** *li* 理; **materialism; Neo-Confucianism;** *qi*; *xin-xue*; **Zhang, Zai**

Further reading: Chan 1963 Ch. 36 (2.2); Liu 2003 (1.10.2)

Wang, Guo-wei (Wang Kuo-wei) 王國維 (style name "Jing-an" 靜安: 1877–1927) is considered the father of modern Chinese **aesthetics**. He is the first Chinese thinker who systematically introduced Western aesthetic thought to the Chinese intellectual circle and made aesthetics an independent subject in China. As one pioneer thinker in the **enlightenment movement in modern Chinese philosophy**, Wang is perhaps the first scholar to introduce Schopenhauer's and Nietzsche's philosophies as "pure" philosophy to the Chinese reader. Furthermore, he used Schopenhauer's philosophy to criticise the Chinese classical novel *Hong-Lou-Meng* (*Dream of the Red Chamber*).

See **aesthetics; enlightenment movement in modern Chinese philosophy**

Further reading: Bonner 1986 (1.11.2); Chou 2003 (1.11.2); Jiang 2009 (1.11.2)

Wang, Shou-ren (Yang-ming) 王守仁 (style name "Bo-an" 伯安; honorific name "Yang-ming" 陽明: 1472–1529) was a representative figure in the *xin-xue* movement (*Lu-Wang-xin-xue*) within **Neo-Confucianism**. In contrast to the *Cheng-Zhu-li-xue* tradition, this movement maintained that *xin*, as the original heart-mind, is identical with *li* 理 and presents itself as *liang-zhi* (innate moral knowledge). Wang is well known for his interpretation of *ge-wu-zhi-zhi* (rectifying things and extending innate knowledge) and his conception of *zhi-xign-he-yi* (the unity of knowledge and action). His major works are *Chuan-Xi-Lu* (*Instructions for Practical Living*) and *Da-Xue-Wen* (*Inquiry on the Great Learning*).

See *ge-wu-zhi-zhi*; *li* 理; *li-xue*; *liang-zhi*; **Neo-Confucianism**; *xin*; *xin-xue*; *zhi-xing-he-yi*

Further reading: Ching 1976 (1.9.2); Cua 2003-(2) (1.9.2); Ivanhoe 2002 (1.9.2); Tu 1976 (1.9.2)

Wei-Shi **Buddhism** 唯識宗 see **Consciousness-Only Buddhism**

"White-Horse-Not-Horse" (*bai-ma-fei-ma*) thesis: Gong-sun Long's well-known thesis "[the] white horse [is] not [the] horse" (*bai-ma-fei-ma*) is the central thesis of his essay "On the White Horse" (*Bai-Ma-Lun*). This essay is considered philosophically interesting and influential for its substantial philosophical points, its articulate rational argumentation, and its sophistication.

The thesis is supported by several arguments in the essay "On the White Horse". Gong-sun Long's crucial argument, which provides his fundamental argument that underlies all the other arguments, is this. Instead of only arguing that the white horse is not the horse, he explained in what sense, or from which perspective, one is entitled (or needs) to claim that the white horse is not identical to (*fei* 非) or different from (*yi* 異) the horse; *and* he also explained in what sense (or from which perspective) one is entitled (or needs) to claim that the white horse is the horse (*bai ma nai ma*) or that the white horse does not differ from (*bu yi*) the horse. On the one hand, he emphasized that what makes a white horse a horse lies in their same (common) aspect given that it is what is sought (*sou qiu yi ye*) and that, if what is sought is the common aspect, a white horse would not differ from (*bu-yi*) a horse with respect to the common aspect. On the other hand, he stressed that *what is sought* in the above case is different from *what is sought* when the white horse is claimed to differ from the horse. In the latter case, what is sought or focused on is a distinct aspect (being white) between the white horse and the horse, which is thus met by neither the yellow horse nor the black horse. It is exactly here that, Gong-sun Long made his crucial point: what the speaker seeks or focuses on concerning the referent of a name (say, "white horse") makes a difference. This crucial point gives the fundamental rationale behind his other major arguments for the thesis, which focus respectively on the following distinctive aspects of the white horse and the horse: the distinctive conceptual contents of their names, their distinctive necessary-identity contributors, and the distinctive extensions of their names.

How to interpret Gong-sun Long's "White-Horse-Not-Horse" thesis, especially in view of its metaphysical implications, has been controversial.

See **Gong-sun, Long; School of Names**

Further reading: Cheng 2007 (1.4.2); Graham 1986a (1.4.2); Hansen 2007 (1.4.2); Fung (Yulan) 1952–53 (1.4.2); Fung (Yiu-ming) 2007 (1.4.2); Im 2007 (1.4.2); Mou 2007 (1.4.2)

world philosophy: Theoretically or conceptually speaking, Chinese *philosophy* is part of the common philosophical enterprise instead of something else; in its reflective practice, modern Chinese philosophy has tended to move toward world philosophy.

Although sometimes the phrases "world philosophy" (*shi-jie-zhe-xue* 世界哲學 as its Chinese counterpart) and "global philosophy" can be used interchangeably, the former is considered more inclusive, while the latter might imply globalizing a certain (particular or "universal") mode of doing philosophy (cf. Searle). To this extent, global philosophy, when associated with the foregoing agenda, might stand as an alternative way of doing world philosophy (at a certain stage).

Generally speaking, world philosophy is construed as a world-wide joint-endeavor of philosophical inquiry that crosses the boundaries of particular traditions, styles or orientations of doing philosophy for the sake of contributing to the common philosophical enterprise. Given that this is one primary goal of world philosophy, a central or crucial issue is how to implement this goal. One strategic way is the **constructive-engagement** methodological strategy. It is to inquire into how distinct modes of thinking, methodological approaches, visions or insights, substantial points of view, or conceptual/explanatory resources from different philosophical traditions and/or from different styles/orientations of doing philosophy (within one tradition or out of different traditions) can learn from each other and make joint contributions to the common philosophical enterprise (i.e., to our understanding and treatment of a series of issues or topics of philosophical significance that can be jointly concerned under philosophical interpretation and/or from a broader philosophical vantage point). World philosophy approached in this way is essentially comparative philosophy aiming at constructive engagement.

See **comparative philosophy; global philosophy; constructive engagement (methodology/purpose)**

Further reading: Angle 2007 (2.1); Fung 1948 (2.1); Mou 2009c (2.1); Searle 2008 (2.1)

wu 無 see *wu-wei*; *you* versus *wu*

wu-wei 無為 **(non-action)**: *Wu-wei* is a seemingly paradoxical slogan in **Lao Zi**'s *Dao-De-Jing* the literal sense of which is non-action. The apparent paradox arises because conforming to *wu-wei* is a kind of action *wei*-ing. The term *wu-wei* means one of the following: (1) do not do those things that are against being **natural**; (2) one should restrict one's activities to what is natural (or what is naturally needed); (3) do not do those things that go beyond natural limitation; for when a thing reaches one extreme, it withdraws from it; (4) act in a natural (effortless or spontaneous) way; (5) act without pretentious "acting"; (6) avoid doing unnecessary things in achieving something; (7) avoid actions based on socialized values or desires, such as status, fame, or rank. What is at issue is what counts as being natural, what is naturally needed, or the natural limitation of a thing. Their identities are context-sensitive.

See *Dao-De-Jing;* **Daoism; Lao, Zi; nature / natural**

Further reading: Fraser 2008 (1.5.2); Lai 2007 (1.2.2); Slingerland 2003 (1.5.2); Zhu 2002 (1.5.2)

wu-xing (*wu-hsing*) 五行 (five phases; five powers): The mature conception of *wu-xing* was first systematically developed by **Zou Yan** (305–240 BCE) of the Warring States Period, and further elaborated by thinkers in the *Han* Dynasty, in combination with the conceptions of **yin-yang** and **qi**.

This conception focuses on working out a **cosmological** framework for the sake of explaining the origin, structure, and changing process of the universe, although the initial conceptions of *yin-yang*, *wu-xin*, and *qi* had been separately suggested before. According to the cosmological framework of *yin-yang* and *wu-xin*, the universe fundamentally consists of five kinds of *qi*, respectively constituting five basic materials or five powers, i.e., water (水 *shui*), fire (火 *huo*), wood (*mu* 木), metal (金 *jin*), and earth (土 *tu*). The interaction and changing process of the five powers results in all things in the universe, including those in human society. Their interaction and changing process fundamentally follows the *yin-yang* model of interaction as characterized in terms of interdependence and mutual complementarity. The interdependence and mutual complementarity of the five basic powers are elaborated and illustrated through their mutual generation (相生 *xiang-sheng*), in the order of wood→ fire→earth→metal→water (→wood . . .), and mutual conquest (相克 *xiang-ke* or 相勝 *xiang-sheng*), in the order of wood→earth→water→ fire→metal (→wood . . .). Their status and functions constitute the five distinct phases of the whole changing/ movement process. In this way, the *yin-yang* and *wu-xin* cosmological framework was to describe and explain the world as an organic cycling whole whose common laws or principles govern both natural phenomena and human affairs (***tian-ren-he-yi***天人合一: the harmonious unity of heaven and human): all things in the universe are unified into the one harmonious whole and are situated in a dynamic cycle of mutual generation and mutual conquest. The way of thinking manifested and illustrated by this kind of worldview is sometimes called "**correlative thinking**" (e.g., by Joseph Needham).

See **corrective thinking**; *qi*; *tian-ren-he-yi*; *yin-yang*; **Zou, Yan**

Further reading: Fung 2008 (1.6.2); Graham 1986 (2.5.3); Hall and Ames 1995 (2.5.3); Henderson 1984 (1.6.2); Hsiao 1979 (2.5.4); Needham 1956 and Schwartz 1985 Ch. 9 (2.5.3).

X

Xi (Ji), Kang (Hsi K'ang) 嵇康 (223–62; '嵇' is pronounced "*ji*" in modern Chinese) was one of the leading figures of **Neo-Daoism** during the *Wei-Jin* Dynasty, also being a musician and poet. He was one of the leaders of the Seven Sages of the Bamboo Grove (*Zhu-Lin-Qi-Xian* 竹林七賢). Although, unlike **Wang Bi** and **Guo Xiang** in Neo-Daoism, he did not leave any commentaries on the **Daoist** classics, Xi set out his thesis of *yang-sheng* (養生 nourishing life) in his essay *Yang-Sheng-Lun* (*On Nourishing Life*). He advocated leading an authentic life which was no longer burdened by the norms of the Confucian tradition but was eventually based on the way of *zi-ran* (naturalness, spontaneity, or what is so of itself).
See **Daoism; Neo-Daoism**
Further reading: Chan 2009 (1.7.2)

xiao (*hsiao*) 孝 (filial piety): *Xiao*, or filial piety (one's affectionate and devoted respect for one's parents and ancestors), is a central virtue emphasized in **classical Confucian** virtue ethics. It was characterized and highlighted in all three classical Confucian texts: the *Lun-Yü*, the *Mencius*, and the *Xun-Zi*.

Methodologically speaking, it is philosophically interesting to look at how Confucius set out to characterize (filial) piety in comparison and contrast to Socrates' approach in "Euthyphro," an early Plato dialogue. Socrates first set up three conditions which any adequate

definition of piety is expected to meet: the property needs
to be shared by all pious behaviors, not shared by any
impious behaviors, and is that which makes all pious
behaviors pious. In contrast, facing the same question
"What is filial piety?", Confucius gave different answers
(concerning distinct aspects or layers of filial piety) to
different interlocutors, depending on who asked the
question, the degree of the person's preliminary understanding of this virtue, in what context the question was
raised, etc. (in 2.5, 2.6, 2.7, 2.8 of the *Lun-Yü*). With
their distinct focuses, Confucius and Socrates respectively took the **becoming**-aspect-concerned and **being**-
aspect-concerned methodological perspectives, which
can be complementary for a complete account of piety.

See **classical Confucianism**; *li*; *Lun-Yü*, *Meng-Zi*; *ren*;
yi 義; *Xun-Zi*

Further reading: Guo 2007 (1.2.2); Liu 2007 (1.2.2);
Rosemont and Ames 2008 (1.2.2); Shun 2003 (3)
(1.2.2)

xin (*hsin*) 心 (heart-mind or mind-heart): The reflective usage of
the Chinese character *xin* in Chinese philosophy, especially
in **Confucianism**, refers to the human agent's faculty of
motivation and guidance that is a blend of emotion/desire
and rationality/belief. This understanding is in contrast to a
dualistic one that relates them respectively to two fundamentally different, separate or even opposed faculties.

See **Confucianism**; **dualism**; *qing* and *li* 理; *xin-xue*

xin-xue 心學 (**study of mind-heart**): *Xin-xue* means *Lu-Wang-
xin-xue* (陸王心學 **Lu Jiu-yuan** and **Wang Shou-ren**'s study
of mind-heart) within **Neo-Confucianism**. It was represented by Lu Jiu-yuan's and Wang Shou-ren's approach to
li 理 and its relation to *xin* (心 heart-mind) for which
Cheng Hao set the stage, in contrast to *Cheng-Zhu-li-xue*.

Like *Cheng-Zhu-li-xue*, *Lu-Wang-xin-xue* also viewed *li* as the ultimate metaphysical principle of the universe. But, according to *Lu-Wang-xin-xue*, *xin* as *ben-xin* (本心 the original heart-mind) is identical with *li* and presents itself as *liang-zhi* (良知 innate moral knowledge); that is, *li* as *liang-zhi* resides in the heart-mind instead of being learnt from outside. *Lu-Wang-xin-xue* did not deny that the state of the heart-mind can be obscured by selfish desires and also believed that through self-cultivation one can recapture to the heart-mind's original state by self-cultivation. However, unlike *Cheng-Zhu-lin-xue*'s approach, Wan emphasized discovering *liang-zi*/innate knowledge through *ge-wu-zhi-zhi* under its interpretation, i.e., *ge-wu* (correcting or overcoming selfish desires within) and *zhi-zhi* (letting one's innate knowledge reach out).

See **Cheng, Hao**; *ge-wu-zhi-zhi*; *li* 理; *liang-zhi*; **Lu, Jiu-yuan**; **Neo-Confucianism**; *xin*; *xin-xue*; **Wang, Shou-ren**

Further reading: Fung 1948, Ch. 26 (2.4); Liu 2009 (1.9.2)

xing (人) 性 see **human nature**

Xiong, Shi-li (Hsiung Shih-li) 熊十力 (alternative name "Zi-zhen" 子真: 1885–1968) is considered the founder of **contemporary Neo-Confucianism** and one of the most innovative thinkers in modern Chinese philosophy. In his major work *Xin-Wei-Shi-Lun* (*A New Treatise on Consciousness-Only Buddhism*, 1932), challenging **Consciousness-Only Buddhism** and resorting to the resources from the *Yi-Jing* and **Neo-Confucianism**, Xiong constructed a metaphysical system that was intended to transcend materialism and idealism. This is done by unifying *ti* (體 substance) and *yong* (用 function) (*ti-yong-bu-er* 體用不二: substance and function are non-dual) and combining mind and matter (*li* 理 and *qi* 氣) into one (*li-qi-he-yi* 理氣合一: the unity of the principle and material force). In this way, Xiong developed Neo-Confucianism by providing a solid metaphysical foundation for the *xin-xue* tradition within Neo-Confucianism.

See **Consciousness-Only Buddhism; contemporary Neo-Confucianism; Neo-Confucianism; *xin-xue*; *Yi-Jing***

Further reading: Liu 2003 (1.13.2); Tan 2009 (1.13.2)

xiu-sheng 修身 see **self-cultivation**

xu (*hsü*) 虛 (empty/emptiness; vacuous/vacuity): The term *xu* in classical Chinese philosophy, generally speaking, is used to indicate the fundamental character of something ultimate that is empty of all relative, non-ultimate attributes. On this characterization, the term is often translated as "empty" or "vacuous". It is sometimes used to refer to the emptiness of the ultimate origin or root of the universe which cannot be adequately identified by any relative or definite predicates and is empty of all the relative or definite attributes characterized by these predicates. This use of the term is given by **Lao Zi** in the *Dao-De-Jing* and **Zhang Zai** in his **Neo-Confucian metaphysics** via the concept of *tai-xu* 太虛. The term is sometimes used to refer to the emptiness of the ultimate state of mind which transcends finite or limited experience (as used in **classical Daoism**) or is absolutely peaceful, pure, and free from (and thus are empty of) worry, selfish desires, and disturbance (as used in Neo-Confucianism).

See **classical Daoism; Lao Zi; metaphysics; Neo-Confucianism; Zhang, Zai; Zhuang, Zi**

Further reading: Liu (Xiaogan) 2003 (1.5.2); Zhang 2002 (2.5.3)

Xuan, Zang (Hsüan-tsang) 玄奘 (596–664) was a master of

the **Consciousness-Only (*Wei-Shi*) School** in **Chinese Buddhism**. He translated major **Buddhist** classics (basically, the Buddhist *Yogacara* texts) into Chinese and developed his interpretation of the central ideas of Buddhism in the Chinese tradition.

See **Buddhism; Chinese Buddhism; Consciousness-Only (*Wei-Shi*) Buddhism**

Xun, Zi (Hsün Tzu) 荀子 (given name "Kuang" 況; style name "Qing" 卿: *c.* 300–230 BCE) was the third of the **Classical Confucians** in pre-*Han* China. His authoritarian and **pragmatic** version of Confucianism dominated Chinese thought during the *Han* Dynasty but fell into disrepute with the rise of post-Buddhist and idealist **Neo-Confucianism** during the *Song-Ming* period. Like other thinkers in the **Confucian** tradition, Xun Zi's primary concern is how to cultivate oneself morally to become Confucian *jun-zi*. Based on his doctrine of the **human nature** in which he argued that human (original) nature is evil, Xun Zi suggested a re-formation model of **self-cultivation**. According to Xun Zi: (1) because of the original evil features of human nature, moral cultivation in terms of the re-formation of human nature within is necessary; (2) the ethical ideal is a re-formation of those incipient evil tendencies in human nature; (3) the morally superior person reaches this state through accumulated effort; (4) with proper education and training all people can become moral sages; (5) goodness is the result of one's conscious effort to transform oneself by diligently applying oneself to the Confucian rites, those guiding principles created and embodied by past sages.

Some of Xun Zi's students were later classed as "**Legalists**" and credited as a major intellectual influence on the emergence of the unified Chinese Empire under the *Qin* "First Emperor." A collection of writings in his name constitute the *Xun-Zi*.

See **classical Confucianism; Confucianism; human (moral) nature;** *jun-zi*; **Legalism; pragmatic; self-cultivation;** *Xun-Zi*

Further reading: Chong 2009 (1.2.2); Cua 2003 (1) (1.2.2); Goldin 1999 (1.2.2)

Xun-Zi (*Hsün Tsu*) 荀子 (*Books of Xun Zi*): The *Xun-Zi* is one of the original texts of classical Confucianism which brings together the writings of **Xun Zi**, one of the major thinkers of Classical Confucianism.

See **classical Confucianism; Confucianism; Xun, Zi**

Y

Yan, Fu (Yen Fu) 嚴复 (style name "Ji-dao" 幾道: 1853–1921) is the first thinker to systematically introduce Western philosophical thought to China (directly from English rather than from Japanese translations). In this sense, his works marked the beginning of the **enlightenment movement in modern Chinese philosophy**. Among others, Yan Fu's best-known works include his translations of Thomas H. Hurley's *Evolution and Ethics*, John Stuart Mill's *On Liberty*, and Mill's *System of Logic* (together with his commentary).

See **Enlightenment Movement in modern Chinese philosophy**

Yan, Yuan (Yen Yüan) 顏元 (style name "Yi-zhi" 易直: 1635–1704) was the founder of the **pragmatic** school of **Confucianism** during the early *Qing* Dynasty. Facing the fall of the *Ming* Dynasty, Yan Yuan emphasized the practical value and function of Confucianism as setting the world in good order and criticized the over-contemplation trend of late *Ming* **Neo-Confucianism.** His major writings were collected in the *Yan-Yuan-Ji* (*Works of Yan Yuan*).

See **Confucianism; Neo-Confucianism; pragmatic;** *Qing* **Confucianism**

yan-yi-zhi-bian 言意之辯 (**the debate on the relation between speech and meaning**): The relation between speech and ideas is a central concern in the so-called *yan-yi-zhi-bian*, that is, the debate on the relationship between speech (*yan* 言) and meaning (*yi* 意). This debate originated in the *Wei-Jin* period (220–20), but this brief introduction will not be limited to a number of representative approaches within **Neo-Daoism** during that time. Instead, other representative approaches in the Chinese tradition will be incorporated. (It is noted that, though using the ready-made translation "speech and meaning" of *yan-yi* here for the sake of convenience, and though *yi* in this debate also means *dao*-like principles in its metaphysical sense and the human understanding of them, *yan-yi* means "speech and ideas in mind" in this context.) In what follows, four representative approaches are focused on: (1) the "meaning-delivery-beyond-speech-capacity" approach; (2) the "forgetting-speech-once-achieving-meaning" approach; (3) the "meaning-delivery-within-speech-capacity" approach; and (4) the context-sensitivity approach. The first three approaches are representative in the *yan-yi-zhi-bian* during the *Wei-Jin* period, while the fourth one is suggested by **Ji Zang**'s **Buddhist** double-truth account (*er-di-lun*).

The "meaning-delivery-beyond-speech-capacity" approach was advocated by **Xi (Ji) Kan.** Its main arguments are these. First, some of our ideas are so refined and sophisticated that speech simply cannot capture them. Second, our ideas are dynamic while speech is static; therefore speech cannot fully capture our ideas. The "forgetting speech once achieving meaning" approach was advocated by **Wang Bi**. This approach acknowledges the important role played by speech as a means to achieve meaning. For example, when one intends to understand someone else's ideas or when one intends to have one's own ideas be understood by another, one has to rely on speech to understand them or express them. But this approach still accepts that, eventually, speech hinders one's understanding of those ideas *per se* and that one should forget speech having captured the meaning. This line of thought sounds like Wittgenstein's well-known metaphor to the effect that, once one has climbed up a building by means of a ladder, one needs to discard the ladder to stay at the top. It is noted that, though the first and second approaches have different emphases and focus, they share basic positions concerning the relation between speech and ideas. Both think that ideas are primary while speech is secondary, that ideas and speech can, and should, be separate and that at most speech serves merely as a means, and makes no contribution to the constitution of thought and ideas.

The "meaning-delivery-within-speech-capacity" approach is suggested by Ouyang Jian (? –300). This view has largely been ignored and is not a strong voice in traditional Chinese philosophy in contrast to the mainstream approach. However, some of the issues it raises deserve close examination. There are two interesting points that seem to engage the two preceding views. First, speech is not merely a means but also a medium of ideas, at least with regard to its contribution to their internal coherent construction. Second, as far as speech as means is concerned, though speech is relatively static and stable, that certainly does not mean that language is static or inert; language itself also keeps changing, in response to changes in what it is supposed to express. This fact is evidenced by the history of the development of natural languages. Although Ouyang's first point is quite vaguely made and expressed, his position makes a distinct contribution to the debate.

The fourth approach, the context-sensitivity approach, suggested by Ji Zang through his *er-di-lun* (i.e., his Buddhist double-truth account), has interesting implications from the point of view of the philosophy of language. It seems to Ji Zang that there are two kinds of truth: truth in the common sense and truth in the higher sense, both of which can be found on each of three levels; what is the truth in the higher sense at a lower level becomes merely truth in the common sense at the higher level. Although Ji Zang as a Buddhist thinker still maintained that the highest truth cannot be captured and delivered via language but has to be contemplated in silence, he emphasized that all those truths, both in the common sense and in the higher sense, and both at the first level and at the second level, can be captured and delivered in terms of language that involves relatively stabilized and fixed conceptual distinctions. As he explicitly distinguished truths in distinct senses and at distinctive levels and acknowledged the important role played by language at the first and second levels, Ji Zang's general point is philosophically interesting: speech needs to be context-sensitive in order to effectively capture and deliver truths, i.e., our understandings and comprehensions of the world.

There are two notes concerning evaluation of the foregoing views. First, one of the reasons why some of the ancient thinkers held that speech is not able to capture meaning (i.e., ideas in mind in this context) is this: some of the available conceptual and explanatory resources in contemporary philosophy that are available to us to capture and deliver sophisticated ideas and thoughts were simply unavailable to those thinkers. Therefore, there is no wonder why they felt that the linguistic means available to them were insufficient to capture sophisticated thoughts and ideas. Second, the term *yi* in *yan-yi-zhi-bian* has much wider coverage than what the term "thought" in the contemporary debate on the relation between language and thought covers: the latter primarily means propositional thoughts while the former includes non-propositional ideas, emotions, and characteristic existential experience; a claim putting into doubt or denying the capacity of speech to capture such non-propositional mental things could be compatible with the positions by those whose primary concern is with the relation between language and propositional thoughts.

See *er-ti* [lun]; **Ji, Zang; Neo-Daoism; Wang, Bi; Xi, Kang**

Further reading: Chan 2009 (1.7.2); Mou 2006 (2.5.2)

Yang, Zhu (Yang Chu) 楊朱 (fifth century BCE?) is sometimes considered to be among the first of the Daoist philosophers. Yang Zhu and his followers are called "Yangist", and their thoughts are called "**Yangism**".

See **Daoism; Yangism**

Yangism / Yangists: In contrast to a general orientation to strive for both sageliness within and kingliness without (*nei-sheng-wai-wang*), Yang Zhu and his followers ("the Yangists") emphasized and enjoyed the comforts of private life instead of the burden and perils of the struggle for power and possessions. Yangist hermits justified the way they lived in terms of preserving life. (Their attitude is different from another kind of withdrawal from politics into private life: one might be ideologically "forced" to retire in protest against the corruption of the times and still maintain one's **Confucian**, or **Mohist**, moral principle.) The Yangist view consists of two basic positions that are intrinsically related in their ideology: (1) Each one for oneself: one's life is the highest good and worthy of preservation at all cost. (The Yangist position in this regard was illustrated in some of the ancient texts by the metaphorical saying: If by plucking out one hair of his shank he could benefit the world, a Yangist would not do it. But this does not amount to saying that, if he could benefit the world without plucking out one hair from of his shank, he would not do it.) (2) Despising external possessions for the sake of valuing one's own life. While the latter shows a general **Daoist** attitude towards the relation between one's natural life and external possessions, the former is considered as the Yangist version of ethical **egoism**, which is not the same as selfishness (or egotism).

See **Daoism; egoism; Yang, Zhu**

Further reading: Fung 1948 Ch. 6 (2.4); Hansen 1992, Part II (1.5.2)

yi 易: A basic philosophical category in the *Yi-Jing* text. The primary meaning of *yi* is changing/changes, becoming, or transformation. However, in the context of the *Yi-Jing* or *Yi-Jing* philosophy, the term has three closely related meanings, though they appear to be unrelated or even incompatible and opposed: (1) changing/**becoming** (*bian-yi* 變易); (2) unchanging/**being** (*bu-yi* 不易); and (3) being simple and easy (*jian-yi* 簡易). The three meanings are intrinsically related from the point of view of the **yin-yang metaphysical vision** (more generally, the **yin-yang way of thinking**) as delivered in the *Yi-Jing* text: (1) changing/becoming (*bian-yi*) and unchanging/being (*bu-yi*) as the two most basic modes of existence and thus the two most basic **metaphysical** categories constitute the most basic pair of **yin-yang** forces in the universe; they are interdependent, interpenetrating, and complementary; they coexist in **harmony**; (2) what makes seemingly chaotic and complicated phenomena of changing/becoming things simple and easy lies in their "unchanging/being" aspect or dimension like their changing patterns, relatively stable identities, or universal components, which exist within changing things, instead of being imposed from without.

See **being versus becoming; harmony;** *Yi-Jing*; *yin-yang*; *yin-yang* **metaphysical vision;** *yin-yang* **way of thinking**

Further reading: Cheng 2009 (1.1.2); Mou 2003 (1.1.2)

yi 義 (**righteousness**): The term *yi* means the morality of righteousness, the right, or the appropriate. Confucius gave one representative account of *yi* in the *Lun-Yü*: *yi* is another important virtue through which *ren* is cultivated. Confucius stressed *yi* as necessary for developing *ren*. Unlike *li* 禮 as external rituals and rules of propriety, *yi* is internal **virtue**, a moral disposition to do what is right and an ability to recognize what is right; *yi* functions as a kind of moral sense or intuition regarding action. Based on *yi*, some actions must be performed only because they are right and not because of what they produce. On the other hand, *yi* is not something that has nothing to do with inclination, disposition, or intuition. As far as the relation between *yi* and *li* is concerned, cultivating *yi* is carried out by observing *li*. **Mencius**, another significant figure in **classical Confucianism**, further elaborated *yi* in this way: *yi* as a moral attribute emphasizes strictness with oneself, a commitment to abide by certain ethical standards that involve both not acquiring things by improper means and not accepting others' improper treatment of oneself.

See **classical Confucianism; Confucius;** *li* 禮; **Mencius;** *ren*; **virtue**

Further reading: Chong 1998 (1.2.2); Cua 2003 (1.2.2); Shun 1997 (1.2.2)

Yi-Jing (I Ching) 易經: The *Yi-Jing* text is one of the basic classical texts of Chinese philosophy, through which the **yin-yang metaphysical vision** and **the yin-yang way of thinking** have developed. The *Yi-Jing* text in the classical sense (the *Zhou-Yi* text) comprises sixty-four **gua** units, each of which consists of three parts: (1) *gua-xiang* 卦象, an ideographical symbol, i.e., a hexagram like ☷, which consists of six divided and/or undivided lines, called "*yao*" 爻 or "*yao* line" (the divided line --, called "*yin-yao*" 陰爻, and undivided lines —, called "*yang-yao*" 陽爻); a hexagram is used to stand for one representative changing pattern; (2) *gua-ci* 卦辭, one explanatory statement that gives the name of the hexagram and the meaning of the whole *gua-xiang*; and (3) *yao-ci* 爻辭, a set of six explanatory statements, each of which respectively gives the meaning of one of the six *yao* lines in the hexagram.

The *Yi-Jing* text in the broad sense is the *Yi-Jing* text in the classical sense of the term, the *Zhou-Yi* text, together with its accompanying commentaries, the "*Yi-Zhuang*" (*Yi* commentaries) 易傳. The *Yi-Zhuang* is also called *Ten Wings* (*Shi-Yi* 十翼); it consists of ten sets of commentaries: two parts of the *Tuan-Zhuan* (彖傳); two parts of the *Xiang-Zhuan* (象傳); the *Wen-Yan* (文言傳); two parts of the *Xi-Ci-Zhuan* (系辭傳); the *Shuo-Gua-Zhuan* (說卦傳); the *Xu-Gua-Zhuan* (序卦傳); and the *Za-Gua-Zhuan* (雜卦傳). Before the *Han* Dynasty (206 BCE–220), *the Ten Wings* were separate from the *Yi-Jing* text; the *Han* **Confucians** combined them with the *Yi-Jing* original text to make the *Yi-Jing* in its broad sense. The views delivered in the *Yi* commentaries are largely later Confucian interpretative elaborations of the *Zhou-Yi* text.

With the foregoing understanding of the structure of the

Yi-Jing text, the identity of the so-called *yin-yang* way of thinking as delivered in the *Yi-Jing* text can thus be given: either that delivered in the *Yi-Jing* text in the classical sense ("the original or classical version of *yin-yang* way of thinking" or simply "the **yin-yang way of thinking**" in this book), or that delivered in the *Yi-Jing* text in the broad sense, which includes many Confucian interpretative elaborations of the former ("Confucian version of *yin-yang* way of thinking").

See *yi* 易; *yin-yang*; *yin-yang* **metaphysical vision**; *yin-yang* **way of thinking**

Further reading: Liu 1998 (1.1.2); Schwartz 1986 (1.1.2); Wilhelm and Wilhelm 1995 (1.1.2)

Yi-Zhuan 易傳 see *Yi-Jing*

yin-yang 陰陽: In its broad sense, it means the unity of two, mutually opposed but correlative and complementary forces that are considered to exist within anything in the universe. The *yang* is considered to be the positive, active, and (manifestly) strong force, while the *yin* is the negative, passive, and yielding force. In a narrow sense, it means two complementary fluid force elements within *qi* whose mix determines the existence of all things in the universe. The *yin* and *yang* are interdependent, interpenetrating and inter-transformational; these features are represented by the dot at the heart of each half of the flowing circle in the *yin-yang* symbol: ☯. In some conventional accounts, the *yang* is depicted in terms of the sun, light, male, summer, dry, dominant, upper, active, etc., while the *yin* in terms of the moon, dark, female, winter, moist, receptive, submissive, lower, passive, etc.

See *Yi-Jing*; *yin-yang* **metaphysical vision**; *yin-yang* **way of thinking**

Further reading: Cheng 2008 (1.1.2); Graham 1986 (1.1.2); Mou 2003 (1.1.2) *yin-yang* **metaphysical vision (in the** *Yi-Jing*): The *yin-yang* metaphysical vision concerning the relation between changing/**becoming** and unchanging/**being,** as delivered in the *Yi-Jing* text in the classical sense, is not a mono-simplex as the changing/becoming-concerned metaphysical perspective alone, but instead is a multilayered metaphysical complex: (1) the *yin-yang* metaphysical vision consists of both its perspective dimension and its guiding principle dimension; (2) its perspective dimension consists of both the changing/becoming-concerned perspective and the unchanging/being-concerned perspective; (3) its guiding principle dimension consists in a reflective guiding polymerization of changing/becoming-concerned and unchanging/being-concerned perspectives which takes neither priority of changing/becoming over unchanging/being nor priority of unchanging/being over changing/becoming, but regards changing/becoming and unchanging/being as complementary *yin-yang* opposites in an organic unity.

The *yin-yang* metaphysical vision has a strong methodological implication and suggests the *yin-yang* **model of interaction and transformation,** a kind of methodological guiding principle. This principle gives a guide toward a balanced, holistic understanding of various aspects or layers of an object of study and renders indispensable and complementary distinctive methodological perspectives that aim to capture the distinctive aspects of the object. This *yin-yang* methodological guiding principle constitutes the reflective core of the *yin-yang* way of thinking.

See **being versus becoming;** *yi* 易; *Yi-Jing*; *yin-yang*; *yin-yang* **way of thinking (***yin-yang* **model of interaction and transformation)**

Further reading: Cheng 2003 (1.1.2); Graham 1986 (1.1.2); Mou 2003 (1.1.2) *yin-yang* **way of thinking (*yin-yang* model of interaction and transformation):** The *yin-yang* way of thinking or, in more theoretic terms, the *yin-yang* model of interaction and transformation, is suggested in the ancient Chinese classical text the ***Yi-Jing*** (*I Ching*), but reflects the collective wisdom of ancient Chinese people on *how* to understand the fundamental way of the world and how to look at events around us. It has profoundly influenced the orientation of mentality, and methodological strategies, of subsequent Chinese thinkers in various schools or movements.

According to the *yin-yang* way of thinking, anything in the universe intrinsically contains two mutually opposed but correlative and complementary forces: **yin** and **yang**. The *yang* is considered to be the positive, active, and strong force, while the *yin* is the negative, passive, and yielding force. The constitution and interaction between *yin* and *yang* are considered to have the following characteristics: (1) universal: *yin* and *yang* coexist within everything in the universe; (2) fundamental: their interaction within is the ultimate source or pushing force for everything's becoming-process (forming, developing, altering, and changing); (3) complementary: they are interdependent; (4) holistic: they are united into one thing within rather than separate without; (5) dynamic: they are not in a static state but in changing process and transform into each other; and (6) **harmonious** equilibrium: they seek balance through cooperation and in accord.

Two notes are due. First, the foregoing *yin-yang* way of thinking was implicitly suggested in the *Yi-Jing* text (in the classical sense) through its **yin-yang metaphysical vision** concerning the relation between changing (*yi*) / becoming and unchanging (*bu-yi*) /being. Second, the term "the *yin-yang* way of thinking of the *Yi-Jing*" here means a group of related fundamental guiding principles or insights as revealed in the *Zhou-Yi* text, i.e., the *Yi-Jing* text in its classical or narrow sense which consists of the sixty-four ideographic symbols, the hexagrams, and their respective explanatory texts (i.e., *gua-ci* and *yao-ci*). In this way, the *yin-yang* way of thinking in the *Yi-Jing* is not exactly the same as the views presented in the commentary elaborations of the *Zhou-Yi* text, i.e., the *Yi-Zhuan* in the *Yi-Jing* text in its broad sense. Those views to large extent are subsequent Confucian interpretative elaborations of the *Zhou-Yi* text.

See **harmonious**; *Yi-Jing*; *yin-yang*; *yin-yang* **metaphysical vision**

Further reading: Allinson 2003 (1.1.2); Cheng 2009 (1.1.2); Graham 1986 (1.1.2); Mou 2003 (1.1.2)

you 有 (**to have, being**) see *you* 有 versus *wu* 無

you 有 versus *wu* 無 (**being versus non-being**): The issue of *you* (being) versus *wu* (non-being) in Chinese philosophy partly overlaps the cross-tradition issue of **being versus becoming** but has distinct aspects that are not fully covered by the latter issue. The term *you* literally means *being* or *there existing* like an existential quantifier, while the term *wu* literally means *non-being*, *non-existence*, or *there being not* (the negation or denial of being), or simply *nothing*. There are three aspects of the issue of *you* versus *wu*, which are well demonstrated and illustrated in **Lao Zi**'s *Dao-De-Jing*. (1) The issue of the constitutional relation between being and non-being as becoming (as the "constitutional-opposite" negation of being) concerning the fundamental constitution and basis of the world. This aspect of the issue of *you* versus *wu* is essentially a Chinese way of delivering the perennial cross-tradition issue of being versus becoming. The *yin-yang* **metaphysical vision** that renders being and non-being (as changing/

becoming) interdependent and complementary is well delivered in such passages in the *Dao-De-Jing* as "*you* (being) and *wu* (non-being/becoming) give rise to each other; difficult and easy complement each other; long and short offset each other; high and low incline turn into each other; sound and tones harmonize with each other; before and after follow each other" (Ch. 2). As indicated in **being versus becoming**, in contrast not merely to Parmenides' line of thought in the Western tradition (taking the absolute priority of being over becoming) but also to the *yin-yang* metaphysical vision, **Buddhism** takes the (absolute) priority of becoming over being. The categories of *you* and *wu* are further used to identify the ontological nature (real or unreal) of becoming phenomena: its **Three-Treatise School** takes it that all (becoming) phenomena are not real or empty of reality (and thus is also called *wu-zon*g 無宗, the School of Non-being), while its **Consciousness-Only School** holds that all (becoming) phenomena are real (and thus is also called *you-zong* 有宗, the School of Being).

(2) The issue of the generational relationship of non-being (as the "origin-tracing" negation of being) to being with regard to the origin of the world. One view takes non-being (or the undifferentiated thing) as the ultimate origin of being (all differentiated existent things, including both being and non-being as constitutional contributors in the sense explained in (1)), as highlighted in the passage "*you* comes from *wu*" (Ch. 40). The Neo-Daoist **Wang Bi** further postulated that *wu* was the "original reality," while *you* was a variety of functions of *wu*. Another view proposed by **Guo Xiang**, also a Neo-Daoist, maintained that *wu* could not be the gateway to anything, but makes sense only relative to *you* (only *not* this being or *not* that being) and that *you* must be self-engendered and eternal.

(3) The issue of the local-global relation between being (as the "local" specific/particular being) and non-being (as the "holistic" negation of "local" being) concerning the dynamic and holistic nature of the world. In this context, "*you*" means some or any "local" specific being, either a specific shape or a specific tone or, in a semantic-ascent way, a specific descriptive name. [The phrase "a semantic-ascent way," simply speaking and understood broadly, means a way of (indirectly) talking about the object(s) under examination through (directly) talking about linguistic or conceptual items that signify the object(s).] *Wu* does not simply mean *having not* but *being not limited to* or *being not exhausted by*, any "local" or "specific" being. One view, as delivered by **Lao Zi**, looks at the relation essentially in terms of the **yin-yang way of thinking** concerning complementarity and **harmonious** balance. On the one hand, the *dao* cannot exist beyond and above, or independently of, *wan-wu* (ten thousand specific/particular things). Lao Zi thus said: "The great *dao* flows everywhere" (Ch. 34) and, expressing the same point but in a semantic-ascent way, "The *dao* can be talked about [in language via specific names]" (the first statement, *dao-ke-dao* 道可道, is the opening sentence of the *Dao-De-Jing*, Ch. 1). On the other hand, "[the *dao* that has been specified via specific descriptive names in language] is not identical with, or do not exhaust, the eternal *dao*" (the second statement, *fei-chang-dao* 非常道, is the opening sentence of Ch. 1); "The great image [as a whole] is not limited to [or cannot be exhausted by] any [specific] shape; the *dao* is hidden [beyond what any specific descriptive names can capture] and cannot be exhausted by any [specific descriptive] names" (*da-xiang-wu-xing*; *dao-yin-wu-ming* 大象無形; 道隱無名, Ch. 41; it is noted that, in this context and in view of Lao Zi's whole thought in the text, *wu* does not means

absolute and indiscriminate denial of any specific being). Nevertheless, another view or interpretation only takes the latter side of Lao Zi's whole vision: it renders the *dao* (or the great image) metaphysically unrelated and irrelevant to specific/particular manifestations (or shapes) and denies the positive and indispensable contribution of specific and particular being to the metaphysical constitution of the *dao*. This view is closely related to the "meaning-delivery-beyond-speech-capacity" approach taken by **Xi Kan** in *yan-yi-zhi-bian* (the debate on the relation between speech and meaning during the *Wei-Jin* period).

See **being versus becoming; Buddhism; Consciousness-Only Buddhism;** *Dao-De-Jing***; Guo, Xiang; harmonious; Lao, Zi; Three-Treatise Buddhism; Wang, Bi; Xi, Kan;** *yan-yi-zhi-bian***;** *yin-yang* **metaphysical vision;** *yin-yang* **way of thinking**

Further reading: Chao 1955 (2.5.3); Hansen 2003 (2.5.3); Graham 1989 (2.5.3); Mou 2003 (1.5.2)

Z

Zen **Buddhism** see *Chan* **Buddhism**

Zhang, Dai-nian 張岱年 (style name "Ji-tong" 季同: 1909–2004) was a modern Chinese philosopher and creative thinker in studying the history of Chinese philosophy. He consciously employed the method of conceptual analysis to examine key concepts in Chinese philosophy, resulting in his influential work *Zhong-Guo-Zhe-Xue-Da-Gang* (*Conceptual Outline of Chinese Philosophy*, 1958), whose English translation is *Key Concepts in Chinese Philosophy* (2002). He also tried to work out a philosophical system that combined **materialism** and Chinese traditional philosophy by means of conceptual analysis.

Zhang, Dong-sun (Chang Tung-sun) 張東蓀 (style name "Sheng-xin" 聖心: 1886–1973) was one of the significant figures in the **enlightenment movement in modern Chinese philosophy**. Unlike his contemporaries in the movement, Zhang based his philosophy more on the assimilation and synthesis of resources (Kantian, **Buddhist**, etc.) from Western and Chinese philosophical traditions to arrive at his own system. This was especially the case for his view on **epistemology** (a subject that had yet to be fully and systematically elaborated in the ancient Chinese philosophy), which resulted in what he called *duo-yuan-ren-shi-lun* (多元認識論 pluralistic epistemology). Zhang's representative works include *Ren-Shi-Lun* (*Epistemology*, 1934) and *Zhi-Shi-Yu-Wen-Hua* (*Knowledge and Culture*, 1946).

See **enlightenment movement in modern Chinese philosophy**

Further reading: Jiang 2009 (1.11.2)

Zhang, Xue-cheng (Chang Hsüeh-ch'eng) 章學誠 (style name "Shi-zhai" 實齋: 1738–1801) was **Dai Zhen**'s contemporary and a leading philosopher during the early *Qing* Dynasty. Dai was famous while Zhang was almost unknown as his major collection of essays, *Weng-Shi-Tong-Yi* (General Principles of Literature and History), was not published until after his death. One of Zhang's distinctive views is his evaluative explanation of a triad of tendencies in Chinese intellectual history: thoughts were originally suggested as functional public learning by teachers; they were then privatized into a number of philosophical schools, each of which captured only one part of the truth; finally, they were followed by the masters of philosophy and then by a flowering of literary art.*

See *Qing* **Confucianism**

Further reading: Nivison 2003 (1.9.2)*

Zhang, Zai (Chang Tsai) 張載 (style name "Zi-hou" 子厚; honorific name "Heng-qu" 橫渠: 1020–77) was an uncle of the Cheng brothers (**Cheng Hao** and **Cheng Yi**). Zhang specialized in the *Yi-Jing* and was also partly influenced by **Daoism**. Zhang developed his **cosmological** ontology which he considered *qi* (氣) to be the most fundamental material force which transforms into the myriad things in the world. He took the idea of *xu* (虛 vacuity) from the Daoists, but transformed it into the ultimate creative ontological principle of **Neo-Confucian** philosophy. *Xu* and *qi* are complementary concepts and are indispensable to the understanding of change. They work together to form the Great Harmony (*Tai-He* 太和) which characterizes the Way. Zhang's representative work is *Zheng-Meng (Rectifying Obscurations)*, notably one of the essays in that book, *Xi-Ming* (Western Inscription). As Wing-tsit Chan pointed out, if **Zhou Dun-Yi**'s short essay on the diagram of the Great Ultimate has become the basis of Neo-Confucian metaphysics, Zhang's *Xi-Ming* has become the basis of Neo-Confucian ethics.

See **Confucianism; Neo-Confucianism; Cheng, Hao;** *qi*; *xu*

Further reading: Chan Ch.30 of 1963 (1.9.1); Liu 2009 (1.9.2)

zheng-ming 正名(**rectification of names**): In the pre-*Qin* period three figures put forward accounts of rectifying names concerning the relation between name and actuality: **Confucius, Gong-sun Long,** and **Xun Zi.** Confucius' and Gong-sun Long's accounts are considered to be more philosophically interesting and thus are considered below, though Xun Zi suggested a much more systematic account of names.

It is known that Confucius' major concern is with

moral and social issues. His doctrine of rectifying names serves his major concern. Nevertheless, the focus here is on those interesting points suggested in this doctrine from the point of view of philosophy of language. The passages in the *Lun-Yü* that are directly related to the issue of name rectification are found in 13.3, 12.11, 12.17. Confucius' doctrine of name rectification can be seen as another way of presenting his teachings on moral cultivation and adequate governance. The teaching delivered in 12.17 concerns how to rectify yourself to fit the meaning (implied prescriptive standards) of the terms that signify rank, duties, functions, and moral attributes, which amount to sageliness within. The teaching delivered in 12.11 is to participate in rectifying others to fit the meaning (implied prescriptive standards) of those terms that signify their ranks, duties, functions, and moral attributes, which amounts to kingliness without. However, what really interests us here are some general points concerning the relationship between language and reality.

Let us start with an apparent puzzle: there appears to be tension between the two suggested kinds of rectification approaches. On the one hand, the trademark title of this doctrine is "rectifying names"; on the other hand, 12.17 and 12.11 indicate that what is rectified is actually the persons who bear the (social-title) name. Which one is the primary goal and which serves as the means? What is the proper relationship between the two kinds of rectification? Why didn't Confucius directly emphasize rectifying the moral agent? The answer seems to be this: in order to rectify the person (self and others) for the sake of **self-cultivation** and for social reform, there needs to be a standard or norm that itself needs language as a means or even a medium in order for it to be carried out, communicated, examined, and passed on. This is a two-level rectification process with the goal of rectifying the agent into a certain, prescriptively specified person. The first step is to take a semantic-ascent strategy: instead of talking directly about how to rectify the agent, first rectify her (social-title) name under examination by assigning it a certain due prescriptive content; this assignment specifies the standard or norm to be met by any eligible referents of the name, thus giving the primary identity condition of such referents. The second step is to rectify the agent based on the primary identity condition of the expected referents of the name that has been established in the preceding semantic-ascent strategy.

An interesting point concerns the relation between name and actuality, which is implicitly suggested by Confucius' account of name rectification. The proper identity condition of the actuality of a thing (say, a ruler) is not simply its status quo or current appearance (say, the ruler-title-bearing person); rather, it consists in the realization of its due place without transgressing its due scope (say, the person who really possesses the moral character that is expected of the ruler). Name rectification will play an important or even indispensable role through the name carrying out and delivering the norm which specifies such a due place of the thing that is normatively denoted by the name (say, through rectifying the name "ruler").

If Confucius' account only implicitly suggests the foregoing point concerning social-title names and their due referents, one of Gong-sun Long's contributions lies in his more sophisticated explication of the point in more general terms concerning any name and its related actuality. In his essay *Ming-Shi-Lun* (On Name and Actuality), Gong-sun Long explained, "What the heaven and earth produce are things. When a thing goes its own way without transgressing its limit, it achieves its actuality (*shi*); when its actuality goes its own way without being out of its track, it achieves its due place (*wei*). If a thing goes beyond its due place, it is in wrong place; if a thing is in its due place, it is in right place. One is expected to rectify a thing in wrong place into right place; one is not expected to challenge a thing in due place by virtue of it being in wrong place. The rectification of a thing is the rectification of its actuality; the rectification of its actuality is implemented through the rectification of its name. Once its name is rectified, the standards for 'that' and 'this' will be formed up and stabilized." Gong-sun Long here emphasized that a thing needs to go its own way without transgressing its limit to achieve its actuality. He further stressed that, once a thing achieves its actuality, there remains the issue of how to keep its actuality in due place. He explicitly pointed out that so-called name rectification lies in rectifying the actuality of a thing in its due place through rectifying the due content of its name. This identifies such due place and thus gives a due identity condition for the thing and its actuality.

See **Confucianism; Confucius; Gong-sun, Long; reference**

Further reading: Makeham 1994 (2.5.2); Mou 2006 (2.5.2)

zhi 知 see **knowledge**

zhi-xing-he-yi (*chih-hsing-ho-i*) 知行合一 (**unity of knowledge and action**): This is the central thesis of **Wang Shou-ren**'s Neo-Confucian account of unity of knowledge (*zhi*) and action (*xing*). As a **Confucian**, Wang was primarily concerned with fulfilling the Confucian mission to become a *jun-zi* (a morally superior person), by achieving moral knowledge and through moral practice. Wang's doctrine of unity of knowledge and action is thus primarily about moral knowledge. Although moral knowledge is practical knowledge rather than purely theoretical or propositional knowledge, it is not purely practical knowledge without theoretical import. Therefore, Wang's doctrine of unity of knowledge and action has a general significance in **epistemology**.

The point of Wang's doctrine of unity of knowledge and action, strictly speaking, is not about applying knowledge or theory to practice, which presupposes that knowledge and action are separate things, but about how (moral) knowledge and action are intrinsically related and unified. Wang highlighted and summarized his doctrine of unity of knowledge and action in terms of two statements: (1) "Knowledge is the direction of action and action the accomplishment of knowledge"; (2) "Knowledge is the beginning of action and action the completion of knowledge." Statement (1) says that prospective (moral) knowledge, by virtue of its cognitive content acquired through learning, provides a direction or leading idea for action, while action is the accomplishment or implementation of prospective (moral) knowledge. Statement (2) says that prospective knowledge is the beginning of action, while action is the completion of retrospective knowledge. Statement (1) emphasizes the process, while Statement (2) stresses (moral) achievement. In this way, prospective knowledge and retrospective knowledge "produce" and benefit each other, and cognitive content and actuating import bring about and promote each other.

For our interpretative purpose, we can further elaborate some implications in these statements and the key terminology employed. Given that Wang emphasized the innate source of knowledge (what he calls *liang-zhi* 良知), what *zhi* (knowledge) means includes an innate and pro-experiential part of the whole knowing process while *xin* (action) means the sense-experiential practice part of the whole knowing process. A Kantian elaboration of the point made in Statement (1) could be this: an innate conceptual apparatus provides the direction or structure of knowledge, while experiential practice is the accomplishment of knowledge. Another implication is a theory–practice relation elaboration. Given that *zhi* means theoretical knowledge or theory while *xing* 行 means practice, an elaboration of the points made in the two statements with regard to the relation between theory and practice is this: theory provides a direction for practice, while practice completes theory. This is meant in the sense that practice provides a test for the viability of theory and practice accomplishes the task set up by theory.

See **Confucianism; epistemology;** *ge-wu-zhi-zhi*; *jun-zi*; **knowledge;** *liang-zhi*; **Neo-Confucianism; Wang, Shou-ren**

Further reading: Cua 1982 (1.9.2)

zhong (*chung*) 忠 (**sincere commitment; loyalty**): The **virtue** *zhong* as characterized in **Confucius'** *Lun-Yü* is one's sincere and devoted commitment to those culturally and historically established social constitutions like the *li* 禮 (rites and rules). In Confucius' version of the **Golden Rule**, *zhong* is the external starting-point for self-examination of one's own desires and one's treatment of others by virtue of those external ritual rules in concrete situations; *zhong* is eventually regulated by the internal starting-point dimension (the substantial aspect of *shu*), but is a way to practice *ren*.

See **Confucius; Golden Rule;** *li* 禮; *Lun-Yü*; *ren*; *shu*; **virtue**

Further reading: Mou 2004 (1.2.2); Shun 2003 (1.2.2)

Zhong-Yong (*Chung Yung*) 中庸 (*Doctrine of the Mean* or *Centrality and Commonality*): The *Zong-Yong* is one of the *Four Books* (*Si-Shu*), along with the *Lun-Yü*

(*Analects*), the *Mencius*, and the *Da-Xue* (*Great Learning*), which **Zhu Xi** (1130–1200) in the *Song* Dynasty identified as the four most important **Confucian** classics.

See **Confucianism**; *Si-Shu*

Zhou, Dun-yi (Chou Tun-i) 周敦頤 (style name "Mao-shu" 茂叔; honorific name "Lian-xi" 濂溪: 1017–73) was the teacher of **Cheng Hao** and **Cheng Yi** and has been considered to be the orginator of **Neo-Confucianism**. Zhou Dun-yi's short essay on the diagram of the great ultimate (*tai-ji* 太極) has become the basis of Neo-Confucian metaphysics. His representative writings are the *Tai-Ji-Tu-Shuo* (*An Explanation of the Diagram of the Great Ultimate*) and the *Tong-Shu* (*Penetrating the Yi-Jing*).

See **Cheng, Hao; Cheng, Yi; Neo-Confucianism**
Further reading: Hon 2003 (1.9.2); Liu 2009 (1.9.2)

Zhu, Xi (Chu Hsi) 朱熹 (style names "Yuan-hui" 元晦; and "Zhong-hui" 仲晦: 1130–1200) was the greatest philosopher of *Song-Ming* **Neo-Confucianism**. His interpretations of **Confucian** works became orthodox and canonical as mastery of them was required for the imperial examinations (Chinese civil service exams). His distinct account of Neo-Confucianism was called *Cheng-Zhu-li-xue* (**Cheng Yi** and Zhu Xi's approach to the study of *li* 理) and was criticized by *Lu-Wang-xin-xue*. His representative works include the *Si-Shu-Ji-Zhu* (*Commentaries on the Four Books*) and *Zhu-Zi-Yü-Lei* (*Classified Conversations of Zhu Xi*).

See **Confucianism**; *ge-wu-zhi-zhi*; *li* 理; *li-xue*; **Neo-Confucianism**; *xin-xue*

Further reading: Chan 1973 (1.9.2); Liu 2003, 2009 (1.9.2)

Zhuang, Zi (Chuang Tzu) 莊子 (given name "Zhou" 周:

375–300 BCE) was born in the *Song* state, a region roughly corresponding to today's Henan province. Along with **Lao Zi,** Zhuang Zi was classified as a founding member of the **classical Daoist** school by Si-ma Qian (145–90 BCE), a historian of the early *Han* Dynasty. The text bearing his name, the *Zhuang-Zi,* consists of three parts, of which only the first, the seven "inner" chapters, are ever seriously credited as writings of the historical person.

A key to understanding Zhuang Zi's thoughts as a whole and his various ideas on different subjects (on identities of things, knowledge, happiness, freedom, etc.) is to understand his basic methodological strategy, a kind of **transcendental perspectivism.** This strategy is explicitly and emphatically delivered in the second chapter of the inner chapters of the *Zhuang-Zi.* There are two closely related basic points. First, each thing has its various aspects, and one can take a finite perspective (as a working perspective) in looking at one aspect: one can look at its *this* aspect, from a *this* aspect-concerned perspective, and see it as a *this,* and one can also look at its *that* aspect, from a *that* aspect-concerned perspective, and see it as a *that.* Its metaphysical foundation is this: various aspects, the *this* aspect and the *that* aspect, ontologically depend on each other; various perspectives, the *this* aspect-concerned perspective and the *that* aspect-concerned perspective, thus are actually complemently. Second, for the purpose of looking at the connection among various aspects of a thing and/or of having a comprehensive understanding of the thing, Zhuang Zi also encouraged us to look at things from a higher point of view which transcends various finite points of view; in this way, those different aspects cease to be viewed as opposite or incompatible but are seen as complementary.

See **classical Daoism; Daoism; knowledge; perspectivism; skepticism; transcendence;** *Zhuang-Zi*

Further reading: Allinson 1989 (1.5.2); Ames 1998 (1.5.2); Hansen 2003 (1.5.2); Mou 2008b, Section 2 (1.5.2); Shen 2009 (1.5.2)

***Zhuang-Zi* (the *Chuang Tzu*)** 莊子: The *Zhuang-Zi* is one of the most important **classical Daoist** texts. The version of the text we have (thirty-three chapters) was compiled around 300 CE and is widely agreed to be the product of multiple authors. The chapters are usually divided into three parts: (1) the inner chapters (Chapters 1–7) whose author is considered to be the historical figure **Zhuang Zi**; (2) the outer chapters (Chapters 8–22); and (3) the miscellaneous chapters (Chapters 23–33). The authors of the chapters in the second and third parts are considered to be Zhuang Zi's followers. The most important chapters to gain an understanding of Zhuang Zi's thought include Inner Chapter 2 *Qi-Wu-Lun* (*On the Equality of Things*). The last chapter (Chapter 33) contains the first philosophical history of classical Chinese thought.

See **classical Daoism; Daoism; Zhuang, Zi**

Further reading: Kjellberg and Ivanhoe 1996 (1.5.2); Liu 2004 (1.5.2); Roth 2003 (1.5.2); Shen 2009 (1.5.2)

zi-ran 自然 see **nature**

Zou, Yan (Tsou Yen) 鄒衍 (305–240 BCE) is considered to be the first thinker of the Warring States Period who systematically developed a **cosmological** framework that combines the conceptions of ***yin-yang*, *wu-xin***, and *qi* in order to explain the origin and structure of the universe. His own writings are lost; all that we know about him comes from a brief account in the *Shi-Ji* (*Records of the Historian*) by Si-ma Qian (145–90 BCE).

See **cosmology; *qi*; *wu-xin*; *yin-yang***

Subject Bibliography: Selected Further Reading

This bibliography offers a further reading list for readers who already have some initial knowledge of Chinese philosophy, from reading this book or other entry-level introductory textbooks. This bibliography does not pretend to be exhaustive but is selective in line with the emphasis and orientation of this book, To be more informative and sensitive to individual readers' needs, the bibliography is not presented in alphabetical order by authors' last names; instead, the entries are organized into various subjects, which is why the bibliography is titled "Subject Bibliography". The subjects into which the entries are organized are of two types: (1) the movements of thought in the historical lines of Chinese philosophy; and (2) a variety of across-the-board subjects which are not limited to any specific period(s) of the history of Chinese philosophy.

Out of consideration to the likely readership of this book, only English language texts are given (with a few exceptions which provide indispensable background knowledge but which are not available in English translation). There is a rich Chinese literature in reflective studies of Chinese philosophy. The reader who is interested in the Chinese original source texts and/or the Chinese literature on Chinese philosophy can consult the selected bibliographies at the end of the chapters in a recent comprehensive volume, *History of Chinese Philosophy* (ed. Bo Mou, Routledge, 2009), which include

Chinese as well as English literature. It is acknowledged that, when compiling part 1 of this subject bibliography, I have consulted some of the bibliographies in the above volume.

1. Movements of Thought in Historical Lines of Chinese Philosophy

Classical Chinese Philosophy (I): Pre-Han Period (c. eleventh-century BCE – 206 BCE)

1.1 The *Yi-Jing* Philosophy and Early Philosophical Ideas in *Zhou* Dynasty

1.1.1 Source Materials

The I Ching, trans. by James Legge, New York: Dover Publications, 1963 (first published by Oxford University Press in 1882).

The I Ching or Book of Change, trans. by Cary F. Baynes from Richard Wilhelm's German translation of the *Yi-Jing*, New York: Bollingen Foundation, 1950; Princeton, NJ: Princeton University Press, 1977.

The Classic of Changes: A New Translation of the I Ching as Interpreted by Wang Bi, trans. by Richard John Lynn, New York: Columbia University Press, 1994.

Source materials as given in Chapter 13 of *A Source Book in Chinese Philosophy*, trans. and comp. Wing-tsit Chan, Princeton, NJ: Princeton University Press, 1963.

Source materials as given in "The Formation of the Classic of Changes" in Chapter 10 of *Sources of Chinese Tradition* (2nd edition), comp. Volumes I and II, Wm. Theodore de Bary and Irene Bloom (1999), New York: Columbia University Press.

1.1.2 *Reflective Studies*

Allinson, Robert (2003), "Hegelian, *Yi-Jing*, and Buddhist Transformational Models for Comparative Philosophy," in *Comparative Approaches to Chinese Philosophy*, ed. Bo Mou, Aldershot: Ashgate, 60–85.

Cheng, Chung-yin (2003), "Inquiring into the Primary Model *Yi-Jing* and Chinese Ontological Hermeneutics," in *Comparative Approaches to Chinese Philosophy*, ed. Bo Mou, Aldershot: Ashgate, 33–59.

— (2009), "The *Yi-Jing* philosophy," in *History of Chinese Philosophy*, ed. Bo Mou, London: Routledge, 71–106.

Graham, A. C. (1986), *Yin-Yang and the Nature of Correlative Thinking*, Singapore: The Institute of East Asian Philosophies.

Guo, Qi (2000), "The Formation of the Philosophical Category *He* in Chinese History," in *Bulletin of the Institute of Chinese Literature and Philosophy* 16, Taipei: Academia Sinica, 451–66 (in Chinese).

Liu, Shu-hsien (1998), Chapter 5, "Book of Changes," of *Understanding Confucian Philosophy*, Westport, CT: Praeger Publishers, 73–97.

Mou, Bo (1998), "An Analysis of the Ideographic Nature and Structure of the Hexagram of the *Yijing*: From the Perspective of Philosophy of Language," *Journal of Chinese Philosophy* 25.3 (September 1998), 305–20.

— (2003), "Becoming–Being Complementarity: An Account of the *Yin-Yang* Metaphysical Vision of the *Yi-Jing*," in *Comparative Approaches to Chinese Philosophy*, ed. Bo Mou, Aldershot: Ashgate, 86–96.

Schwartz, Benjamin (1986), Section "The Book of Changes," *The World of Thought in Ancient China*, Cambridge, MA: Harvard University Press, 390–7.

Wilhelm, Hellmut and Richard Wilhelm (1995), *Understanding the I Ching*, Princeton, NJ: Princeton University Press.

1.2 Classical Confucianism

1.2.1 Source Materials:

The Analects / the Lun-Yü 論語
  Confucian: Confucian Analects, The Great Learning and The Doctrine of the Mean, trans., with critical and exegetical notes, by James Legge, Oxford: Clarendon Press, 1893; New York: Dover Publications, 1971.
  Confucius: The Analects, trans. and with an introduction by D. C. Lau, New York: Penguin Books, 1979; bilingual edition, Hong Kong: Chinese University of Hong Kong, 1983.
  The Analects of Confucius: A Philosophical Translation, trans., with explanatory notes, by Roger Ames and Henry Rosemont, New York: Ballantine Books, 1998.
  The Original Analects: Sayings of Confucius and His Successors, trans. and commenting by E. Bruce Brooks and A. Taeko Brooks, (1998), New York: Columbia University Press, 1998.
  Confucius: Analects, with selections from traditional comments, trans. Edward Slingerland, Cambridge, MA: Hackett, 2003.

The Meng-Zi (The *Mencius*) 孟子
  The Works of Mencius, trans., with critical and exegetical notes, by James Legge, Oxford: Clarendon Press, 1895; New York: Dover Publications, 1970.
  Mencius; trans. and with an introduction by D. C. Lau, New York: Penguin Books, 1970, 1979; bilingual edition, Hong Kong: The Chinese University Press, 1984.

The Xun-Zi (*Hsun Tzu*) 荀子
  Hsun Tzu: Basic Writings, trans. Burton Watson, New York: Columbia University Press, 1963, 1996.
  Xun Zi – A Translation and Study of the Complete Works,

3 volumes, trans. John Knoblock, Stanford, CA: Stanford University Press, 1988, 1990, 1994.

Source materials as given in Chapters 2–6 of *A Source Book in Chinese Philosophy*, trans. and comp. Wing-tsit Chan (1963), Princeton, NJ: Princeton University Press.

Source materials as given in Chapters 3 and 6 of *Sources of Chinese Tradition* (2nd edition), comp. Volumes I and II, Wm. Theodore de Bary and Irene Bloom, New York: Columbia University Press, 1999.

Source materials as given in Chapters 1, 3, and 6 of *Readings in Classical Chinese Philosophy,* eds. Philip J. Ivanhoe and Bryan W. Van Norden, Indianapolis: Hackett, 2001, 2006.

1.2.2 Reflective Studies

Allinson, Robert E. (1992), "The Golden Rule as the Core Value in Confucianism and Christianity: Ethical Similarities and Differences," *Asian Philosophy* 2.2: 173–85.

Ames, Roger T. and David L. Hall (1987), *Thinking Through Confucius*, Albany, NY: SUNY Press.

— (2003), Confucianism: Confucius," in *Encyclopedia of Chinese Philosophy*, ed. Antonio S. Cua, New York and London: Routledge, 58–64.

Bai, Tongdong (2009), "The Price of Serving Meat – on Confucius's and Mencius's Views of Human and Animal Rights," *Asian Philosophy* 19:1, 85–99.

Brooks, E. Bruce and A. Taeko Brooks (trans. and commentary) (1998), *The Original Analects: Sayings of Confucius and His Successors*, New York: Columbia University Press, 1998.

Chan, Alan (1984), "Philosophical Hermeneutics and the *Analects*: the Paradigm of 'Tradition'," *Philosophy East & West* 34:4, 421–36.

Chan, Sin Yee (2000), "Can *Shu* be the One Word that Serves as the Guiding Principle of Caring Action?" *Philosophy East and West* 50:4, 507–24.

Chan, Wing-tsit (1955), "The Evolution of the Confucian Concept *Jen*," *Philosophy East & West* 4:1, 295–319.

Chang, Chun-shu (2007), *The Rise of the Chinese Empire: Nation, State, and Imperialism in Early China*, Ann Arbor, MI: University of Michigan Press.

Cheang, Alice (2000), "The Master's Voice: On Reading, Translating and Interpreting the *Analects* of Confucius," *The Review of Politics* 62:3, 563–81.

Chen, Ning (1997), "Confucius' View of Fate (*Ming*)," *Journal of Chinese Philosophy* 24, 323–59.

Cheng, Chung-ying (2003), "Mencius," in *Encyclopedia of Chinese Philosophy*, ed. Antonio S. Cua, New York and London: Routledge, 440–8.

Chong, Kim Chong (1998), "Confucius' Virtue Ethics: *Li, Yi, Wen* and *Chih* in the *Analects*," *Journal of Chinese Philosophy* 25, 101–30.

— (2007), *Early Confucian Ethics*, Chicago, IL: Open Court.

— (2008), "Xunzi on Capacity, Ability and Constitutive Rules," in *Searle's Philosophy and Chinese Philosophy: Constructive Engagement*, ed. Bo Mou, Leiden and Boston, MA: Brill, 295–310.

— (2009), "Classical Confucianism (II): Meng Zi and Xun Zi," in *History of Chinese Philosophy*, ed. Bo Mou, London and New York: Routledge, 189–208.

Cline, Erin (2007), "Two Senses of Justice: Confucianism, Rawls, and Comparative Philosophy", *Dao* 6:4, 361–82.

Creel, H. G (1960), *Confucius and the Chinese Way*, New York: Harper & Row.

Cua, Antonio S. (2003), (1) "Xunzi," (2) "*Yi* and *Li*: Rightness and Rites," in *Encyclopedia of Chinese Philosophy*, ed. Antonio S. Cua, New York and London: Routledge, 821–9, 842–6.

— (2005a), "Philosophy of Human Nature," in *Human Nature, Ritual, and History – Studies in Xunzi and Chinese Philosophy*, Washington, DC: The Catholic University of America Press.

— (2005b), "Dimensions of *Li* (Propriety)," in *Human Nature, Ritual, and History – Studies in Xunzi and Chinese Philosophy*, Washington, DC: The Catholic University of America Press.

Eno, Robert (1990), *The Confucian Creation of Heaven*, Albany, NY: SUNY Press.

Fan, Ruiping (2003), "Social Justice: Rawlsian or Confucian?" in *Comparative Approaches to Chinese Philosophy*, ed. Bo Mou, Aldershot: Ashgate, 144–68.

Finazzo, Giancarlo (1967), *The Principle of T'ien: Essays on its Theoretical Relevancy in Early Confucian Philosophy*, Taipei: Mei-ya.

Fingarette, Herbert (1972), *Confucius: Secular as Sacred*, New York: HarperTorchbooks.

Fu, Pei-jung (2003), "*Tian (T'ien)*: Heaven," in *Encyclopedia of Chinese Philosophy*, ed. Antonio S. Cua, New York and London: Routledge, 726–8.

Gier, Nicholas (2001), "The Dancing *Ru*: A Confucian Aesthetics of Virtue," *Philosophy East & West* 51:2, 280–305.

Goldin, Paul Rakita (1999), *Rituals of the Way: The Philosophy of Xunzi*, Chicago, IL: Open Court.

Graham, A. C. (1986), "The Background of the Mencian Theory of Human Nature," in *Studies in Chinese Philosophy and Philosophical Literature*, A. C. Graham, Singapore: The Institute of East Asian Philosophies.

Guo, Qiyong (2007), "Is Confucian Ethics 'Consanguinism'?," *Dao* 6:1, 21–38.

Hansen, Chad (1992), *A Daoist Theory of Chinese Thought*, Chs. 3, 5, 9, and 10, New York: Oxford University Press.

— (1994), "*Fa* (Standards: Laws) and Meaning Changes in

Chinese Philosophy," *Philosophy East and West* 44:3, 433–88.

Hsu, Hsei-Yung (2000), "Confucius and Act-Centered Morality," *Journal of Chinese Philosophy* 27:3, 331–44.

Ihara, Craig K. (1991), "David Wong on Emotions in Mencius," *Philosophy East and West* 41, 45–53.

Ivanhoe, Philip J. (1990), "Reweaving the 'One Thread' of the *Analects*," *Philosophy East & West* 40:1, 17–33.

— (2000), *Confucian Moral Self Cultivation*, Indianapolis, IN: Hackett.

— (2002), "Whose Confucius? Which *Analects*?" in *Confucius and the* Analects: *New Essays*, ed. Bryan Van Norden, 119–33, New York: Oxford University Press.

Kupperman, Joel (1968), "Confucius and the Problem of Naturalness," *Philosophy East & West* 18, 175–85.

— (2002), "Naturalness Revisited: Why Western Philosophers Should Study Confucius," in *Confucius and the* Analects: *New Essays*, ed. Bryan Van Norden, New York: Oxford University Press, 39–52.

Lai, Karyn (2006), "*Li* in the *Analects*: Training in Moral Competence and the Question of Flexibility," *Philosophy East & West* 56:1, 69–83.

Lau, D.C. (2000), "Theories of Human Nature in *Mencius* and *Xunzi*," in *Virtue, Nature, and Moral Agency in the Xunzi*, ed. T. C. Kline III and Philip J. Ivanhoe, Indianapolis, IN: Hackett.

Lee, Sang-Im (1999), "The Unity of Virtues in Aristotle and Confucius," *Journal of Chinese Philosophy* 26:2, 203–23.

Li, Chenyang (ed.) (2000), *The Sage and the Second Sex: Confucianism, Ethics, and Gender*, Chicago, IL: Open Court.

— (2006), "The Confucian Ideal of Harmony," *Philosophy East & West* 56:4, 583–603.

Li, Youzheng (2003), "Towards a Minimal Common Ground for Humanist Dialogue: A Comparative Analysis of

Confucian Ethics and American Ethical Humanism," in *Comparative Approaches to Chinese Philosophy*, ed. Bo Mou, Aldershot: Ashgate, 169–84.

Liu, Qingping (2007), "Confucianism and Corruption," *Dao* 6:1, 1–20.

Liu, Shu-hsien (1998), Chapters 1–3 of *Understanding Confucian Philosophy*, Westport, CT: Praeger Publishers, 3–72.

Liu, Yuili (2004), *The Unity of Rule and Virtue: A Critique of a Supposed Parallel Between Confucian Ethics and Virtue Ethics*, Singapore: Eastern Universities Press.

MacIntyre, Alasdair (1981), *After Virtue*, Notre Dame, IL: University of Notre Dame Press.

— (1991), "Incommensurability, Truth, and the Conversation between Confucians and Aristotelians about the Virtues," In *Culture and Modernity: East–West Philosophical Perspectives*, ed. Eliot Deutsch, Honolulu: University of Hawaii Press, 104–22.

Mahood, George (1974), "Human Nature and the Virtues in Confucius and Aristotle," *Journal of Chinese Philosophy* 1, 295–312.

Mou, Bo (2004), "A Reexamination of the Structure and Content of Confucius' Version of the Golden Rule," *Philosophy East & West* 54:2, 218–48.

Munro, Donald (1969), *The Concept of Man in Early China*, Stanford, CA: Stanford University Press.

— (1996), "A Villain in the *Xunzi*," in *Chinese Language, Thought, and Culture: Nivison and His Critics*, ed. Philip J. Ivanhoe, Chicago, IL: Open Court.

Neville, Robert Commings (2003), "The Project of Boston Confucianism," in *Comparative Approaches to Chinese Philosophy*, ed. Bo Mou, Aldershot: Ashgate, 185–201.

Nivison, David (1996), *The Ways of Confucianism*, ed. Bryan Van Norden. La Salle, IL: Open Court.

Nuyen, A. T. (2008), "Confucianism and Is–Ought Question,"

in *Searle's Philosophy and Chinese Philosophy: Constructive Engagement*, ed. Bo Mou, Leiden and Boston, MA: Brill, 273–89.

Richey, Jeffrey (2000), "Ascetics and Aesthetics in the *Analects*," *Numen* 47:2, 161–74.

Roetz, Heiner (1993), *Confucian Ethics of the Axial Age*, Albany, NY: SUNY Press.

Rosemont, Henry and Roger T. Ames (2008), "Family Reverence (*xiao*) as the Source of Consummatory Conduct (*ren*)," *Dao* 7:1, 9–20.

Ryan, James (2001), "Conservatism and Coherentism in Aristotle, Confucius, and Mencius," *Journal of Chinese Philosophy* 28:3, 275–84.

Sahleen, Joel (2002), "An Annotated Bibliography of Works on Confucius and the *Analects*," in *Confucius and the Analects: New Essays*, ed. Bryan Van Norden, New York: Oxford University Press, 303–20.

Shen, Vincent (2003), "*Ren*: Humanity," in *Encyclopedia of Chinese Philosophy*, ed. Antonio S. Cua, New York and London: Routledge, 643–6.

Shun, Kwong-loi (1997), *Mencius and Early Chinese Thought*, Stanford, CA: Stanford University Press.

— (2002), "*Ren* and *Li* in the *Analects*," in *Confucius and the Analects: New Essays*, ed. Bryan Van Norden, New York: Oxford University Press, 53–72.

— (2003), (1) "*Cheng*," (2) "*Chengyi*," (3) "*Xiao*," (4) "Xiushen: Self-Cultivation," (5) "*Zhong (Chung)* and *Xin (Hsin)*," in *Encyclopedia of Chinese Philosophy*, ed. Antonio S. Cua, New York and London: Routledge, 37–9; 47–8; 793–5, 807–9, 885–8.

— (2005), "Chinese Philosophy: Confucianism," in *Encyclopedia of Philosophy* (2nd edition) ed. Donald M. Borchert (2006), Thomson-Gale/Macmillan Reference USA, 170–80.

Slingerland, Edward (1996), "The Conception of *Ming* in Early Chinese Thought," *Philosophy East & West* 46:4, 567–81.

— (2000), "Why Philosophy Is Not 'Extra' in Understanding the *Analects*, a Review of Brooks and Brooks, *The Original Analects*," *Philosophy East and West* 50:1, 137–41, 146–7.

— (2009), "Classical Confucianism (I): Confucius and the *Lun-Yü*," in *History of Chinese Philosophy*, ed. Bo Mou, London and New York: Routledge, 107–36.

Tan, Sor-Hoon (2001), "Mentor or Friend? Confucius and Aristotle on Equality and Ethical Development in Friendship," *International Studies in Philosophy* 33:4, 99–123.

— (2005), "Imagining Confucius: Paradigmatic Characters and Virtue Ethics," *Journal of Chinese Philosophy* 32:3, 409–26.

Taylor, Charles (1989), *Sources of the Self: The Makings of Modern Identity*, Cambridge, MA: Harvard University Press.

Taylor, Rodney (1990), *The Religious Dimensions of Confucianism*, Albany: SUNY Press.

Tiwald, Justin (2008), "A Right of Rebellion in the Mengzi?", *Dao* 7:3, 269–82.

Van Norden, Bryan (ed.) (2002), *Confucius and the* Analects: *New Essays*, New York: Oxford University Press.

— (2003), "Virtue Ethics and Confucianism," in *Comparative Approaches to Chinese Philosophy*, ed. Bo Mou, Aldershot: Ashgate, 99–121.

Wan, Junren (2004), "Contrasting Confucian Virtue Ethics and MacIntyre's Aristotelian Virtue Theory" (trans. Edward Slingerland), in *Chinese Philosophy in an Era of Globalization*, ed. Robin Wang, Albany, NY: SUNY Press.

Wang, Qingjie (1999), "The Golden Rule and Interpersonal Care – From a Confucian Perspective," *Philosophy East and West* 49:4, 415–38.

Wang, Robin (2003), "The Principled Benevolence: A Synthesis of Kantian and Confucian Moral Judgment," in *Comparative Approaches to Chinese Philosophy*, ed. Bo Mou, Aldershot: Ashgate, 122–43.

Wong, David (1991), "Is There a Distinction between Reason

and Emotion in Mencius?" *Philosophy East and West* 41, 31–44.

Xiao, Yang (2006), "Reading the *Analects* with Davidson: Mood, Force, and Communicative Practice in Early China," in *Davidson's Philosophy and Chinese Philosophy: Constructive Engagement*, ed. Bo Mou, Leiden and Boston, MA: Brill, 247–68.

Yao, Xinzhong (2000), *An Introduction to Confucianism*, Cambridge: Cambridge University Press.

Yu, Jiyuan (2007), *The Ethics of Confucius and Aristotle: Mirrors of Virtue*, London: Routledge.

1.3 The Mohist School

1.3.1 Source Materials

The Mo-Zi / The Mo Tzu 墨子

Mo Tzu: Basic Writings, trans. by Burton Watson (1963), New York: Columbia University Press.

"Mo Tzu's Doctrines of Universal Love, Heaven, and Social Welfare", trans., with an introduction and commentary, by Wing-tsit Chan (1963), in Wing-tsit Chan (comp. and transl.), *A Source Book in Chinese Philosophy*, Princeton, NJ: Princeton University Press, 1963, 1969.

"Mozi" (excerpts), trans. by Philip J. Ivanhoe, in Philip J. Ivanhoe and Bryan W. Van Norden (eds.), *Readings in Classical Chinese Philosophy,* Indianapolis, IN: Hackett, 2001, 2006, Chapter 2.

Source materials as given in Chapter 9 of *A Source Book in Chinese Philosophy*, trans. and comp. Wing-tsit Chan, Princeton, NJ: Princeton University Press, 1963.

Source materials as given in Chapter 4 *Sources of Chinese Tradition* (2nd edition), comp. Volumes I and II, Wm. Theodore de Bary and Irene Bloom, New York: Columbia University Press, 1999.

Source materials as given in Chapter 2 of *Readings in Classical Chinese Philosophy,* eds. Philip J. Ivanhoe and Bryan W. Van Norden, Indianapolis, IN: Hackett, 2001, 2006.

1.3.2 Reflective Studies

Ahern, Denis (1976), "Is Mo Tzu a Utilitarian?" *Journal of Chinese Philosophy* 3:2, 185–93.

Duda, Kristopher (2001), "Reconsidering Mo Tzu on the Foundations of Morality," *Asian Philosophy* 11:1, 23–31.

Fraser, Chris (2002), "Mohism," in *Stanford Encyclopedia of Philosophy,* ed. Edward Zalta, http://plato.stanford.edu/entries/mohism/.

— (2009), "The Mohist School," in *History of Chinese Philosophy,* ed. Bo Mou, London and New York: Routledge, 137–63.

Garrett, Mary (1993), "Classical Chinese Conceptions of Argumentation and Persuasion," *Argumentation and Advocacy* 29:3, 105–15.

Graham, A. C. (1989), Part II, Ch. 2 of *Disputers of the Tao,* LaSalle, IL: Open Court.

Graham, A. C. (2003/1978), *Later Mohist Logic, Ethics and Science,* Hong Kong: Chinese University Press.

Hansen, Chad (1992), Ch. 4 of *A Daoist Theory of Chinese Thought,* Oxford: Oxford University Press.

— (2003), "Mohism: Later," in *Encyclopedia of Chinese Philosophy,* ed. Antonio S. Cua, New York and London: Routledge, 461–9.

Lai, Whalen (1993), "The Public Good That Does the Public Good: A New Reading of Mohism," *Asian Philosophy* 3:2, 125–41.

Lum, Alice (1977), "Social Utilitarianism in the Philosophy of Mo Tzu," *Journal of Chinese Philosophy* 4:2, 187–207.

Mei, Yi-pao (trans.) (1929), *The Ethical and Political Works of Motse,* London: Probsthain.

Mei, Yi-pao (1934), *Mo-tse, the Neglected Rival of Confucius,* London: Probsthain.

Soles, David (1999), "Mo Tzu and the Foundations of Morality," *Journal of Chinese Philosophy* 26:1, 37–48.

Van Norden, Bryan W. (2003), "A Response to the Mohist Arguments in 'Impartial Caring'," in Kim-chong Chong et al. (eds.), *The Moral Circle and the Self: Chinese and Western Approaches,* La Salle, IL: Open Court, 41–58.

Vorenkamp, Dirck (1992), "Another Look at Utilitarianism in Mo-Tzu's Thought," *Journal of Chinese Philosophy* 19:4.

Wong, David (1989), "Universalism vs. Love with Distinctions: An Ancient Debate Revived," *Journal of Chinese Philosophy* 16:3/4, 251–72.

— (2003), "Mohism: The Founder, Mozi," in *Encyclopedia of Chinese Philosophy*, ed. Antonio S. Cua, New York and London: Routledge, 453–61.

Yates, Robin D. S. (1980), "The Mohists on Warfare: Technology, Technique, and Justification," *Journal of the American Academy of Religion* 47:3, 549–603.

1.4 School of Names

1.4.1 Source Materials

Source materials as given in Chapter 10 of *A Source Book in Chinese Philosophy*, trans. and comp. Wing-tsit Chan, Princeton, NJ: Princeton University Press, 1963.

1.4.2 Reflective Studies

Chen, Cheng-yih (1987), "A Comparative Study of Early Chinese and Greek Work on the Concept of Limit," in *Science and Technology in Chinese Civilization*, ed. Cheng-yih Chen, Singapore: World Scientific Publishing.

Cheng, Chung-ying (1983), "Kung-sun Lung: White Horse and Other Issues," in *Philosophy East and West*, 33:1, 341–54.

— (2007), "Reinterpreting Gongsun Longzi and Critical Comments on Other Interpretations," *Journal of Chinese Philosophy* 34:4, 537–60.

Chmielewski, Januz (1962), "Notes on Early Chinese Logic (I)," in *Rocznik Orientalistyczny* 26:1, 7–21.

Fung, Yiu-ming (2007), "A Logical Perspective on 'Discourse on White-Horse'," *Journal of Chinese Philosophy* 34:4, 515–36.

— (2009), "School of Names," in *History of Chinese Philosophy*, ed. Bo Mou, London and New York: Routledge, 164–88.

Fung, Yu-lan (1934), *A History of Chinese Philosophy*, 2 volumes, trans. Derk Bodde (1952, 1953), Princeton, NJ: Princeton University Press.

Graham, A. C. (1978), *Later Mohist Logic, Ethics and Science*, Hong Kong: The Chinese University Press.

— (1986a), "The Disputation of Kung-sun Lung as Argument about Whole and Part," *Philosophy East and West* 36:2, 89–106.

— (1986b), "Three Studies of Kung-Sun Lung," in *Studies in Chinese Philosophy and Philosophical Literature*, Singapore: The Institute of East Asian Philosophies, 125–215.

— (1989), Part I, Ch. 5 of *The Disputer of Tao*, La Salle, IL: Open Court.

Im, Manyul (2007), "Horse-parts, White-parts, and Naming: Semantics, Ontology, and Compound Terms in the White Horse Dialogue," *Dao* 6:2, 167–85.

Le Poidevin, Robin (2003), *Travels in Four Dimensions: The Enigmas of Space and Time*, Oxford: Oxford University Press.

Hansen, Chad (1983), *Language and Logic in Ancient China*, Ann Arbor, MI: University of Michigan Press.

— (2007), "Prolegomena to Future Solutions to 'White-Horse Not Horse'," *Journal of Chinese Philosophy* 34:4, 473–91.

Hu, Shih (1922), *The Development of the Logical Method in Ancient China*, Shanghai: The Oriental Book Company.

Mou, Bo (1999), "The Structure of the Chinese Language and Ontological Insight: A Collective-Noun Hypothesis," *Philosophy East and West* 49:1, 45–62.

— (2007), "A Double-Reference Account: Gongsun Long's 'White-Horse-Not-Horse' Thesis," *The Journal of Chinese Philosophy* 34:4, 493–513.

Needham, Joseph (1956), *Science and Civilisation in China* Volume II, *History of Scientific Thought*, Cambridge: Cambridge University Press.

— (1998), *Science and Civilisation in China* Volume VII: 1, *Part 1: Language and Logic*, by Christoph Harbsmeier, Cambridge: Cambridge University Press.

1.5 Classical (Philosophical) Daoism

1.5.1 Source Materials

The Dao-De-Jing (Lao Tzu) 道德經

Daodejing: A Philosophical Translation, trans. Roger T. Ames and David L. Hall, New York: Ballantine Books, 2003.

Lao Tzu's Tao Te Ching: A Translation of the Startling New Documents Found at Guodian, trans. Robert G. Henricks, New York: Columbia University Press, 2000.

Lao-Tzu Te-Tao Ching: A Translation of the Ma-wang-tui Manuscripts, trans. Robert G. Henricks, London: Rider, 1991.

The Daodejing of Laozi, trans. Philip J. Ivanhoe, Indianapolis: Hackett, 2002.

Lao Tzu: Tao Te Ching, trans. D. C. Lau (1963), London: Penguin Books; Hong Kong: The Chinese University Press, 2001 (bilingual edition).

The Classic of the Way and Virtue: A New Translation of the Tao-te Ching of Laozi as Interpreted by Wang Bi, trans. Richard John Lynn, New York: Columbia University Press, 1999.

The Zhuang-Zi (*Chuang Tzu*) 莊子
Chuang Tzu: The Inner Chapters, trans. by Angus C. Graham, London: George Allen & Unwin, 1981; Indianapolis, IN: Hackett, 2001 (with textual ntoes).
The Complete Works of Chuang Tzu, trans. by Burton Watson, New York: Columbia University Press, 1968.

Source materials as given in Chapters 7 and 8 of *A Source Book in Chinese Philosophy*, trans. and comp. Wing-tsit Chan (1963), Princeton, NJ: Princeton University Press.
Source materials as given in Chapter 5 of *Sources of Chinese Tradition* (2nd edition), comp. Volumes I and II, Wm. Theodore de Bary and Irene Bloom, New York: Columbia University Press, 1999.
Source materials as given in Chapters 4 and 5 of *Readings in Classical Chinese Philosophy,* eds. Philip J. Ivanhoe and Bryan W. Van Norden, Indianapolis, IN: Hackett, 2001, 2006.

1.5.2 *Reflective Studies*

Allinson, Robert E. (1989), *Chuang-Tzu for Spiritual Transformation: An Analysis of the Inner Chapters*, Albany, NY: SUNY Press.
Ames, Roger T. (ed.) (1998), *Wandering at Ease in the Zhuangzi*, Albany, NY: SUNY Press.
Cheng, Chung-ying (2003), "*Dao*: The Way," in *Encyclopedia of Chinese Philosophy*, ed. Antonio S. Cua, New York and London: Routledge, 202–6.
Fraser, Chris (2008), "*Wu-Wei*, the Background, and Intentionality," in *Searle's Philosophy and Chinese*

Philosophy: Constructive Engagement, ed. Bo Mou, Leiden and Boston, MA: Brill, 63–92

Fu, Charles Wei-Hsun (1976), "Creative Hermeneutics: Taoist Metaphysics and Heidegger," *Journal of Chinese Philosophy* 3, 115–43.

Fung, Yu-lan (1948), Chapters 6, 9, and 10, *A Short History of Chinese Philosophy*, New York: The Free Press.

Graham, A. C. (1987), Sections II.3 and III.1, *Disputers of the Tao: Philosophical Argument in Ancient China*, La Salle, IL: Open Court.

— (1990), *Studies in Chinese Philosophy and Philosophical Literature*, Albany, NY: SUNY Press.

Hadot, Pierre (2002), *What is Ancient Philosophy*, trans. Michael Chase, Cambridge, MA: Harvard University Press.

Hansen, Chad (1992), *A Taoist Theory of Chinese Thought: A Philosophical Interpretation*, New York: Oxford University Press.

— (2003), "Zhuangzi," in *Encyclopedia of Chinese Philosophy*, ed. Antonio S. Cua, New York and London: Routledge, 911–18.

— (2003), "The Metaphysics of *Dao*," in *Comparative Approaches to Chinese Philosophy*, ed. Bo Mou, Aldershot: Ashgate, 205–24.

— (2006), "Chinese Philosophy: Daoism," in *Encyclopedia of Philosophy* (2nd edition), ed. Donald M. Borchert, Thomson-Gale/Macmillan Reference USA, 184–94.

Ivanhoe, Philip J.(1999), "The Concept of *de* (Virtue) in the Laozi," in *Religious and Philosophical Aspects of the Laozi*, eds. Mark Csikeszentmihalyi and Philip J. Ivanhoe, Albany, NY: SUNY Press, 211–37.

Kjellberg, Paul and Philip J. Ivanhoe (1996), *Essays on Skepticism, Relativism, and Ethics in the Zhuangzi*, Albany, NY: SUNY Press.

Krueger, Joel W. (2008), "A Daoist Critique of Searle on Mind and Action," in *Searle's Philosophy and Chinese*

Philosophy: Constructive Engagement, ed. Bo Mou, Leiden and Boston: Brill, MA, 97–123.

Lai, Karyn (2007), "Ziran and Wuwei in the Daodejing: An Ethical Assessemnt," *Dao* 6:4, 323–38.

Li, Chenyang (2003), "Zhuang Zi and Aristotle on What A Thing Is," in *Comparative Approaches to Chinese Philosophy*, ed. Bo Mou, Aldershot: Ashgate, 263–77.

Li, Xue-qin (2002), "Walking out of the 'Doubting of Antiquity' Era," *Contemporary Chinese Thought* Winter 2002–3, 26–49.

Liu, JeeLoo (2003), "The Daoist Conception of Truth: Lao Zi's Metaphysical Realism and Zhuang Zi's Internal Realism," in *Comparative Approaches to Chinese Philosophy*, ed. Bo Mou, Aldershot: Ashgate, 278–93.

Liu, Xiaogan (2003a), "From Bamboo Slips to Received Versions: Common Features in the Transformation of the *Laozi*," *Harvard Journal of Asiatic Studies* 63:2, 337–82.

— (2003b), "*Xu*: Emptiness," in *Encyclopedia of Chinese Philosophy*, ed. Antonio S. Cua, New York and London: Routledge, 807–9.

— (2004), *Classifying the Zhuangzi Chapters*, Ann Arbor, MI: Center for Chinese Studies, University of Michigan.

— (2009), "Daoism (I): Lao Zi and the *Dao-De-Jing*," in *History of Chinese Philosophy*, ed. Bo Mou, London and New York: Routledge, 209–36.

Moeller, Han-Georg (2004), *Daoism Explained*, Chicago, IL: Open Court.

— (2006), *The Philosophy of the* Daodejing, New York: Columbia University Press.

Mou, Bo (2002), "Moral Rules and Moral Experience: A Comparative Analysis of Dewey and Laozi on Morality," *Asian Philosophy* 11:3, 161–78.

— (2003), "Eternal *Dao*, Constant Names, and Language Engagement," in *Comparative Approaches to Chinese Philosophy*, ed. Bo Mou, Aldershot: Ashgate, 245–62.

— (2006), "Truth Pursuit and *Dao* Pursuit: from Davidson's Approach to Classical Daoist Approach in View of the Thesis of Truth as Strategic Normative Goal," in *Davidson's Philosophy and Chinese Philosophy: Constructive Engagement*, ed. Bo Mou, Leiden and Boston, MA: Brill, 309–49.

— (2008), "Searle, Zhuang Zi, and Transcendental Perspectivism," in *Searle's Philosophy and Chinese Philosophy: Constructive Engagement*, ed. Bo Mou, Leiden and Boston, MA: Brill, 405–30.

Roth, Harold D. (ed.) (2003), *A Companion to Augus C. Graham's Chuang Tzu*, Honolulu: University of Hawaii Press.

Schwartz, Benjamin I. (1985), *The World of Thought in Ancient China*, Cambridge, MA: Harvard University Press.

Shen, Vincent (1994), "Daoism: Classical," in *Encyclopedia of Chinese Philosophy*, ed. Antonio S. Cua, New York and London: Routledge, 206–14.

— (2009), "Daoism (II): Zhuang Zi and the *Zhuang-Zi*," in *History of Chinese Philosophy*, ed. Bo Mou, London and New York: Routledge, 237–65.

Slingerland, Edward (2003), *Effortless Action: Wu-wei as Conceptual Metaphor and Spiritual Ideal in Early China*, New York: Oxford University Press.

Smith, Kidder (2003), "Sima Tan and the Invention of Daoism, 'Legalism,' *et cetera*," *Journal of Asian Studies* 62:1, 129–56.

Smullyan, Raymond (1977), *The Tao is Silent*, San Francisco: Harper.

Waley, Arthur (1958), *The Way and Its Power: A Study of the* Tao Te Ching *and Its Place in Chinese Thought*, New York: Grove Press.

Wang, Qingjie (2003), "'It-self-so-ing' and 'Other-ing' in Lao Zi's Concept of *Zi Ran*," in *Comparative Approaches to Chinese Philosophy*, ed. Bo Mou, Aldershot: Ashgate, 225–44.

Williams, Raymond (1985), *Keywords: A Vocabulary of Culture and Society*, revised edition, New York: Oxford University Press.

Zhu, Rui (2002), "*Wu-Wei: Lao-Zi, Zhuang-Zi* and the Aesthetic Judgment," *Asian Philosophy* 12:1, 53–63.

Classical Chinese Philosophy (II): From Han Through Tang (206 BCE–907)

1.6 *Han* Philosophy

1.6.1 Source Materials

Source materials as given in Chapters 14–17 of *A Source Book in Chinese Philosophy*, trans. and comp. Wing-tsit Chan, Princeton, NJ: Princeton University Press, 1963.

Source materials as given in Chapter 10 of *Sources of Chinese Tradition* (2nd edition), comp. Volumes I and II, Wm. Theodore de Bary and Irene Bloom, New York: Columbia University Press, 1999.

1.6.2 Reflective Studies

Ames, Roger T. (2003), "Dong Zhongshu," in *Encyclopedia of Chinese Philosophy*, ed. Antonio S. Cua, Routledge, 238–40.

Fung, Yiu-ming (2009), "Philosophy in the Han Dynasty," in *History of Chinese Philosophy*, ed. Bo Mou, London and New York: Routledge, 269–302.

Henderson, John B. (1984), *The Development and Decline of Chinese Cosmology*, New York: Columbia University Press.

Nylan, Michael (2003), "Wang Chong," in *Encyclopedia of Chinese Philosophy*, ed. Antonio S. Cua, New York and London: Routledge, 745–8.

Note: Also see Hall and Ames 1995, Graham 1986, Needham 1956, and Schwartz 1985 Ch. 9 in 2.5.3, Hsiao 1979 in 2.5.4.

1.7 Neo-Daoism

1.7.1 Source Materials

Source materials as given in Chapter 19 of *A Source Book in Chinese Philosophy*, trans. and comp. Wing-tsit Chan, Princeton, NJ: Princeton University Press, 1963.

Source materials as given in Chapter 13 of *Sources of Chinese Tradition* (2nd edition), comp. Volumes I and II, Wm. Theodore de Bary and Irene Bloom, New York: Columbia University Press, 1999.

1.7.2 Reflective Studies

Berkowitz, Alan (2000). *Patterns of Disengagement: The Practice and Portrayal of Reclusion in Early Medieval China*. Stanford, CA: Stanford University Press.

Cai, Zong-qi (ed.) (2004) *Chinese Aesthetics: The Ordering of Literature, the Arts, and the Universe in the Six Dynasties*. Honolulu: University of Hawaii Press.

Twitchett, Denis and Michael Loewe (eds.) (1986), *The Cambridge History of China*. Volume 1. *The Ch'in and Han Empires, 221 B.C.–A.D. 220*. Chapter 16, "Philosophy and Religion from Han to Sui," Cambridge: Cambridge University Press, 808–78.

Chan, Alan K. L. (1991), *Two Visions of the Way: A Study of the Wang Pi and Ho-shang Kung Commentaries on the Lao-tzu*, Albany, NY: SUNY Press, 1991.

— (2003), "Zhong Hui's *Lao-Zi* Commentary and the Debate on Capacity and Nature in Third-Century China," *Early China* 28, 101–59.

— (2009), "Neo-Daoism," in *History of Chinese Philosophy*, ed. Bo Mou, London and New York: Routledge, 303–23.

Dien, Albert E. (ed.) (1990), *State and Society in Early Medieval China*, Stanford, CA: Stanford University Press.

Graham, A. C. (1960), *The Book of Lieh-tzu*, London: A. Murray.

Henricks, Robert G. (trans.) (1983), *Philosophy and Argumentation in Third-Century China: The Essays of Hsi K'ang*. Princeton, NY: Princeton University Press.

Holcombe, Charles (1994), *In the Shadow of the Han: Literati Thought and Society at the Beginning of the Southern Dynasties*, Honolulu: University of Hawaii Press.

Holzman, Donald (1976), *Poetry and Politics: The Life and Works of Juan Chi, A.D. 210–263*, Cambridge: Cambridge University Press.

Kohn, Livia (1992), *Early Chinese Mysticism: Philosophy and Soteriology in the Taoist Tradition*, Princeton, NJ: Princeton University Press.

Lin, Paul J. (trans.) (1977), *A Translation of Lao-tzu's Tao-te ching and Wang Pi's Commentary*, Ann Arbor, MI: Center for Chinese Studies, University of Michigan.

Mather, Richard B. (1969–70), "The Controversy over Conformity and Naturalness during the Six Dynasties," *History of Religions* 9:2–3, 160–80.

Wagner, Rudolf G. (2000), *The Craft of a Chinese Commentator: Wang Bi on the Lao-Zi*, Albany, NY: SUNY Press.

Wagner, Rudolf G. (2003), *Language, Ontology, and Political Philosophy in China: Wang Bi's Scholarly Exploration of the Dark (Xuan-xue)*, Albany, NY: SUNY Press.

Yü Ying-shih (1985), "Individualism and the Neo-Taoist Movement in Wei-Chin China," in *Individualism and Holism: Studies in Confucian and Taoist Values*, ed. Donald Munro, Ann Arbor, MI: Center for Chinese Studies, University of Michigan, 121–55.

Ziproyn, Brook (2003), *The Penumbra Unbound: The Neo-Taoist Philosophy of Guo Xiang*, Albany, NY: SUNY Press.

1.8 Chinese Buddhist Philosophy from *Han* Through *Tang*

1.8.1 Source Materials

Source materials as given in Chapters 20–26 of *A Source Book in Chinese Philosophy*, trans. and comp. Wing-tsit Chan, Princeton, NJ: Princeton University Press, 1963.

Source materials as given in Chapters 15–17 of *Sources of Chinese Tradition* (2nd edition), comp. Volumes I and II, Wm. Theodore de Bary and Irene Bloom, New York: Columbia University Press, 1999.

Cleary, Thomas and J. C. (trans.) (1992), *The Blue Cliff Record*. 3 volumes. Boston, MA: Shambala.

1.8.2 Reflective Studies

Allinson, Robert E. (2008), "The Philosopher and the Sage: Searle and the Sixth Patriarch on the Brain and Consciousness," in *Searle's Philosophy and Chinese Philosophy: Constructive Engagement*, ed. Bo Mou, Leiden and Boston, MA: Brill, 131–67.

Buswell, Robert E. (ed.) (1990), *Chinese Buddhist Apocrypha*, Honolulu: University of Hawaii Press.

Buswell, Robert E., Jr. (1992), *The Zen Monastic Experience*, Princeton, NJ: Princeton University Press.

Chang, Chung-yuan (1971), *Original Teachings of Ch'an Buddhism*, New York: Vintage.

Chang, Garma Chen-chi (1971), *The Buddhist Teaching of Totality: The Philosophy of Hwa-yen Buddhism*, University Park PN: Pennsylvania State University Press.

Chappell, David W. (ed.) (1987), *Buddhist and Taoist Practice in Medieval Chinese Society*, Honolulu: University of Hawaii Press.

Chappell, David W. (ed.) (1983), *T'ien-t'ai Buddhism*, Tokyo: Daiichi-Shobo.

Ch'en, Kenneth 1964), *Buddhism in China, A Historical Survey*, Princeton, NJ: Princeton University Press.

Cheng, Chung-ying (1973), "On Zen (Ch'an) Language and Zen Paradoxes," *Journal of Chinese Philosophy* 1, 77–99.

Cheng, Hsueh-li (1981), "The Roots of Zen Buddhism," *Journal of Chinese Philosophy* 8, 451–78.

— (2005), "Chinese Philosophy: Buddhism," in *Encyclopedia of Philosophy* (2nd edition), ed. Donald M. Borchert (2006), Thomson-Gale/Macmillan Reference USA, 160–70.

Cook, Francis H. (1977), *Hua-yen Buddhism: The Jewel Net of India*, University Park, PN: Pennsylvania State University Press.

— (1979), "Causation in the Chinese Hua-yen Tradition," *Journal of Chinese Philosophy* 6, 367–85.

Donner, Neal and Daniel B. Stevenson (1993), *The Great Calming and Contemplation: A Study and Annotated Translation of the First Chapter of Chih-i's Mo-ho Chih-Kuan*, Honolulu: University of Hawaii Press.

Dumoulin, Heinrich (1988), *Zen Buddhism: A History*, 2 volumes, New York: Macmillan.

Faure, Bernard (1993), *Chan Insights and Oversights: An Epistemological Critique of Chan/Zen Buddhism*, Princeton, NJ: Princeton University Press.

— (1991), *The Rhetoric of Immediacy: A Cultural Critique of Chan/Zen Buddhism*, Princeton, NJ: Princeton University Press.

Fung, Yiu-ming (2008), "How to do Zen (Chan) with Words? An Approach of Speech Act Theory," in *Searle's Philosophy and Chinese Philosophy: Constructive Engagement*, ed. Bo Mou. Leiden and Boston, MA: Brill, 229–42.

Garfield, Jay L. (2001), *Empty Words: Buddhist Philosophy and Cross-Cultural Interpretation*, Oxford: Oxford University Press.

Gernet, Jacques (1995), *Buddhism in Chinese Society: An*

Economic History (5th to 10th c.), trans. Franciscus Verellen, New York: Columbia University Press.

Gimello, Robert (1976), "Apophatic and Kataphatic Discourse in Mahayana: A Chinese View," *Philosophy East and West* 26, 117–36.

Gimello, Robert and Peter N. Gregory (1983), *Studies in Ch'an and Hua-yen,* Honolulu: University of Hawaii Press.

Gomez, Luis O. (1996), *The Land of Bliss: The Paradise of the Buddha of Measureless Light,* Honolulu: University of Hawaii Press.

Gregory, Peter N. (trans.) (1996), *Inquiry into the Origin of Humanity: An Annotated Translation of Tsung-mi's Yuan Jen Lun with a Modern Commentary,* Honolulu: University of Hawaii Press.

— (1991), *Tsung-mi and the Sinification of Buddhism,* Princeton, NJ: Princeton University Press.

Gregory, Peter N. (ed.) (1987), *Sudden and Gradual: Approaches to Enlightenment in Chinese Thought,* Honolulu: University of Hawaii Press.

Hakeda, Yoshito (1967), *The Awakening of Faith,* New York: Columbia University Press.

Hirakawa, Akira (1990), *A History of Indian Buddhism: From Sakyamuni to Early Mahayana,* trans. Paul Groner, Honolulu: University of Hawaii Press.

Holcombe, Charles (1994), *In the Shadow of the Han: Literati Thought and Society at the Beginning of the Southern Dynasties,* Honolulu: University of Hawaii Press.

Hongladaron, Soraj (2008), "Searle and Buddhism on the Mind and the Non-Self," in *Searle's Philosophy and Chinese Philosophy: Constructive Engagement,* ed. Bo Mou, Leiden and Boston, MA: Brill, 169–88.

Hurvitz, Leon (1963), *Chih-i (538–597): An Introduction to the Life and Ideas of a Chinese Buddhist Monk,* Mélanges Chinois et Bouddhiques, XII, Bruges, Belgium.

Jiang, Tao (2006), *Contexts and Dialogue: Yogacara Buddhism and Modern Psychology on the Subliminal Mind*, Honolulu: University of Hawaii Press.

King, Sallie B. (1991), *Buddha-Nature*, Albany, NY: SUNY Press.

Lai, Whalen (1977), "The Meaning of Mind Only: An Analysis of a Sinitic Mahayana Phenomenon," *Philosophy East and West* 27:1, 65–83.

— (1980), "The I-Ching and the Formation of the Hua-yen Philosophy," *Journal of Chinese Philosophy* 7, 245–58.

— (1982), "Sinitic Speculation on Buddha-Nature: The Nirvana School (420–589)," *Philosophy East and West* 32:2, 135–49.

— (1987a), "Tao-sheng's Theory of Sudden Enlightenment Re-examined," in *Sudden and Gradual: Approaches to Enlightenment in Chinese Thought*, ed. Peter Gregoryu Honolulu: University of Hawaii, 169–200.

— (1997), "Buddhism in Chinese Philosophy," in *Companion Encyclopedia of Asian Philosophy*, eds. Brian Carr and Indira Mahalingam, London: Routledge, 575–92.

— (with assistance from Yu-Yin Cheng) (2009), "Chinese Buddhist Philosophy from *Han* through *Tang*," in *History of Chinese Philosophy*, ed. Bo Mou, London and New York: Routledge, 324–61.

Lancaster, Lewis and Whalen Lai (eds.) (1983), *Early Ch'an in China and Tibet*, Berkeley, CA: Asian Humanities Press.

Liu, JeeLoo (2006), Part II, "Chinese Buddhism," of *An Introduction to Chinese Philosophy*, Oxford: Blackwell, 209–331.

Liu, Ming-Wood (1994), *Madhyamaka Thought in China* Leiden and Boston, MA: Brill,

Lusthaus, Dan (2003), *Buddhist Phenomenology: A Philosophical Investigation of Yogacara Buddhism and the Ch'eng Wei-shih Lun*, New York: RoutledgeCurzon.

McRae, John R. (1986), *The Northern School and the Formation of Early Ch'an Buddhism*, Honolulu: University of Hawaii Press.

Ng Yu-Kwan (1993), *T'ien-t'ai Buddhism and Early Madhyamika*, Honolulu: University of Hawaii Press.

Paul, Diana Y. (1984), *Philosophy of Mind in the Sixth-Century China: Paramartha's Evolution of Consciousness*, Stanford, CA: Stanford University Press.

Robinson, Richard H. (1967), *Early Madhyamika in India and China*, Madison, WI: University of Wisconsin.

Swanson, Paul L. (1989), *Foundations of T'ien-t'ai Philosophy: The Flowering of the Two Truths Theory in Chinese Buddhism*, Berkeley, CA: Asian Humanities Press.

Suzuki, Teitaro (1976), *Asvaghosa's Discourse on the Awakeining of Faith in the Mahayana*. Reissued, San Francisco: Chinese Materials Center.

Takakusu, Junjiro (1956), *The Essentials of Buddhist Philosophy*, 3rd edition, Honolulu: Office Appliance Co.

Tanaka, Kenneth K. (1990), *The Dawn of Chinese Pure Land Buddhist Doctrine*, Albany, NY: SUNY Press.

Teiser, Stephen F. (1988), *The Ghost Festival in Medieval China*, Princeton, NY: Princeton University Press.

Tsukamoto, Zenryu (1985), *History of Early Chinese Buddhism: From its Introduction to the Death of Hui-Yuan*, trans. Leon Hurvitz, Tokyo and New York: Kodansha International.

Weinstein, Stanley (1987), *Buddhism under the T'ang*, Cambridge: Cambridge University Press.

Williams, Paul (1989), *Mahayana Buddhism: The Doctrinal Foundations*, London and New York: Routledge.

Wright, Arthur F. (1959), *Buddhism in Chinese History*, Stanford, CA: Stanford University Press.

Wright, Dale (2000), *Philosophical Meditations on Zen Buddhism*, Cambridge: Cambridge University Press.

Yampolsky, Philip (trans.) (1967), *The Platform Sutra of the Sixth Patriarch*, New York: Columbia University Press.

Zeuschner, Robert B. (1981), "The Understanding of Karma in Early Ch'an Buddhism," *Journal of Chinese Philosophy* 8, 399–425.

Zurcher, Erik and Stephen F. Teiser (1972), *The Buddhist Conquest of China: The Spread and Adaptation of Buddhism in Early Medieval China*, Leiden: E. J. Brill.

Classical Chinese Philosophy (III): From Song Through Early Qing (960–1838)

1.9 *Song-Ming* Neo-Confucianism

1.9.1 *Source Materials*

Source materials as given in Chapters 28–35 of *A Source Book in Chinese Philosophy*, trans. and comp. Wing-tsit Chan, Princeton, NJ: Princeton University Press, 1963.

Instructions for Practical Learning and Other Neo-Confucian Writings of Wang Yang-ming [Wang Yang-ming's *Chuan-Xi-Lu*], trans. Wing-tsit Chan, New York: Columbia University Press, (1936b).

Zhu Xi and Lu Zu-qian (comp.), *Reflections on Things at Hand* [*Jin-Si-Lu*], trans. Wing-tsit Chan, New York: Columbia University Press, (1967).

The Philosophical Letters of Wang Yang-ming, trans. Julia Ching, Columbia: University of South Carolina Press, (1972).

The Records of Ming Scholars: A Selected Translation, ed. Julia Ching, Honolulu: University of Hawaii Press, (1987).

1.9.2 Reflective Studies

Chan, Wing-tsit (1973), "Chu Hsi's Completion of Neo-Confucianism," in *Études Song-Sung Studies in Memoriam*

Étienne Balazs, ser. 2, no. 1, ed. Francoise Aubin Paris: Mouton.

Chang, Carsun (1957, 1962), *The Development of New Confucian Thought*, 2 volumes New York: Bookman Associates.

Cheng, Chung-ying (2008), "Analysis of Searle's Philosophy of Mind and Critique from a Neo-Confucian Point of View," in *Searle's Philosophy and Chinese Philosophy: Constructive Engagement*, ed. Bo Mou, Leiden and Boston, MA: Brill, 33–56.

Ching, Julia (1974), "The Goose Lake Monastery Debate (1175)," *Journal of Chinese Philosophy* 1:2, 161–78.

Ching, Julia (1976), *To Acquire Wisdom: The Way of Wang Yang-ming*, New York: Columbia University Press.

Cua, A. S. (1982), *The Unity of Knowledge and Action: A Study in Wang Yang-ming's Moral Psychology*, Honolulu: University of Hawaii Press.

— (2003), (1) "Quan: Weighing Circumstances," (2) "Wang Yangming," in *Encyclopedia of Chinese Philosophy*, ed. Antonio S. Cua New York and London: Routeldge, 625–7, 760–75.

de Bary, Wm. Theodore (ed.) (1975), *The Unfolding of Neo-Confucianism*, New York: Columbia University Press.

Fung, Yu-lan (1934), Chapters 12–14 of *A History of Chinese Philosophy*, 2 volumes, trans. Derk Bodde, Princeton, NJ: Princeton University Press, 1952, 1953.

Fung, Yu-lan (1948), Chapters 23–26 of *A Short History of Chinese Philosophy*, New York: Free Press.

Graham, A. C. (1992), *Two Chinese Philosophers: The Metaphysics of the Brothers Cheng*, LA Salle, IL: Open Court.

Hon, Tzc-ki (2003), "Chen Hao," "Chen Yi," and "Zhou Dunyi," in *Encyclopedia of Chinese Philosophy*, ed. Antonio S. Cua, New York and London: Routledge, 39–46, 891–5.

Ivanhoe, Philip J. (2002), *Ethics in the Confucian Tradition: The Thought of Mencius and Wang Yang-ming* (2nd edition), Indianapolis, IN: Hackett.

Liu, Shu-hsien (1998), "Sung-Ming Neo-Confucian Philosophy," Part II, of *Understanding Confucian Philosophy*, Westport, CT: Praeger.

— (2003), "*Liyi fenshu*: Principle and Manifestations" and "Zhu Xi," in *Encyclopedia of Chinese Philosophy*, ed. Antonio S. Cua, New York and London: Routledge, 409–10, 895–902.

— (2003), *Essentials of Contemporary Neo-Confucian Philosophy*, Westport, CT and London: Praeger.

— (2009), "Neo-Confucianism (I): From Cheng Yi to Zhu Xi" and "Neo-Confucianism (II): From Lu Jiu-yuan to Wang Yang-ming," in *History of Chinese Philosophy*, ed. Bo Mou, London and New York: Routledge, 365–95, 396–428.

Needham, Joseph (1956), *Science and Civilization in China*, volume 2, Cambridge: Cambridge University Press.

Shun, Kwong-loi (2003), "*Gewu* and *Zhizhi*," in *Encyclopedia of Chinese Philosophy*, ed. Antonio S. Cua, New York and London: Routledge, 267–9.

Tillman, Hoyt (1992), "A New Direction in Confucian Scholarship: Approaches to Examining the Differences between Neo-Confucianism and Tao-hsüeh", *Philosophy East and West* 42:3, 455–74.

Tu, Wei-ming (1976), *Neo-Confucian Thought in Action: Wang Yang-ming's Youth (1472–1509)*, Berkeley, CA: University of California Press.

Wilson, Thomas (1995), *Genealogy of the Way: The Construction and Uses of the Confucian Tradition in Late Imperial China*, Stanford, CA: Stanford University Press.

1.10 Philosophical Development in Late *Ming* and Early *Qing*

1.10.1 Source Materials

Source materials as given in Chapters 36–38 of *A Source Book in Chinese Philosophy*, trans. and comp. Wing-tsit Chan, Princeton, NJ: Princeton University Press, 1963.

1.10.2 Reflective Studies

Cheng, Chung-yi (2009), "Philosophical Development in Late *Ming* and Early *Qing*," in *History of Chinese Philosophy*, ed. Bo Mou, London and New York: Routledge, 429–69.

Cheng, Chung-ying (2003), "Dai Zen," in *Encyclopedia of Chinese Philosophy*, ed. Antonio S. Cua, New York and London: Routledge, 195–202.

Chin, Ann-ping and Mansfield Freeman (trans. and with a critical introduction) (1990), *Tai Cheng on Mencius: Explorations in Words and Meaning*, New Haven, CT and London: Yale University Press.

Ching, Julia (trans. with the collaboration of Fang, Chao-ying) (1987), *The Records of Ming Scholars*, Honolulu: University of Hawaii Press.

Chow, Kai-wing (1994), *The Rise of Confucian Ritualism in Late Imperial China: Ethics, Classics and Lineage Discourse*, Stanford, CA: Stanford University Press.

de Bary, W. T. (1991), *Learning for One's Self: Essays on the Individual in Neo-Confucian Thought*, New York: Columbia University Press.

Dewey, John (1929), *The Varieties of Religious Experience: A Study in Human Nature*, New York: The Modern Library.

Kim, Young-oak (1982), "The Philosophy of Wang Fu-chih

(1619–1692)", PhD dissertation. Cambridge, MA: The Department of East Asian Languages and Civilization, Harvard University.

Liu, JeeLoo (2003), "Wang Fuzhi," in *Encyclopedia of Chinese Philosophy*, ed. Antonio S. Cua, New York and London: Routledge, 748–55.

Liu, Shu-hsien (1988), *Understanding Confucian Philosophy: Classical and Sung-Ming*, Westport, CT and London: Praeger.

— (2003), *Essentials of Contemporary Neo-Confucian Philosophy*, Westport, CT and London: Praeger.

Nivison, David (2003), "Zhang Xuecheng," in *Encyclopedia of Chinese Philosophy*, ed. A. S. Cua, New York and London: Routledge, 861–4.

Modern Chinese Philosophy: From Late Qing (1839–) through Twenty-first Century

1.11 Enlightenment Movement

1.11.1 Source Materials

Source materials as given in Chapters 39–41 of *A Source Book in Chinese Philosophy*, trans. and comp. Wing-tsit Chan, Princeton, NJ: Princeton University Press, 1963.

1.11.2 Reflective Studies

Bonner, Joey (1986), *Wang Kuo-wei: An Intellectual Biography*, Cambridge, MA: Harvard University Press.

Chang, Hao (1971), *Liang Ch'i-ch'ao and Intellectual Transition in China 1890–1907*. Cambridge, MA: Harvard University Press.

Cheng, Chung-ying and Nicholas Bunnin (eds.) (2002), Part

I of *Contemporary Chinese Philosophy*, Oxford: Blackwell.

Chou, Min-chih (2003), "Wang Guowei," in *Encyclopedia of Chinese Philosophy*, ed. Antonio S. Cua, New York and London: Routledge, 755–60.

Hu, Xinhe (2002), "Hu Shi's Enlightenment Philosophy," in Cheng and Bunnin (eds) (2002), 82–101.

Huang, Phillip C. (1972), *Liang Ch'i-ch'ao and Modern Chinese Liberalism*, Seattle, WA: University of Washington Press.

Jiang, Xinyan (2002), "Zhang Dongsun: Pluralist Epistemology and Chinese Philosophy," in Cheng and Bunnin (eds.) (2002), 57–81.

— (2009), "Enlightenment Movement," in *History of Chinese Philosophy*, ed. Bo Mou, London and New York: Routledge, 473–511.

Rickett, Adele (1977), *Wang Kuo-wei's Jen-Chien Tz'u-Hua*, Hong Kong: Hong Kong University Press.

Schwartz, Benjamin (1964), *In Search of Wealth and Power: Yen Fu and the West*, Cambridge, MA: Harvard University Press.

Tan, Chester C. (1971), *Chinese Political Thought in the Twentieth Century*, Garden City, NY: Anchor Books, Doubleday.

Xiao, Yang (2002), "Liang Qichao's Political and Social Philosophy," in Cheng and Bunnin (eds.) (2002), 17–36.

1.12 Development of Marxist Philosophy in China

1.12.1 Source Materials

Source materials as given in Chapters 36–38 of *A Source Book in Chinese Philosophy*, trans. and comp. Wing-tsit Chan, Princeton, NJ: Princeton University Press, 1963a.

1.12.2 Reflective Studies

Briere, O. (1965), *Fifty Years of Chinese Philosophy: 1898–1948*, London: George Allen & Unwin.

Cheng, Chung-ying and Nicholas Bunnin (eds.) (2002), Part III of *Contemporary Chinese Philosophy*, Oxford: Blackwell.

Dirlik, Arif (1997), "Mao Zedong and 'Chinese Marxism'," in *Companion Encyclopedia of Asian Philosophy* eds. Brian Carr and Indira Mahalingam, London and New York: Routledge.

Fogel, Joshua A. (1987), *Ai Ssu-chi'i's Contribution to the Development of Chinese Marxism*, Harvard Contemporary China Series: 4. Cambridge, MA: Harvard University Press.

Guo, Zhanbo (1965), *Chinese Thought in the Past Fifty Years*, Honolulu: Dragon Gate Bookstore.

Knight, Nick (ed.) (1990), *Mao Zedong on Dialectical Materialism: Writings on Philosophy*, Armonk, NY: M. E. Sharpe.

— (2005), *Marxist Philosophy in China: From Qu Qiubai to Mao Zedong, 1923–1945*, Dordrecht: Springer.

Li, Yu-ning (1971), *The Introduction of Socialism into China*, New York: Columbia University Press.

Luk, Michael Y. L. (1990), *The Origins of Chinese Bolshevism, An Ideology in the Making, 1920–1928*, Hong Kong: Oxford University Press.

Mao, Zedong (Mao Tse-tung) (1937), "On Contradiction," in Knight, Nick (ed.) (1990), *Mao Zedong on Dialectical Materialsm: Writings on Philosophy*, Armonk, NY: M. E. Sharpe.

Meissner, Werner (1990), *Philosophy and Politics in China: The Controversy over Dialectical Materialism in the 1930's*, Stanford, CA: Stanford University Press.

Ollman, Bertell (1993), *Dialectical Investigations*, New York: Routledge.

Schram, Stuart (1989), *The Thought of Mao Tse-Tung*, Cambridge: Cambridge University Press.

Tian, Chenshan (2005), *Chinese Dialectics: From Yijing to Marxism*, Lexington, MA: Lexington Books.

— (2009), "Development of Dialectical Materialism in China," in *History of Chinese Philosophy*, ed. Bo Mou, London and New York: Routledge, 512–38.

1.13 Contemporary Neo-Confucian Philosophy

1.13.1 Source Materials

Source materials as given in Chapters 42 and 43 of *A Source Book in Chinese Philosophy*, trans. and comp. Wing-tsit Chan, Princeton, NJ: Princeton University Press, 1963.

Source materials as given in "The New Confucians," in Chapters 39 of *Sources of Chinese Tradition* (2nd edition), comp. Volumes I and II, Wm. Theodore de Bary and Irene Bloom New York: Columbia University Press, 1999.

1.13.2 Reflective Studies

Chan, Sin Yee (2002), "Tang Junyi: Moral Idealism and Chinese Culture," in Chung-ying Cheng and Nicholas Bunnin (eds.), 2002, 305–26.

Chang, Hao (1976), "New Confucianism and the Intellectual Crisis of Contemporary China," in *Limits of Change: Essays on Conservative Alternatives in Republican China*, ed. Charlotte Furth, Cambridge, MA: Harvard University Press.

Cheng, Chung-ying (1991), *New Dimensions of Confucian and Neo-Confucian Philosophy*, Albany, NY: SUNY Press.

— with Nicholas Bunnin (eds.) (2002), Parts II and IV of *Contemporary Chinese Philosophy*, Oxford: Blackwell.

Li, Chenyang (2002), "Fang Dongmei: Philosophy of Life,

Creativity, and Inclusiveness," in Cheng and Bunnin (eds.) (2002), 263–80.

Liu, Shu-hsien (2003), *Essentials of Contemporary Neo-Confucian Philosophy*, Westport, CT: Praeger.

Makeham, John (ed.) (2003), *New Confucianism: A Critical Examination*, New York: Palgrave.

Ni, Peimin (2002), "Practical Humanism of Xu Fuguan," in Cheng and Bunnin (eds.) (2002), 281–304.

Tan, Sor-hoon (2004), *Confucian Democracy: A Deweyan Reconstruction*, Albany, NY: SUNY Press.

— (2009), "Contemporary Neo-Confucian Philosophy," in *History of Chinese Philosophy*, ed. Bo Mou, London and New York: Routledge, 539–70.

Tang, Refeng (2002), "Mon Zongsan on Intellectual Intuition," in Cheng and Bunnin (eds.) (2002), 327–46.

Tu Wei-ming (1979), *Humanity and Self-Cultivation*, Berkeley, CA: Asian Humanities Press.

— (1989), *Confucianism in Historical Perspective*, Singapore, Institute of East Asian Philosophies.

Yu, Jiyuan (2002), "Xiong Shili's Metaphysics of Virtue," in Cheng and Bunnin (eds.) (2002), 127–46.

2. Across-the-Board Subjects

2.1 Identity of Chinese Philosophy, its Methodological Issues, and its Comparative Engagement with Other Philosophical Traditions

Allinson, Robert E. (2001), "The Myth of Comparative Philosophy or the Comparative Philosophy *Malgré Lui*," in Mou (ed.) (2001a), 269–91.

Ames, Roger T. and David L. Hall (1995), *Anticipating China: Thinking through the Narratives of Chinese and Western Culture*, Albany, NY: SUNY Press.

Angle, Stephen C. (2006), "Making Room for Comparative

Philosophy: Davidson, Brandom, and Conceptual Distance," in Mou (ed.) (2006a), 73–100.

— (2007), "Chinese Philosophers and Global Philosophy," in *Chinese Philosophy and Culture*, 1:1, 239–56 (in Chinese).

Bunnin, Nicholas (2003), "Contemporary Chinese Philosophy and Philosophical Analysis," *Journal of Chinese Philosophy* 30:3 & 4, 341–56.

Cheng, Chung-ying (2001), "Onto-Hermeneutical Vision and Analytic Discourse: Interpretation and Reconstruction of Chinese Philosophy," in Mou (ed.) (2001a), 87–129.

Cua, Antonio S (2000, 2003), "Emergence of the History of Chinese Philosophy," in *International Philosophical Quarterly*, 40:4, 441–64; revised version in Mou (ed.) (2003), 3–30.

Davidson, Donald (1977), "Radical Interpretation," in Donald Davidson (2001), *Inquiries into Truth and Interpretation* (2nd edition), Oxford: Clarendon Press, 199–214.

— (2001), "Foreword" [on analytic method and cross-cultural understanding] to Mou (ed.) (2001a), v–vi.

Defoort, Carine (2001), "Is There Such a Thing as Chinese Philosophy? Arguments of an Implicit Debate," *Philosophy East & West* 51:3, 393–413.

Fung, Yu-lan (1948), Chapter 1 "The Spirit of Chinese Philosophy," *A Short History of Chinese Philosophy*, London: Macmillan; New York: The Free Press, 1976.

— (1948), "Chinese Philosophy and a Future World Philosophy," *The Philosophical Review* 57:6, 539–49.

Fung, Yu-ming (2006), "Davidson's Charity in the Context of Chinese Philosophy," in Mou (ed.) (2006a), 117–62.

Graham, Angus C. (1985), *Reason and Spontaneity*, London: Curzon Press.

— (1992), *Unreason with Reason*, LaSalle, IL: Open Court.

Hall, David L. and Roger T. Ames (1995), *Anticipating China: Thinking through the Narratives of Chinese and Western Culture*, Albany, NY: SUNY Press.

— (2001), "The Import of Analysis in Classical China," in Mou (ed.) (2001a), 153–67.

Hansen, Chad (1991), "Should the Ancient Masters Value Reason?" in Henry Rosemont (ed.), *Chinese Texts and Philosophical Contexts*, La Salle, IL: Open Court, 179–207.

— (1992),Chapter 1 of *A Daoist Theory of Chinese Thought: A Philosophical Interpretation*, New York and Oxford: Oxford University Press, 1992, 1–29.

— (2001), "Metaphysical and Moral Transcendence in Chinese Thought," in Mou (ed.) (2001a), 197–227.

Krausz, Michael (2006), "Relativism and its Scheme", in Mou (ed.) (2006a), 37–53.

Leiter, Brian (2006), "Analytic and Continental Philosophy," in his *The Philosophical Gourmet Report (2006–08)* at http:www.philosophicalgourmet.com/analytic.asp.

Li, Chenyang (1999), *The Tao Encounters the West: Explorations in Comparative Philosophy*, Albany, NY: SUNY Press.

Li, Youzheng (2001), "Chinese Philosophy and Semiotics," in Mou (ed.) (2001a), 169–94.

Littlejohn, Ronnie (2006), "Comparative Philosophy," in *The Internet Encyclopedia of Philosophy* at http://www.iep.utm.edu/c/comparat.htm

Liu, Shu-hsien (2001), "Philosophical Analysis and Hermeneutics: Reflections on Methodology via an Examination of the Evolution of My Understanding," in Mou (ed.) (2001a), 131–52.

Mou, Bo (ed.) (2001a), *Two Roads to Wisdom? —Chinese and Analytic Philosophical Traditions*, Chicago, IL: Open Court.

— (2001b), "An Analysis of the Structure of Philosophical Methodology: In View of Comparative Philosophy," in Mou (ed.) (2001a), 337–64.

— (ed.) (2003), *Comparative Approaches to Chinese Philosophy*, Aldershot: Ashgate.

— (ed.) (2006a), *Davidson's Philosophy and Chinese Philosophy: Constructive Engagement*, Leiden and Boston, MA: Brill.

— (2006b), Section 2 of "How Constructive Engagement of Davidson's Philosophy and Chinese Philosophy is Possible: A Theme Introduction," in Mou (ed.) (2006a), 1–33.

— (ed.) (2008a), *Searle's Philosophy and Chinese Philosophy: Constructive Engagement*, Leiden and Boston, MA: Brill.

— (2008b), "Searle, Zhuang Zi, and Transcendental Perspectivism," in Mou (ed.) (2008d), 405–35.

— (ed.) (2009a), *History of Chinese Philosophy*, London and New York: Routledge.

— (2009b), "On Some Methodological Issues Concerning Chinese Philosophy," in Mou (ed.) (2009a), 1–39.

— (2009c), "Constructive Engagement of Chinese and Western Philosophy: A Contemporary Trend Towards World Philosophy," in Mou (ed.) (2009a), 571–608.

— (2010), "On Constructive-Engagement Methodological Strategy in Comparative Philosophy," forthcoming in *Comparative Philosophy* 1:1.

Neville, Robert C. (2001), "Methodology, Practices, and Discipline in Chinese and Western Philosophy," in Mou (ed.) (2001a), 27–44.

Ragland, C. P. and Sarah Heidt (eds.) (2001), *What is Philosophy?* New Haven, CT and London: Yale University Press.

Rescher, Nicholas (1994), "Philosophical Methodology," in his *A System of Pragmatic Idealism. Volume III: Metaphilosophical Inquiries*, Princeton, NJ: Princeton University Press, 36–58; reprinted in Mou (ed.) (2001a), 3–25.

Searle, John (2008), "The Globalization of Philosophy," in Mou (ed.) (2008a), 17–30.

Shun, Kwong-loi (2001), Section 1.2 "Some Methodological Issues" of *Mencius and Early Chinese Thought*, Stanford, CA: Stanford University Press, 5–13.

— (2009), "Studying Confucian and Comparative Ethics: Some Methodological Reflections," forthcoming in *Journal of Chinese Philosophy* 36.3 (September 2009).

Van Norden, Bryan (2001), "Mencius and Augustine on Evil: A Test Case for Comparative Philosophy," in Mou (ed.) (2001a), 313–36.

Wang, Hao (1988), Chapter 5 "Methodological Observation" of *Beyond Analytic Philosophy*, Cambridge, MA: MIT Press, 191–213.

Wheeler, Samuel (2006), "Davidsonian Rationality and Ethical Disagreement between Cultures," in Mou (ed.) (2006a), 165–88.

Wong, David (2005), "Comparative Philosophy: Chinese and Western," in Edward Zalta, (ed.), *Stanford Encyclopedia of Philosophy*, at http://plato.stanford.edu/entries/compar-phil-chiwes/.

— (2006), "Where Charity Begins?" in Mou (ed.) (2006a), 103–16.

Yu, Jiyuan and Nicholas Bunnin (2001), "Saving the Phenomena: An Aristotelian Method in Comparative Philosophy," in Mou (ed.) (2001a), 293–312.

Zhang, Xianglong (2006), "Studies of Continental Philosophy in China and its Comparative Engagement of Traditional Chinese Philosophy," in *APA Newsletter* Vol. 5, No. 2, 19–22.

— (2010), "Comparison Paradox and Comparative Situation—A Methodological Reflection on Philosophical Comparison," forthcoming in *Comparative Philosophy* 1:1.

Zheng, Yujian (2006), "A Davidsonian Approach to Normativity and the Limits of Cross-Cultural Interpretation," in Mou (ed.) (2006a), 189–203.

2.2 Source Books

Chan, Wing-tsit (comp. and trans.) (1963), *A Source Book in Chinese Philosophy*, Princeton, NJ: Princeton University

Press. [Though published several decades ago, this is still a good comprehensive source book of Chinese philosophy. It covers ancient times to the first half of the twentieth century.]

de Bary, Wm. Theodore and Irene Bloom (comp.) (1999), *Sources of Chinese Tradition* (2nd edition), Volumes I and II, New York: Columbia University Press. [Though this book is intended to capture the Chinese tradition as a whole instead of being focused on Chinese philosophy, its coverage is comprehensive from ancient times to the whole of the twentieth century.]

Ivanhoe, Philip J., and Bryan W. Van Norden (eds.) (2001), *Readings in Classical Chinese Philosophy* (2nd edition), Indianapolis, IN: Hackett. [Covers the pre-*Han* period.]

2.3 Reference Books

Cua, Antonio S. (ed.) (2002), *Encyclopedia of Chinese Philosophy*, New York and London: Routledge.

Zhang, Dainian (2002), *Key Concepts in Chinese Philosophy*, trans. Edmund Ryden, Beijing: Foreign Language Press and New Haven, CT: Yale University Press.

Also see relevant entries concerning Chinese philosophy in some recent philosophy encyclopedias, such as:

Borchert, Donald M. (ed.) (2006), *Encyclopedia of Philosophy* (2nd edition), Chicago, IL: Thomson-Gale/Macmillan Reference USA.

Honderich, Ted (ed.) (2005), *The Oxford Companion to Philosophy* (2nd edition), Oxford: Oxford University Press.

Zalta, Edward (ed.), *Stanford Encyclopedia of Philosophy,* an online encyclopedia of philosophy at http://plato.stanford.edu/.

2.4 Authoritative but Accessible (Advanced) Introduction to Chinese Philosophy

Note: There are various entry-level introductory textbooks available written for beginners. In view of the purpose and function of this bibliography, the books listed below are authoritative but accessible, and that can be used for more advanced studies as well as being an introduction to (the whole history, or some of its major periods, of) Chinese philosophy.

Cheng, Chung-ying and Nicholas Bunnin (eds.) (2002), *Contemporary Chinese Philosophy*, Oxford: Blackwell.

Fung, Yu-lan (1948), *A Short History of Chinese Philosophy*, New York: The Free Press.

Fung, Yu-lan (1952/1953), *A History of Chinese Philosophy: Volume I and II*, trans. Derek Bodde, Princeton, NJ: Princeton University Press, 1952 and 1953. (Original work: *Zhong-Guo-Zhe-Xue-Shi, Shang-Ce*, 1931 and 1934.) [An abridged version, *A Short History of Chinese Philosophy*, ed. Derek Bodde (1948) (London: Macmillan, 1948; New York: The Free Press, 1976) is more accessible and readily available.]

Graham, Angus (1989), *Disputers of the Tao: Philosophical Argument in Ancient China*, La Salle, IL: Open Court.

Mou, Bo (ed.) (2009), *History of Chinese Philosophy*, London and New York: Routledge.

Schwartz, Benjamin I. (1985), *The World of Thought in Ancient China*, Cambridge, MA: Harvard University Press.

2.5 Subject Studies of Chinese Philosophy

2.5.1 Aesthetics

Cai, Zong-qi (ed.) (2004), *Chinese Aesthetics*, Honolulu: University of Hawaii Press.

Dale, Corinne H. (ed.) (2004), *Chinese Aesthetics and Literature*, Albany, NY: SUNY Press.

Li, Zehou (1995), *The Path of Beauty: A Study of Chinese Aesthetics*, trans. Lizeng Gong, Oxford: Oxford University Press.

Saussy, Haun (1995), *The Problem of a Chinese Aesthetic*, Stanford, CA: Stanford University Press.

2.5.2 *Language, Mind, and Logic*

Ames, Roger T. and David L. Hall (1987), Part V, Section 2 of *Thinking Through Confucius*, Albany, NY: SUNY Press, 261–83.

Chao, Y. R. (1955), "Notes on Chinese Grammar and Logic," *Philosophy East and West* 5:1, 31–41.

Cheng, Chung-ying (1987), "Logic and Language in Chinese Philosophy," *Journal of Chinese Philosophy* 14: 85–307.

— (2006), "From Donald Davidson's Use of 'Convention T' to Meaning and Truth in Chinese Language," in *Davidson's Philosophy and Chinese Philosophy: Constructive Engagement*, ed. Bo Mou, Leiden and Boston, MA: Brill, 271–308.

Chong, Kim-chong (2006), "Metaphorical Use versus Metaphorical Essence: Examples from Chinese Philosophy," in *Davidson's Philosophy and Chinese Philosophy: Constructive Engagement*, ed. Bo Mou, Leiden and Boston, MA: Brill, 229–46.

Graham, A. C. (1989), Appendix 2 "The Relation of Chinese Thought to Chinese Language," in his *Disputers of Tao*, La Salle, IL: Open Court, 389–428.

Hansen, Chad (1983), *Language and Logic in Ancient China*, Ann Arbor, MI: University of Michigan Press.

— (1985), "Chinese Language, Chinese Philosophy, and 'Truth'," *Journal of Asian Studies* 44:3, 491–519.

— (1992), *A Daoist Theory of Chinese Thought,* New York: Oxford University Press.

Harbsmeier, Christoph (1989), "Marginalia Sino-Logica," in *Understanding the Chinese Mind: The Philosophical Roots*, ed. Robert E. Allinson, Hong Kong: Oxford University Press, 125–66.

— (1998), Part 1, "Language and Logic in Traditional China," *Science and Civilisation in China. Volume 7, The Social Background*, ed. Joseph Needham, Cambridge: Cambridge University Press.

Hu, Shih (1922), *The Development of the Logical Method in Ancient China*, Shanghai, NY: Commercial Press.

Makeham, John (1994), *Name and Actuality in Early Chinese Thought*, Albany: SUNY Press.

Mou, Bo (1999), "The Structure of Chinese Language and Ontological Insights: A Collective-Noun Hypothesis," *Philosophy East and West* 49:1, 45–62.

— (2006), "Chinese Philosophy: Language and Logic," in *Encyclopedia of Philosophy* (2nd edition), ed. Donald M. Borchert, Chicago, IL: Thomson-Gale/Macmillan Reference, 202–15.

— (2009), Chapter 5 "A Cross-Tradition Examination – Philosophical Concern with Truth in Classical Daoism," in Bo Mou, *Substantive Perspectivism: An Essay on Philosophical Concern with Truth* ("Synthese Library" monograph series vol. 344), Dordrecht: Springer.

Smith, Huston (1980) "Western and Comparative Perspectives on Truth," *Philosophy East and West* 30 (4): 425–37.

Willman, Marshall D. (2008), "Searle, *De Re* Belief, and the Chinese Language," in *Searle's Philosophy and Chinese Philosophy: Constructive Engagement*, ed. Bo Mou, Leiden and Boston, MA: Brill, 247–63.

[Note: Section A "Mind" of the anthology *Searle's Philosophy and Chinese Philosophy: Constructive Engagement* (ed. Bo Mou, Leiden and Boston: Brill, 33–194) consists of five essays examining Confucian, Daoist, and Buddhist approaches to mind, four of which are respectively included in (1.9.2), (1.5.2) and (1.8.2).]

2.5.3 *Metaphysics and Epistemology*

Ames, Roger T. et al. (eds.) (1994), *Self as Person in Asian Theory and Practice*, Albany, NY: SUNY Press.

Cheng, Chung-ying (1989), "Chinese Metaphysics as Non-metaphysics: Confucian and Daoist Insights into the Nature of Reality," in *Understanding the Chinese Mind: The Philosophical Roots*, ed. Robert E. Allinson, Hong Kong: Oxford University Press, 167–208.

Geaney, Jane (2002), *On the Epistemology of the Senses in Early Chinese Thought*, Honolulu: University of Hawaii Press.

Graham, A. C. (1989), Part IV, Chapter 1 "The Cosmologists," in his *Disputers of the Tao*, La Salle, IL: Open Court, 315–70.

Hall, David L. and Roger T. Ames (1998), *Thinking from the Han: Self, Truth, and Transcendence in Chinese and Western Culture*, Albany, NY: SUNY Press.

— (1997): "The Way and the Truth," in *A Companion to World Philosophies*, eds. Eliot Deutsch and Ron Bontekoe, Oxford: Blackwell, 214–24.

Hans, Lenk and Gregor, Paul (eds.) (1993), *Epistemological Issues in Classical Chinese Philosophy*, Albany, NY: SUNY Press.

Hansen, Chad (2003), "*Youwu*: Being and Nonbeing," in *Encyclopedia of Chinese Philosophy*, ed. Antonio S. Cua, New York and London: Routledge, 847–9.

Munro, Donald J. (1969), *The Concept of Man in Early China*, Stanford, CA: Stanford University Press.

Needham, Joseph (1956), *Science and Civilisation in China*. Volume II, *History of Scientific Thought*, Cambridge: Cambridge University Press.

Schwartz, Benjamin (1985), relevant chapters in *The World of Thought in Ancient China*, Cambridge, MA: Harvard University Press.

Shen, Vincent (2005), "Chinese Philosophy: Metaphysics and Epistemology," in *Encyclopedia of Philosophy* (2nd edition), ed. Donald M. Borchert (2006), Chicago: Thomson-Gale/Macmillan Reference USA, 215–23.

Smith, Huston (1980), "Western and Comparative Perspectives on Truth," *Philosophy East and West* 30:4, 425–37.

Wu, Kuang-Ming (1996), *On Chinese Body Thinking*, Leiden and Boston, MA: Brill.

Zhang, Dainian (2002), Part One, "Metaphysics," and Part Three, "Epistemology," in his *Key Concepts in Chinese Philosophy*, trans. Edmund Ryden, Beijing: Foreign Language Press and New Haven, CT: Yale University Press, 3–281, 421–85.

2.5.4 Moral Philosophy and Social and Political Philosophy

Ames, Roger (1993), *The Art of Rulership: A Study of Ancient Chinese Political Thought*, Albany, NY: SUNY Press.

Becker, Gerhold (ed.) (1996), *Ethics in Business and Society: Chinese and Western Perspectives*, New York: Springer.

Ci, Jiwei (1994), *The Dialectic of the Chinese Revolution: From Utopianism to Hedonism*, Stanford, CA: Stanford University Press.

Cua, Antonio S. (1998), *Moral Vision and Tradition: Essay in Chinese Ethics*, Washington, DC: Catholic University of America Press.

Hansen, Chad, "*Fa* (Standards: Laws) and Meaning Changes in Chinese Philosophy," *Philosophy East and West* 44:3, 433–88.

Hsiao, Kung-chuan (1979), *A History of Chinese Political*

Thought, trans. F. W. Mote, Princeton, NJ: Princeton University Press.

Ivanhoe, Philip J. (2000), *Confucian Moral Self Cultivation* (2nd edition), Indianapolis, IN: Hackett.

Jiang, Xinyan (ed.) (2002), *The Examined Life – Chinese Perspective: Essays on Chinese Ethical Traditions*, Binghamton, NY: Global Publications.

Munro, Donald J. (2005), *A Chinese Ethics for the New Century*, Hong Kong: The Chinese University Press.

Van Norden, Bryan (2007), *Virtue Ethics and Consequentialism in Early Chinese Philosophy*, Cambridge: Cambridge University Press.

Wong, David (2006): "Chinese Philosophy: Ethics," in *Encyclopedia of Philosophy* (2nd edition), ed. Donald M. Borchert, Thomson-Gale/Macmillan Reference USA, 194–202.

Yan, Jinfen (1998), *Utilitarianism in Chinese Thought*, Quebtt: World Heritage Press.

Zhang, Dainian (2002), Part Two, "Anthropology" (on Moral Ideals, Ethical Concepts, Human Nature, etc.), in his *Key Concepts in Chinese Philosophy*, trans. Edmund Ryden, Beijing: Foreign Language Press and New Haven, CT: Yale University Press, 285–418.

Appendix 1:
Comparative Chronology
of Philosophers

Chinese Philosophy	Western Philosophy
2200 BCE *Xia Dynasty (2070–1600 BCE)*	
2000 BCE *Shang Dynasty (1600–1046 BCE)* *Zhou Dynasty (1046–256 BCE)*	
800 BCE *Spring and Autumn Period (722–481 BCE)* Confucius (551–479 BCE)	Thales (640–546 BCE)
	Founding of Rome (508 BCE)
	Heraclitus (535–475 BCE)
500 BCE *Warring States Period (480–222 BCE)*	Parmenides (515–450 BCE)

Mo Zi (470–391 BCE)	Anaxagoras (500–428 BCE)
Yang Zhu (5th century BCE?)	Empedocles (c. 495–435 BCE)
Lao Zi (before 4th century BCE?)	Protagoras (485–415 BCE)
	Zeno of Elea (c. 470 BCE)
400 BCE	Socrates (470–399 BCE)
Zhuang Zi (375–300 BCE)	Democritus (460–370 BCE)
Mencius (371–289 BCE)	Plato (427–347 BCE)
Hui Shi (350–260 BCE)	Aristotle (384–322 BCE)
Gong-sun Long (320–250 BCE)	
300 BCE	Pyrrho (360–270 BCE)
Xun Zi (298–238 BCE)	
Han Fei (280–233 BCE)	
Qin Dynasty (221–206 BCE)	
Han Dynasty	
(206 BCE–220 AD)	
200 BCE	
Dong Zhong-shu	
(c. 179–104 BCE)	
Huai-Nan-Zi Text (?)	
100 BCE	
Commm Eia	
Wang Chong (27–97?)	Jesus Christ (c. 6 BCE –30)
100 CE	
200 CE	
The Period of Three-Kingdoms (220–80):	Sextus Empiricus (second/third centuries)

Wei (220–265) / *Shu-Han* (221–63)/ *Wu* (222–80)	Plotinus (204–70)
He Yan (c. 207–49)	
Xun Can (c. 212–40)	
Xi Kang (223–62)	
Wang Bi (226–49)	
Jin Dynasty (265–420)	
Ou-yang Jian (late third century)	
300 CE	
Guo Xiang (d. 312)	
Dao An (312–85)	Augustine (354–430)
Hui Yuan (336–416)	
400 CE	
The Northern and Southern Dynasties (420–589)	*Fall of Roman Empire* (476)
Seng Zhao (384–414)	Boethius (c. 480–c. 526)
Fan Zhen (450–515)	
Bodhidharma (fl. 460–534)	
500 CE	
Sui Dynasty (581–618)	
Zhi Yi (538–97)	
Ji Zang (549–623)	
Du Shun (557–640)	
600 CE	
Xuan Zang (596–664)	
Fa Zang (643–712)	
Tang Dynasty (618–907)	

Shen Xiu (c. 605–706)
Hui Neng (638–713)
 	
700 CE
 	
900 CE
The Five Dynasties (907–60)
Song Dynasty (960–1279)
 	
1000 CE
Shao Yong (1011–77)
Zhou Dun-yi (1017–73)
Cheng Hao (1032–85)
Zhang Zai (1020–77)
Cheng Yi (1033–1107)
 	
1100 CE
Zhu Xi (1130–1200)
Lu Jiu-yuan (1139–93)
 	
1200 CE
Yuan Dynasty (1206–1368)
 	
1300 CE
Ming Dynasty (1368–1644)
 	
1400 CE
Wang Shou-ren (Yang-ming)
  (1472–1529)
1500 CE
	
	Anselm (1033–1109)
	
	Thomas Aquinas (1224–74)
	Renaissance begins in Italy
	  (1215)
	
	William of Ockham (1285–
	  1347)
	
	Copernicus (1473–1543)

1600 CE	Francis Bacon (1561–1626)
Qing Dynasty (1616–1911)	Galileo Galilei (1564–1642)
Huang Zong-xi (1610–95)	Thomas Hobbes (1588–1679)
Wang Fu-zhi (1619–92)	René Descartes (1596–1650)
	Baruch Spinoza (1632–77)
	John Locke (1632–1704)
	Gottfried Leibniz (1646–1716)
1700 CE	
Dai Zhen (1723–77)	George Berkeley (1685–1753)
	David Hume (1711–76)
	Immanuel Kant (1724–1804)
	French Revolution (1789–91)
1800 CE	
Opium Wars (1839–42)	George Hegel (1770–1831)
Tai-Ping Revolution (1851–64)	Arthur Schopenhauer (1788–
Yan Fu (1854–1921)	1860)
Liang Qi-chao (1873–1929)	John Stuart Mill (1806–73)
Wang Guo-wei (1877–1927)	Søren Kierkegaard (1813–55)
	Karl Marx (1818–83)
	Friedrich Engels (1820–95)
	American Civil War (1861–5)
	William James (1842–1910)
	Friedrich Wilhelm Nietzsche
	(1844–1900)
	Gottlob Frege (1848–1925)
	Aexius Meinong (1853–1920)
	Edmund Husserl (1859–1938)
1900 CE	
The Boxer Movement (1900)	
Republic of China (1912–)	*World War I* (1914–17)

May Fourth Movement (1919)	*Russian Revolution* (1917)
Xiong Shi-li (1885–1968)	John Dewey (1859–1952)
Zhang Dong-sun (1886–1973)	Alfred North Whitehead (1861–1947)
Hu Shi (1891–1962)	
Mao Ze-dong (1893–1976)	Bertrand Russell (1872–1970)
Liang Shu-ming (1893–1988)	Moritz Schlick (1882–1936)
People's Republic of China (1949–)	Martin Heidegger (1889–1976)
	Ludwig Wittgenstein (1889–1951)
Jin Yue-lin (1895–1984)	
Fung yu-lan (1895–1990)	*World War II* (1939–45)
Fang Dong-mei (1899–1977)	Gilbert Ryle (1900–76)
"Cultural Revolution" (1966–77)	Hans Georg Gadamer (1900–2002)
He Lin (1902–92)	Alfred Tarski (1902–83)
Xu Fu-guan (1903–82)	Karl Popper (1902–94)
Hong Qian (1909–92)	Jean-Paul Sartre (1905–80)
Tang Jun-yi (1909–78)	W. V. Quine (1908–2000)
Mou Zong-san (1909–95)	Paul Ricoeur (1913–2005)
Zhang Dai-nian (1909–2004)	Donald Davidson (1917–2003)
	John Rawls (1921–2002)
	Richard Rorty (1931–2007)

(Studies of) Chinese Philosophy in Global Context during the twentieth and twenty-first centuries

Angus Charles Graham (1919–91)

Appendix 2:
Note on Transcription and Guide to Pronunciation

Because of its official status in China, its relative accuracy in transcribing actual pronunciation in Chinese common speech, and consequent worldwide use, the *pinyin* romanization system is employed in this book for transliterating Chinese names and terms. However, I have left transliterations of Chinese names and terms as originally published (typically in the Wade-Giles system) in the following cases: (1) the titles of cited publications; (2) the names whose Latinizations have become quite conventional (such as "Confucius" and "Mencius"); and (3) the names of the writers who have had their authored English publications under their regular non-*pinyin* romanized names (such as "Fung Yu-lan"). The titles of cited Chinese books and essays are given in their *pinyin* transcriptions with their paraphrases given in parentheses. The following rule of thumb has been used in dealing with the order of the surname (family) name and given name in romanized Chinese names: (1) for the name of a historical figure in Chinese history, the surname appears first, and the given name second (such as "Zhu Xi"); and (2) for contemporary figures, their own practice is followed when writing in English (typically, those who have had their English publications tend to have their given name appear first and surname second). In the *pinyin* versions of Chinese publication titles and those proper

phrases that contain two or more than two Chinese characters, hyphens may be used to indicate separate characters.

Transcription Conversion Table

Wade-Giles	*Pinyin*
ai	ei
ch	zh
	j
ch'	ch
	q
hs	x
ien	ian
-ih	-i
j	r
k	g
k'	k
p	b
p'	p
szu	si
t	d

t'	t
ts, tz	z
ts', tz'	c
tzu	zi
ung	ong
yu	you